THE BILLBOARD GUIDE TO

Home Recording

REVISED EDITION

THE BILLBOARD GUIDE TO

Home Recording

REVISED EDITION

Ray Baragary

BILLBOARD BOOKS
An imprint of Watson-Guptill Publications/New York

Senior Editor: Bob Nirkind
Edited by: Amy Handy
Technical art: Play-It Publishing, Ltd.
Line illustrations: Pat Welch
Book design and composition: Bob Fillie, Graphiti Graphics

First published 1996 by Billboard Books,
an imprint of Watson-Guptill Publications,
a division of BPI Communications, Inc.
1515 Broadway, New York, NY 10036

Library of Congress Cataloging-in-Publication Data
Baragary, Ray
   The billboard guide to home recording/ Ray Baragary.
—Rev. and enl. ed.
       p. cm.
   Includes index.
   ISBN 0-8230-8300-4
   1. Sound—Recording and reproducing—Amateurs' manuals.
I.Title.
TK9968.B368   1996
621.389'3'02478—dc20   96–23985
                                              CIP

Manufactured in the United States of America
First printing, 1996

3 4 5 6 7 8 9 / 99 98

*For Nancy and Danny;
in memory of Joe and Helen*

Acknowledgments

I'd like to thank the following people for helping to make this book possible: Tad Lathrop, Jackson Braider, David Moulton of Berkelee College of Music, Bill Mohrhoff and David Oren of TAS-CAM, Jim Mothersbaugh and Chuck Vandeman and Thomas Beckmen of Roland, the Boddickers (Michael, Gerald, and Arlene), and the musicians, family, and friends who encouraged me to write this book.

Additional thanks to the following people: Bette Burton of Shure Brothers, Larry DeMarco of Korg USA, David Jensen of Ampex, Sherry Kahn of Scholz Research, Bob Lowig of Beyerdynamic, Chuck Thompson of J. L. Cooper Electronics, and Diane Zedicker of AEG.

Thanks also to Akai Electronic Co., Crown International Inc., Fostex, and Mark of the Unicorn, Inc.

Contents

Preface to the Second Edition

As I prepared the second edition of this book, I came away from the task both pleased and apprehensive. I was very happy that our focus on the fundamentals of capturing pure music and sound rather than straying into the murk of techniques for specific instruments and machines proved to be correct. The general recording tips and most of the specific techniques held up well and survived into the second edition without too many changes. I have, of course, included in this edition references to digital recorders, both tape and hard disk systems.

I feel very strongly that the book will be a big help to your recording success no matter what type of recorder you use. Feedback from readers of the first edition has been very positive, particularly about the "Recording Techniques" and "Specifications" sections. To all of you who took the time and trouble to communicate with me about the book, I want to say thank you.

The recording industry has undergone profound changes in the last decade and a half. As mentioned in the first edition, the big-buck album-oriented studios of the seventies are gone. In their place has come the "project" or home studio. Now that we have entered fully into the digital revolution in recording, more and more power has come to the people. With digital multitracks, DAT machines, and affordable CD mastering machines, the recording industry has truly become a cottage industry. The internet and other open communication forums also offer the promise of a distribution system available to these same cottage artisans.

What will we do with this new power? Will we fritter it away, allowing the politicians and phone companies to carve up and possess our access and our creative outlet? Or will we seize the day? Will we fill the world with our diverse music and voices? Or will we simply use the net to browse the shopping network and our digital recorders to copy the latest pop pap? This is the source of my apprehension. Already big business and big government are preparing to assimilate the digital revolution and turn the information superhighway into a closed oval of consumerism.

I want to challenge the readers of this book to become music and media activists. I am unconcerned whether I will agree with the specifics of your message or muse. I simply want to enjoy the glory of your right to express it well and widely. So learn the techniques and get out there and spread your good news!

Introduction

Anyone who has ever recorded in a large commercial recording studio knows the feeling.

It's Take 15 of a piercing lead guitar solo. You're manning the fretboard, blazing toward the final measures of a moment of glory. The drums-bass-keyboard accompaniment of the basic tracks is pumping through the headphones, and you approach the song's climax with that special devil-may-care confidence of someone who's spent far too many coffee-driven hours in the recording room. You hit the final note dead on the money and give it a last bit of body english, letting it hang there in space until it disappears into the track. A voice cuts into the headphones:

"Sounds like we've got a take."

The engineer peers at you from the control booth, giving the "thumbs up" signal. It's time to listen to the playback.

A feeling of relief settles in. This solo was the very last part that needed to be recorded for the song-in-progress. The basic rhythm tracks were committed to tape days ago. Now, or so you think, it's time for the fun to begin: hear the rough playback and start working on the mix. You untangle yourself from the guitar strap, effects boxes, and cords and head for the control room door.

The other members of the band are all there, wild about your solo and turned on by the anticipation of hearing the final song with all its component parts. While the tape rewinds, the engineer is busy preparing the levels of all the tracks for a rough mix. Too excited to sit down, all you want to do is hear the guitar solo played back so you can be sure that what you just performed was every bit as perfect as you imagined it to be.

The engineer hits Playback and the climate-controlled quiet in the booth is obliterated by the sound of a full-volume guitar power chord. It hangs in midair while bass drum and tom-toms roll into the soaring strains of a solo guitar—*your* guitar. The first impact is powerful; you are all lifted by the richness of what you hear yet you're impatient to hear what's coming up.

Relief is now tinged with anxiety: Is it all there? Does the recording sustain the power and glory of the arrangement, or will the music somehow fall flat? The feeling continues for the entire length of the playback. As the end nears you sense your own pulse rate quickening; Take 15 is roaring into the crescendo that caps the tune. It has to be just right.

Hold it. What was *that?* Rewind. Replay the end of the take. A mistake, where your finger slipped from the string. It's too obvious to ignore because it comes right at the climax of the crucial phrase. Your stomach flops. There goes that moment of glory. At the end of an otherwise perfect take, you hit a note so bad that even your own mother couldn't love you.

Take comfort, though; You don't have to re-record the entire solo. Too much of the take is too good to send the whole thing into magnetic oblivion. With the help of electronics and a good, friendly engineer you can fix the portion of the track that you had flubbed. All you have to do is "punch in" the correct notes and "punch out" to save the rest.

Back in the recording room you strap on the guitar and match the volume and sound with the guitar track playing back into your headphones. When you're set, the engineer rewinds the tape and begins playing back the song well before the point where the guitar gears up for the big ending. As the guitar track kicks into your headphones, you begin playing along, though the engineer hasn't hit Record yet. You're trying to match the feeling and intensity of the original take so that the "patch" will sound seamless.

The bad section approaches. You play into it. Just before reaching the sour note, the engineer presses Record and captures you soaring beautifully, cleanly, through the last several measures of the song, the break between the old take and the new one all but imperceptible to even the most discerning ear. The music fades away and you return to the control booth to make certain everything came out right.

Mistake? What mistake?

A second runthrough of the recording indicates that the hard part is indeed over—the individual tracks are all strong. It's just a matter of equalization, signal processing, balancing, and panning before you have what everyone in the room *knows* will be a hit. The time has finally come to relax and celebrate before you go back to work on fixing the mix.

Up until a few years ago, this couldn't have happened anywhere outside a large commercial recording studio. To get that big, clean, impressive sound you needed multiple track recording; to get multiple tracks you needed professional equipment; to record a number of musicians you needed adequate space and the patience of a saint; to handle equipment of daunting complexity you needed a professional engineer.

And to afford all this you needed money. Lots of it.

Fortunately, the recording climate has changed—and changed profoundly. Thanks to the amazing advances in technology we've all been experiencing in recent years, the machines so big that they required a room of their own have been replaced by little wonders that can sit comfortably on a tabletop and still do many of the same things. This has been true of computers, and it's been true of recording equipment as well. Today you can experience the ecstasy, the agony, and the fleeting glory inherent in the creation of professional-quality recording *in your own home* with your own high-quality equipment—and all without having to move into a bigger apartment or adding a wing onto your house.

What is more, you can do it on the cheap. For the price of a few weeks of serious recording time, you can outfit yourself with all the rig you need to get that incredible recording studio sound. Take it one step further, and you can do it all yourself: you may never again have to bring in another musician.

The question is knowing what you want to do and what you need in order to do it. People have a variety of reasons for wanting to record their music at home. To some, their music is a personal expression that they want to arrange for a group of instruments; they may just want a permanent record of their composition. To others, perhaps members of a band, the home multitrack is a tool for working out the arrangement to their songs. It allows them the space to hear the music clearly without playing it; it lets them hear how well they're doing. Professional songwriters, as another example, need multitrack recording to make their demonstration tapes—*demos,* in the jargon—that are sent to their music publisher. Still others may actually want to produce and distribute their own recordings on a commercial basis.

Regardless of your particular reasons for choosing home recording, it allows you to experience your music in a way that is quite different from simply playing it over and over again. Rather than wishing you could have harmonies backing the main vocal in the chorus, you can now actually hear them in action. And where you always used to imagine that this was the spot in the song where the fiery guitar came in, home multitrack allows you to realize just that—bringing in the fiery guitar, playing the notes you want because *you're* the one playing it.

As you become better acquainted with the multitracking process, you will also develop a new awareness of sound. Witness the change in the Beatles' music in the short time between 1963, when they were recording essentially live, and 1966, when John Lennon started working with backward tapes—all done on machines incapable of achieving many of the techniques available on homebound technology today.

But the question will come up time and time again: What do you want to do with your material? At some point, you are going to experience frustration unless your goals are consistent with your means and equipment.

The hobbyist who wants a permanent record of his music will be perfectly content with a basic cassette-based portable studio, as long as the tapes he makes sound good to him. The professional songwriter, on the other hand, is sending his tapes to people who spend their lives listening to demos. Their ears are "tuned" to the quality of the recording and the techniques used. While, in the ideal world, the song is the most important thing, the fact remains that "the medium is the message." *How* you say things can be as important as *what* you say. If the professional songwriter is using the same bare-bones system as the hobbyist, he won't go very far in impressing people who have very high standards.

What about those who want to make and distribute their own recordings? The proliferation of great recording equipment at low prices has instigated a decline in the "mega-studio" recording business. While Michael Jackson will spend a great deal of time in a big-name studio, there has been a lot of activity at the "project studio" level. Many performing artists and songwriters are now equipped to produce multitrack tapes good enough to distribute commercially.

Finally, many performers and songwriters may opt to record some of the basic tracks in their home studios and later have these tracks "bumped up" to more sophisticated machines at a big studio. By working arrangements out at home, you can avoid costly experimentation in the studio—and when the meter is going at $300 per hour at one of these places, you begin to understand why Jack Benny had such a hard time answering the robber:

"Hurry up! Your money or your life!"

"I'm thinking! I'm thinking!"

What I've been trying to illustrate with these examples is the fact that there are all kinds of issues involved in home recording. You will be happiest if your level of equipment, your level of knowledge, and the level of professionalism you want to have in your finished product are all consistent with one another. The latest multi-effects digital processor will not make your recordings sound better if you don't know how to record effects properly. Using a very expensive microphone to record your operatic vocals on a cheap cassette machine that has not had its heads cleaned or degaussed for months will be a complete waste of a terrific microphone. And just as it's a waste of time to use a state-of-the-art digital multitrack and mastering facility to record a simple song demo, it's foolish to record a demo for the president of Capitol Records on mediocre equipment with poor production.

Basic? Yes. But sometimes, it's important to remember the obvious. A chain is only as strong as its weakest link. This applies to an audio chain, too. Your recordings can only be as good as the worst piece of gear in your system.

You are also an important link in this chain. Unless you know how to wring every last bit, or dB, of performance from your equipment, you won't be getting the best of either your machinery or your work. Knowledge, experience, and persistence can accomplish great things with simple tools. Just as David put Goliath down for the count with a pebble and a piece of leather, Bruce Springsteen and his associates recorded the basic tracks for the *Nebraska* album on a cassette portable studio.

The assumption here is that you're ready to present your work to people, peers, and powerbrokers. You're tired of the commercial studio money pit and are ready to invest in high-quality home recording gear so you can take full creative control of your sound. You may not be active in the professional music arena—you may not even plan to be—but either way, the information in this book will steer you on the path to a sensible home studio setup and show you how to make the best use of it.

In what follows, I will always attempt to present the various options available to you—not just in terms of equipment, but also in terms of techniques. I will make suggestions based on my experiences in the recording field and the experiences of the very fine professionals whom I have worked with through the years.

Every profession has a vocabulary that protects it from the prying ears of "outsiders." The recording industry certainly has its share of unusual words and phrases that identify the people that use them as "in" or "out." You will pick up a lot of these buzz words by reading this book. My intention is to demystify these terms so that we can understand them in common language. The terms in this book will, wherever possible, be tied to production techniques rather than to idiosyncratic terms developed by individual manufacturers. On those occasions when you need to know specific manufacturer labels to accomplish a particular task, I will tell you the names given that function by the major manufacturers.

Wherever possible, I will also give you a basis for understanding the "hows" and "whys" of the machines under discussion. Any technophiles should be advised that many of the perverse bends and sophistications of technologies and techniques presented in this book have been left out, but they have not been forgotten entirely. I just want to get to the "doing" as fast and as simply as possible.

In my years at TASCAM, we used to say that "recording is an art as well as a science." We intended this to be a warning as well as a reminder that art is in the mind of the beholder. Your postmodern interpretations of tribal war chants or "Tug Boats at Dawn" may certainly be worth recording, but they quite possibly might not inspire rave reviews. I can't guarantee that others will love or understand your muse's message.

I can assure you, however, that what I will try to do is take the romance and mystery away from the equipment and techniques so that you can put it back where it belongs—in your music. When you are done reading and practicing the techniques presented in this book, you will be able to record your music well. You will know the tools and understand the basics of the technologies relevant to recording. And, I personally hope, you will come away from this with an attitude that will allow you to approach new technologies boldly and ask:

"That's great, but what can it do for me?"

PART ONE

RECORDING STUDIO COMPONENTS

In the next seven chapters, we are going to look at the basic hardware you will need to assemble your home studio. As you read through this section, keep asking yourself the basic question, "What do I want to do with my recording?" Because the kind of equipment you have should be consistent with what you want to do.

Don't be afraid to shoot low at the beginning. Say you just want to put your material down on tape, taking advantage of multitrack technology to add some harmonies or another instrument so the piece just sounds different from the way it usually does when you're playing it by yourself. That's fine: You can always change your mind and upgrade your equipment from time to time.

And there's a good aspect to starting with the most basic of basics: Simple machines, because of their limitations, have a way of driving you toward creativity and innovation to capture the best collection of sounds possible, whether it's getting a gigantic sound out of your acoustic guitar or trying to make room for one more track when your tape is already full. Home recording is a study in economy in more ways than just dollars and cents. By learning how to deal with these fundamental issues, when you upgrade, you'll be adding more than just tracks or outboards. You'll have the added advantage of a lot of hard-earned knowledge.

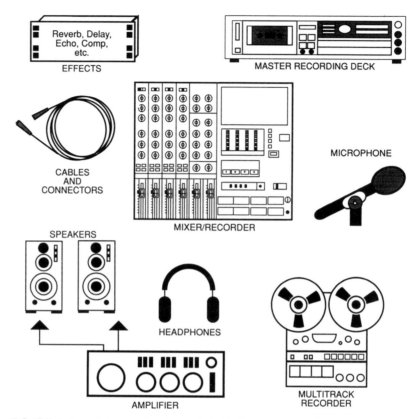

FIGURE 1-1.   An array of multitrack recording components.

When considering the options for your own studio, you should think about five different but equally important elements: the recorders (a multitrack and mixdown); a mixer; sources (that is, the microphones and instruments); a monitor system, made up of speakers, headphones, and amplification; signal processors; and the cables and doodads that tie them all together (Figure 1-1). This section will outline the way these various parts of the recording system work together.

Depending on your individual preferences, your studio budget may be weighted more heavily toward particular items. No matter what your priorities are, however, you will need all of the basic elements to have a working system.

CHAPTER 1

Recorders

Alexander Graham Bell was responsible for inventing the telephone; Thomas Edison was the first to record sound when he invented the cylinder recorder. The first words uttered over the telephone are probably unprintable, since Bell had just spilled some chemicals on his suit and was none too pleased about it. The first recorded sound, however, was Edison reciting "Mary Had a Lamb."

A LITTLE BACKGROUND

In the end, musicians probably owe more to Bell than to Edison, primarily because what Edison recorded were actually sound vibrations captured in a hearing trumpet and etched with a needle onto a wax cylindrical surface, while Bell was busy turning sound into *signal*—sound transformed through a microphone into electrical impulses that passed along a set of wires to a receiver where the impulses were transformed back to sound.

More than a century has passed since then, and while technology has brought us refinements that probably would have astounded both gentlemen, the essential principle of transforming sound into signal and back again remains the same.

While the history of recording followed a tortuous path from cylinders to disks and even, briefly, to wire before arriving at tape and, most recently, digital recording, the impetus for the development of the multitrack recorder came from people like you searching for a better way to record their music. The forefathers of the multitrack were the unlikely trio of Les Paul, Bing Crosby, and, very indirectly, Adolph Hitler.

The very first tape recorders were developed by German scientists for military work before and during the Second World War. One of these machines, the Magnetophon (Figure 1-2), was captured by the Allies in 1943 and later brought to the United States.

The Magnetophon offered many advantages over previous methods of recording. In 1943, music was still being recorded directly to a phonographic disc. A player's mistake would ruin not only the take, but the disk as well. The Magnetophon, by contrast, had extremely high fidelity, great dynamic range, and the tape itself could be edited with a razor blade and some scotch tape.

After several years of development following the war, a magnetic tape recorder was demonstrated to Bing Crosby (Figure 1-3). Impressed by the machine's performance, Crosby immediately started recording using the new technology. Others quickly followed his example: if it was good enough for a big star like

FIGURE 1-2. A 1938 AEG Magnetophon (right), and the more recent Magnetophon M20 (left). Early tape recorders made it possible to change or fix recordings by editing and cutting. (Courtesy of AEG Corporation)

FIGURE 1-3. Bing Crosby with the prototype of the Ampex Model 600 (1950s). (Courtesy of Ampex)

Bing, then it must be all right. Soon, phonographic disk recording was a thing of the past.

Just as American engineers were learning how to come to grips with tape, an enterprising musician named Les Paul (Figure 1-4) was experimenting with the recording process. Recording one guitar part to disk, Paul would then play the recorded part back, while laying down another take on his guitar. The signals from the first disk and the live guitar would be mixed and sent to another phonographic disk machine where they were recorded together. It sounded like two guitars, but there was only one guitarist.

The process of recording from one recorder to another is called *dubbing*. What Les Paul invented was, and still is, called *overdubbing*—adding to the original take while dubbing to another recorder. But Les Paul wasn't finished revolutionizing recording when he invented overdubbing. Working with the Ampex Corporation, Paul was responsible for creating the first eight-track multitrack recorder. Christened the Octopus, Paul's recorder could put eight tracks on a reel of one-inch tape (Figure 1-5). But in essence, it was still the kind of overdubbing Paul had been doing with the phonographic disk machines; the only differ-

FIGURE 1-4.   Les Paul in the late 1940s. (Courtesy of Ampex)

ence was that he was using one machine where he previously had used two.

The problem revolved around the way in which the record and playback *heads* were set up in the tape recorder. As originally designed, the tape first comes into contact with the record head—that is, the head that imprints the signal onto the magnetic tape. Only after it has passed the record head does the imprinted tape come into contact with the playback head, the head that "reads" the imprinted tape and reproduces the signal imbedded in it.

This separation of the two heads allows the engineer to monitor the quality of a recording even as it is being made. The problem it presented overdubbing enthusiasts was the slight lag time between the point of recording and the moment of playback. Depending on the speed with which the tape was moving, there was always going to be a delay between the material played back on one track and that recorded on another. Moreover, overdubbing in this fashion created a double problem involving the dissolution of the original recorded signal and development of *hiss,* the accumulation of sound emanating from the tape itself.

FIGURE 1-5. Ampex MM-1000 (1967), a commercial version of the "Octopus." (Courtesy of Ampex)

The solution was deceptively simple—creating a new type of head, one that could both record and play back (Figure 1-6). Because the individual recording the new material was performing with what was on the same location on the tape, the two parts would sound simultaneously in playback. And not only did the new recording not have the annoying delay between the different parts, it did not increase the generation of accumulated tape noise or lead to the dissolution of the original track.

Thus was born the original multitrack recorder, capable of compiling up to four independent tracks recorded at different times but played back as if they were all done simultaneously.

Although brilliant work was done by engineers on four-track machines (most notably George Martin and Geoff Emerick's work with the Beatles, especially on the *Sgt Pepper* album), eight-track, one-inch recorders became the studio standard for

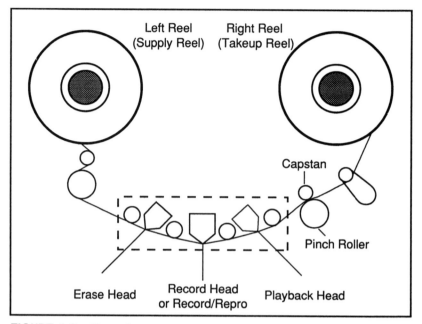

FIGURE 1-6. Recorders use separate heads for the record and playback functions. A multitrack recorder must have a head that records and plays back simultaneously.

the late 1960s. Soon there were two-inch 16-track recorders; then two-inch 24-track recorders.

By the mid-seventies, recording had become a multitrack, megabuck mess. Million-dollar albums became commonplace, and the little guy was being squeezed out by technology. To be competitive, you needed lots of tracks, and channels, and processors, and bucks.

Several companies recognized a market when they saw one and began to develop multitrack for the masses. The open-reel, quarter-inch, four-track recorders were born. These were followed by the cassette-based four-, six-, and eight-track machines. These machines didn't perform to the level of the 24-track studios of the time, but they brought a level of performance to the home studio that would have been sufficient to record a top-selling album only a few short years before.

The level of performance of the proletarian multitrack has continued to soar while the price has dropped. A tremendous array of formats and performance levels are now available for the home. Digital formats on tape and hard disk have brought even

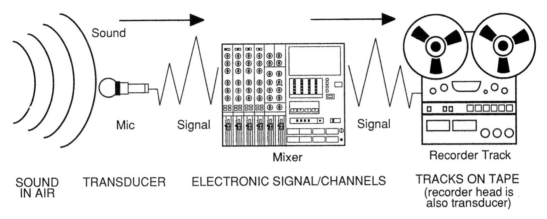

Sound

Mic Signal Signal

Mixer Recorder Track

SOUND IN AIR TRANSDUCER ELECTRONIC SIGNAL/CHANNELS TRACKS ON TAPE (recorder head is also transducer)

FIGURE 1-7. A microphone changes acoustic energy into an electronic signal. The path of an electronic signal through the mixer and other processors is called a *channel*. A recorder head converts the energy in a channel to magnetic energy that can be imprinted on a *track* of the recording tape.

more performance into the hands and homes of creative musicians. It is now possible to outfit a studio capable of CD-quality recording on a budget that, not long ago, would not have bought a week of recording time in a professional studio.

Before we look at these different formats, let's examine a few more basic terms. You'll notice that the chapter title "Recorders" is plural; you are going to need at least two of them for your system. You will use a multitrack recorder to put your music together, laying down *tracks* in much the same way an artist paints a picture by adding the colors and forms together until achieving a completed work.

Unlike the painter, the recording artist must then take his or her *multitrack master* (the tape containing the final tracks of the recording) and mix it down to a two-channel *stereo master* (the finished product).

When people talk about the recording process, they often get tracks and channels confused. The problem is that recorders use both channels and tracks, so there's a certain logic to the mistake. As I use the term here, *channel* can refer to one of two things: channel is an electronic signal, regardless of whether it's passing through your mixer, processors, or any of the other electronics in your system. Channel can also mean the designated path that the signal follows as it goes from the source—you might plug a microphone, for example, into Channel 1.

Track, on the other hand, quite simply refers to the physical place upon which the signal is recorded or stored, whether it's on tape (Figure 1-7) or the vinyl of a record. Even in the digital world these designations still hold. Tracks are still tracks on hard disks and digital tape. Channels are still channels in digital processors and digital mixers.

So, though you may hear of a "24-track mixer," this is either a misnomer referring to a board that carries 24 channels, or else it is a mixer that goes with a 24-track recorder.

THE MULTITRACK RECORDER

Okay. Now you know the track is the portion of the tape upon which the signal is imprinted—not unlike the footprint you leave as you walk in soft sand. Although the term *multitrack* (meaning "many track") might describe any machine capable of recording and playing back more than one track at a time (for example, a stereo recorder plays one track for the left side and another track for the right), it generally refers to machines that do so on four or more tracks *in a single direction*.

Why do you need multiple tracks? So that you can do two things that separate recording from live performance:

1. You can record yourself singing and playing guitar, and then at a later time, you can record yourself playing another instrument, say a piano, for the same song. When you finally play it all back, the guitar, vocal, and piano parts will sound as if they were recorded at the same time.

2. You can return to your recording and fix small parts or record whole new parts. After you have recorded the piano with the guitar, for example, you may decide the guitar part is too busy. Or you may find that you made a mistake. You may simply record the part again, or fix a small section of it by using the *sync* or *punch-in* capabilities of the multitrack recorder.

Standard Cassette versus Multitrack

The cassette machine in your home stereo system or car is a four-track, two-channel deck. Whether it records or only plays back sound, this machine does so using four-track tape just as a four-track multitrack recorder does. But the fact that the cassette player is a two-channel means it only uses two tracks of the tape at a time—two tracks in each direction. Side A of the tape contains two tracks, which are played back through the machine's

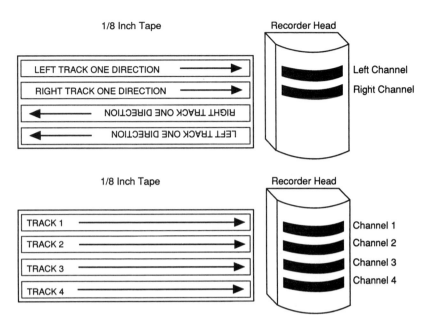

FIGURE 1-8. A standard cassette machine records and plays back using two tracks at a time (two tracks in one direction, then two tracks in the other when the tape is flipped over). A multitrack machine uses four tracks at a time, all in one direction.

left and right channels. When the tape is turned over to Side B, it plays the other two tracks on the tape.

A multitrack, on the other hand, can record or play back all four tracks on tape simultaneously in a single direction. The heads of the multitrack read all the tracks, while those on the stereo machine read only two tracks at a time (Figure 1-8).

Multitrack Heads

As we saw in our capsule history, the heads of a multitrack are special in that they can both record and play back. This means that you will be able to record a track today while listening to something you played yesterday, so that, on playback, both tracks will sound as if they were recorded at the same time. This differs from recorders that have separate record and *repro* (playback) heads, like your cassette machine.

Multitrack technology goes by various trademarked aliases, but these usually share the abbreviation for synchronize: *sync*. Regardless of the name and regardless of the brand, however, the essential format is the same—a single head that is able to record on some tracks while playing back on others at the same time. Digital multitrack heads operate this same way on the surface (as far as the user can see, even though their technology operates in a different way from analog tape recorders).

MULTITRACK FORMATS

There are four basic multitrack formats: open-reel, cassette, digital tape, and hard disk systems (computer-based systems usually use hard disk storage). Tape is simply a medium of storage for your audio signals. Magnetic tape, including digital tape and floppy disks, uses magnetic particles to store your music. The heads impregnate the tape in the recording process with patterns that the same type heads can later return to and read back as your music. You put your music on tape and it stays there, undisturbed, until you are ready to use it again. Although the physics are different, the function remains the same with digital formats—you put your music into the storage system until you need to come back and use it later.

The Open-Reel Format

In appearance, open-reel tape has not changed too much since the days of the Magnetophon, though tape formulas and the mechanical tape handling of recorder transports have improved dramatically. Reel tapes are comparatively expensive and unwieldy. You have to thread the tape onto the machine and the tape can break if you are not careful. And the machines themselves are *big*. As you will see, though, they do have their advantages.

The Cassette Format

What we commonly know as the cassette is a tape format developed and marketed by the Phillips Corporation. The Phillips cassette won a hard-fought victory over many manufacturers who were trying to develop the tape system that would replace the open reel on the consumer audio market. The makers were responding to the public's demand for a tape type that was easy to use (didn't require threading) and was inexpensive. Developed initially as a tape for dictation purposes, the cassette filled the bill nicely.

Technical Drawbacks   Perhaps "nicely" is a bit of an over-statement. As a dictation device, the cassette was a low-fidelity instrument not too well suited to the demands of high-fidelity music recording. The tape was narrow and moved slowly across the tape heads. The mechanism of the cassette itself didn't guide the tape accurately enough to the heads, and it was noisy to boot. So how could it win a popularity contest against better-performing contestants? It was cheaper and easier. Convenience and cost won the day.

Eventually, companies became committed to improving the audio quality of the cassette format. They developed better tape formulas capable of delivering a broader spectrum of musical sound. They made the cassettes themselves more accurate and quiet deliverers of tape. And finally, they developed noise-reduction technologies to mitigate that most annoying aspect of the cassette.

Cassette multitrack was still a few years away. The performance disparity between open-reel machines and the cassette was still too broad and too much of a crucial factor to dedicated musicians and enthusiasts.

One of the solutions to the problem of cassette sound quality was to increase the tape speed. When the cassette multitrack was developed, its tape ran past the heads at twice the speed of the ordinary cassette, $3\,^3/_4$ inches-per-seconds (ips). The early models also demanded that the highest quality tape be used to ensure acceptable performance.

Just as the artist can put more paint on a bigger canvas, a machine running at higher speeds gives the recorder a larger section of tape on which to imprint any given sound. The more tape allotted to a particular sound, the greater the aural fidelity. In simple terms, if a single sound event were to last one second, a consumer audio cassette would imprint the track for $1\,^7/_8$ inches, while a high-speed cassette multitrack would imprint tape for $3\,^3/_4$ inches with the same sound.

Open-reel multitracks do much the same thing, only they do it on a much grander scale. Since the open-reel tape is generally twice as wide as cassette tape, it has twice the space to devote to each signal. Moreover, while the high-speed cassette multitrack rips along at $3\,^3/_4$ inches per second, the open reel can hit velocities of $7\,^1/_2$, 15, or even 30 ips. And because audio signals imprinted on tape achieve a measure of physical existence, this means that signals on open reel get a lot more room to breathe. It's easy to see why open-reel, high-speed recorders remain the machine of choice for many audio purists. This remains true even in the face of the growing popularity of digital multitrack machines.

Cassette Multitracks

Still, in terms of sheer popularity, ease of use, and the unstinting support of record companies who release pre-recorded cassettes by major artists, the cassette is the medium of choice. In an effort to combine the convenience of the cassette with the fidelity of larger and faster format tape, several manufacturers have put a great deal of effort into developing the cassette as a suitable multitrack medium.

Through innovative head, transport, and noise-reduction technology, manufacturers are at last wringing every last bit of performance from the cassette format. Today, even the harshest critics of the format admit astonishment at the level of performance attained by four- and even eight-track cassette multitracks.

Digital Multitracks

Digital recorders store the sound sent their way in the form of binary data, in much the same way a computer stores your letters or financial files on its disk drives. Once esoteric and incredibly expensive, digital multitracks have evolved into affordable machines about the size of a video cassette recorder. In fact, two of the most popular digital multitracks use tape transports originally designed for consumer video recorders. Alesis, Fostex, Panasonic, and others use the VHS video transport. TASCAM and Sony, among others, use an 8-millimeter video transport in their digital multitracks.

Large "hard" disk drives such as those used in computers are also used instead of tape in digital multitracks. Akai, Vestax, Emu, Roland, Fostex, and other companies currently make hard-disk-based multitracks. The personal computer itself has also been utilized as a platform for digital multitrack recording through add-on hardware and software from a variety of companies.

THE MIXDOWN RECORDER

Why do you need this second recorder? The basic idea is that even though you'll be doing your recording work on a multitrack machine, you'll ultimately have to prepare a simplified, stereo product for distribution. You wouldn't want to give away your only multitrack master, now would you?

So you need a second machine to make a stereo master—if only to make copies to give to your significant other. Joe Consumer, the music fan, uses a stereo deck, as does the record company A&R exec who listens to demos in his office. If you intend to send tapes of your music to a record company or your Aunt Sarah, you will probably do so on the standard stereo cassette.

Most cassette and open-reel stereo recorders are "quarter-track" machines. Apart from serving as a mixdown deck, a high-quality cassette deck—or an additional two-track open-reel machine—can also be used to help complete your multitrack tape. It can be used for "bouncing" tracks, as a tape echo, flanger, or a variety of other processing uses in addition to that of mix-down deck. At the time of this writing, digital audio tape (DAT) machines, also sometimes called R-DAT (Rotary-head Digital Audio Tape) machines are finding a broader place as mixdown decks in home studios. They are also showing up in those same A&R offices; in the near future, DAT machines may totally replace the venerable cassette as the preferred medium in the music industry. In later chapters, we will explore some of this digital technology. We will also take a look at how you might prepare yourself and your studio to implement the technology in your home studio.

CHAPTER 2

Mixers and Recorder/Mixers

Now that I've convinced you of the need for not one, but *two* recording machines, you might as well face the fact that you will probably also have to get a mixer or two. Yes, yes, I know you have been perfectly happy plugging a pair of mics straight into your cassette machine and capturing the true essence of your soul on tape.

But that was back in the bad old days, before you had to start thinking of all the logistics of dealing with four individual tracks.

In a recording system, the mixer is the audio command center. It receives incoming signals, processes them for level and tone, sends them to various external processors, receives the returning signals from the processors, and routes all the inputs and returns to their final destinations via the output *busses*. Most mixers designed specifically for recording also provide various ways to listen to your recording. These functions—*mixes*—are called *monitor, cue,* and *solo.*

You can see in Figure 2-1 that a mixer is a very busy place. The word *mixer* comes from the most elementary function that the machine accomplishes—that is, taking two or more signals (i.e., voices, instruments, or any sound input) and combining them in proper proportion to create a single and, hopefully, pleasing sound.

Indeed, the mixer enables you to combine sound elements together just as a cook mixes ingredients to make a dish. And just as the taste of a meal depends on the cook's ability to mix the proper amounts of spices and ingredients, the sound-taste of the audio meal will depend upon the skill of the person doing the mixing of

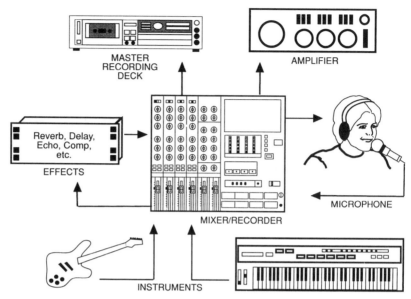

FIGURE 2-1. The mixer is the command center that controls the routing of audio signals to and from numerous components.

the signals. So the most important and elementary function of the mixer is to control how much of any given signal goes into the mix.

The best way to think of the mixer is actually as a system of submixers combining the *main mixer,* the *monitor submixer,* and the *effects* or *auxiliary (aux) submixer.* The function of each is described in greater detail below.

THE MAIN MIXER

In the early days of mixers, there was really only one destination for the sound signals. They went from the instruments/microphones to the phonographic recorder. This basic function is the *main mix.*

As multitrack techniques were developed, the role played by the mixer in the recording process became increasingly complex. Where the mixer once coordinated live signals from source, with overdubbing, it now is required to coordinate prerecorded tracks with the live signal.

And we saw in our discussion of the need for a mixdown recorder, the main mixer enables you to blend the individual sounds

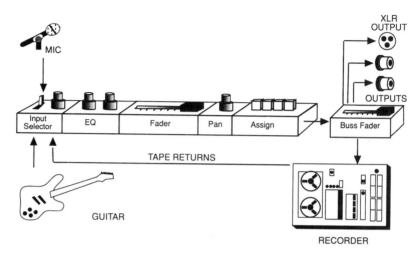

FIGURE 2-2. The main mixer receives signals from microphones, instruments, or tape recorders. The signal is processed for level and tone and then assigned to busses, which can then go to outputs or the tape recorder.

of pre-recorded tracks through the manipulation of their volume (*gain*), tone and timbre (*equalizing*), and their relative location in the stereo field between left and right (*panning*) (Figure 2-2).

THE MONITOR SUBMIXER

The mixer must also enable the performer to hear the previous track so that he may play his new part with it. Similarly, the engineer (the person running the mixer) must hear both parts to be sure that they will both be printed to the tape properly. The overdubbing process demands that mixers include a submixer section to the main mixer called the *monitor mixer*.

The word *monitor* means to hear or oversee, and that's precisely what the monitor submixer does as a subsystem in our larger mixer. Figure 2-3 shows the path of a signal through the monitor mixer into the speaker and headphones.

THE EFFECTS OR AUXILIARY SUBMIXER

In the '60s, recording artists began to work a great deal with sound effects. Taking a hint from John Cage and other electronic music

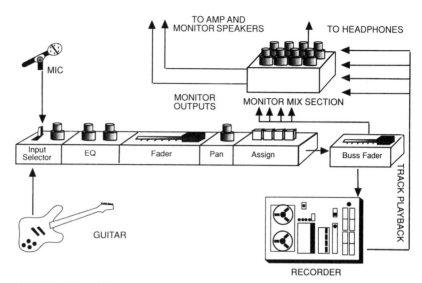

FIGURE 2-3. The monitor mixer enables the user to listen to channels and/or track playback.

pioneers, engineers started manipulating tape and signals in many exciting ways—anything from playing tape backwards to cutting tape into strips and splicing it together in no particular order or creating *slapback echo* (internal echo made with the recorder itself). Pushed on by creative artists and a consuming public looking for more far-out musical sounds, the use of effects in recording became standard practice.

For our purposes, an effect is anything that processes the signal or tape in such a way as to change the sound. We generally think of effects as devices with labels such as *flanger, reverb, chorus, delay, phase shifter,* or *distortion.* We will deal with effects in greater detail later.

Vis-à-vis the mixer, the predominance of effects called for the development of yet another submixer system geared toward coordinating the traffic between the source, the processors, and the tape. The result, logically enough, is called *effects* or *auxiliary submixers* (Figure 2-4).

Using effects extensively means that the engineer has to send taped or live signals through the mixer out to these external processors—the effects. The effects will do their magic to the signal and send it to their own outputs. The signal from the effect must then be routed back into the main mixer where it is combined with the other signals. The use of effects is so pervasive that many mixers now have eight, ten, or even more aux systems.

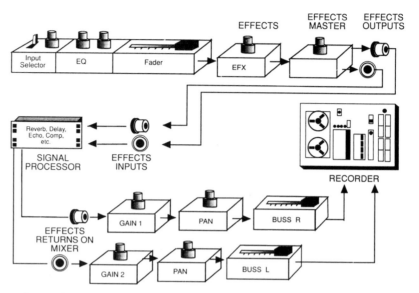

FIGURE 2-4. The effects and aux mixers are used for a variety of tasks such as adding signal processing and setting up cue mixes for talent. Effects outputs are brought back to the mixer via aux/effects returns.

No matter how large or seemingly complicated a mixer is, it will always be a combination of these three submixer systems: the main mixer, the monitor mixer, and the aux mixers. Each of these submixers have the same basic parts: inputs, channels with processors, and busses that lead to outputs.

INPUTS

An input is more than just a connector that receives the cable from your instrument or microphone. A truly effective mixer must be able to accept a wide variety of levels and impedances. It must be switchable to accept the inputs from your recorders. And it should process the incoming signals without discoloring or distorting them.

The types, impedances, and levels of the signals coming from your instruments and microphones vary greatly (Figure 2-5). Every electrical signal that comes into your mixer will have three basic attributes: *level, impedance,* and *balanced* or *unbalanced wiring.*

We know that every signal has some kind of *level* or strength: some are strong or "hot," while others are low or weak.

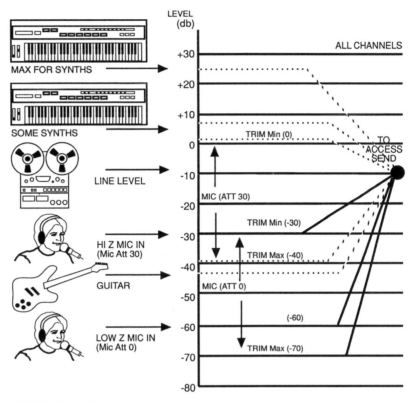

FIGURE 2-5. Input sources for the mixer vary greatly in level and impedance. The various lines that converge on -10 dB show how each signal is attenuated or amplified to create a level consistent with the needs of the mixer.

Similarly, every signal must obey the laws of physics and encounter some kind of *resistance* or *impedance*. For the moment, all we need to know about impedance is that it exists, and that impedances of inputs and outputs should match.

A *balanced signal* requires three wires, so the connector for a balanced signal is three-pronged. Unbalanced signals, on the other hand, use two wires, so the connectors have two points instead of three. For example, most recording microphones send a low-impedance, balanced signal that has a relatively low level. The cable for this mic has a male three-pronged connector (sometimes called a *cannon*). Your mixer should have the corresponding female balanced three-prong connector at its input. The signals coming from microphones must be bumped up to the level of the signals that will be used inside the mixer, so your input stage must have some amplifier (*gain stage*) circuitry to do this.

But microphones are not the only input sources you'll be using with your mixer. Most musical instruments use quarter-inch phone connectors that offer connections for wires at the tip and the sleeve. They send signals that are high-impedance with signal levels that can vary tremendously from instrument to instrument—and sometimes within the same instrument as well, as is the case when you're using a quiet string voice on a synthesizer. A piezo pickup in an acoustic guitar, for example, sends a signal that is not much higher than a low-impedance microphone, but the pickup uses a quarter-inch connector. A synthesizer, sampler, or drum machine, on the other hand, may use the same connector, but they will send much higher levels of signal to your mixer.

The quarter-inch inputs on your mixer must be able to deal with all these signals, from extremely hot to extremely low, with equal efficiency, while the amplifier circuits must have the headroom necessary for these signal extremes. A *pad* that helps dampen the level of the hotter signals is a very useful feature of many mixers. Located at the input stage of a mixer, this pad allows manufacturers to use amplifier circuits that are more sensitive to the lower level signals.

In addition to your instruments and microphones, your mixer must accept signals from your recorders and other "line-level" sources. (The general levels in decibels (dB) of the sources is shown in Figure 2-5 on page 21.) Although it sounds like a standardized level, line-level varies from −10 dBV to +4 dBm.* When home stereos and recorders became popular, the manufacturers chose a low signal level as the standard. This was primarily for economic reasons; it is more expensive to make the circuits that send, receive, and support higher signal levels. Technology had advanced to the point that the audio quality could be maintained fairly well with a lower signal level, so −10 dBV was selected as the standard. (The "+" and "−" are related to "0" dB.)

Although this was supposed to be the standard, it just didn't work out that way. So you will now see all three line levels (−10 dB, 0 dB, and +4 dB) as you shop for components for your studio.

In addition to the different line levels, manufacturers use different connectors for the various levels. −10 dBV signals use RCA connectors exactly like those on your home stereo and video products. Professional broadcast audio products use +4 dBm levels with balanced three-pin connectors like those on your low-impedance microphones. Many recorders offer not only both types of connectors and levels, but quarter-inch jacks as well. 0 dB signals are

---

*The "dB" is more complicated to describe than this section warrants. For the moment, just think of the "dee-bee" as a way to measure signal levels.

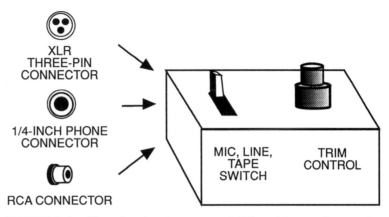

FIGURE 2-6. The mixer input can accept different types of connectors. It has a selector switch that allows only one source to proceed down the channel strip. The trim control and an amplifier circuit process the signal for level before it proceeds.

often found with quarter-inch connectors like the ones on your guitar cables or high-impedance mic cables.

To mix down your multitrack tapes or use a recorder as a source while building tracks, your mixer needs convenient connections for line-level sources (Figure 2-6). Ideally, you shouldn't have to disconnect/reconnect cables every time you want to use a recorder signal.

An ideal mixer for our recording purposes should have RCA connectors and either a separate monitor section to accept and reroute the signals or tape inputs in the channels next to the mic and instrument inputs. If the tape inputs are located at the channel input stage, the mixer should have a switch to activate whichever input you want to use—high-impedance, low-impedance, or line level.

You can see that the input stage of a mixer has to deal with a wide variety of characters: soft-speaking microphones, loud and aggressive drum machines, moderate-speaking recorders. The input stage must be able to select the character and then respond to its individual traits appropriately.

At the end of the input stage, the signal that proceeds down the mixer channel strip must be conditioned to the internal line-level that the mixer itself uses throughout its electronics.

THE CHANNEL STRIP

By simple definition, the word *channel* means a groove or path of conveyance. The channel in our mixer is the path the audio signal

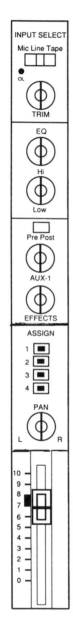

FIGURE 2-7.
A typical mixer "channel strip."

follows after it has been selected and amplified or attenuated (reduced/padded/trimmed) by the input stage. As the signal flows along the channel strip, we can manipulate it in several ways: by changing its volume with the fader, by changing its tone and timbre with an equalizer; by routing the signal through one of the aux submixers for processing; by placing the signal within the stereo landscape (*panning*), and by monitoring and measuring the strength of the signal (VU meters and LED read-outs).

The channel strip lets you check out an individual signal before it is combined (*summed*) with other signals in the mixer busses. The normal components in most mixer channels are: the equalizer, some kind of meter or LED to indicate overload or signal level, an insert point, a series of entry points to the aux, monitor, or effects submixers, the channel fader, a pan control, and the channel assignment switches (Figure 2-7).

The Equalizer

Though an equalizer is a signal processor, it is so commonly used in the recording process that it has become an integral part of most mixer channel strips. The equalizer emphasizes or reduces specific portions of a signal known as "bands" or frequency bands. When you *equalize* a signal, then (some people call it "EQ-ing"), you are manipulating its tone and timbre. Any emphasis of a frequency band is done by means of an amplifier circuit; reduction is achieved through an attentuating circuit.

The frequency bands are described in terms of their relative "highness" or "lowness." The notes made by a bass or a tuba are low, while those of a piccolo or a mandolin are high. The notes of the tuba are more affected by adjustments made to the low frequency equalizer control, while the piccolo is more affected by the high frequency control.

But though an equalizer is a pitch-related device, it doesn't change the actual pitches of notes. An equalizer makes notes that fall into its control area louder or softer, and by doing so it changes the relative brightness or bassiness of the signal. The term *Hertz* means a single vibration per second. The lowest note produced by a string bass vibrates at a rate of approximately 35 times per second. So a low bass note E would be called 35 Hertz (Hz) by cold-hearted scientists. The highest note of a piccolo vibrates at approximately 4,200 times per second or 4.2 kHz (1,000 hertz is equal to 1 *kilohertz,* or 1 kHz).

But well you might ask, "Gee, Mr. Science, if instruments only play notes between 35 Hz and roughly 5 kHz, why are there equalizer controls for ranges 10 kHz and above?"

The answer has to do with *harmonics,* also called *overtones.* A note played on an instrument is made up of not just one vibration frequency, but many. These are generated around the basic pitch that you play. It is the harmonics that determine the unique "voice" or character of an individual sound and distinguish the pitch A (440 Hz on your tuning dial) on the piano and on the violin.

From a recording standpoint, then, there are many vital musical frequencies above the 4.2 kHz limit of our piccolo. Frequencies four or five times the piccolo's limit are still useful for adding brightness, brilliance, or life to our music. The healthy human ear, before age or heavy metal music set in, is capable of perceiving frequencies as high as 20 kHz.

An equalizer is not unlike the color, tint, and brightness controls on a typical television. These controls don't change the channels or the program, but they can add definition, clarity, and excitement to the picture—or they can transform the nature of the picture entirely (ever seen green newscasters?). We'll discuss specific uses and techniques for equalizers in later chapters.

Overload Indicators and Meters

At some point in every channel strip there will be a meter or LED (*l*ight-*e*mitting *d*iode) overload indicator. An indicator or meter is usually placed after the EQ circuitry in the channel.*

Because they let you see the strength and characteristic fluctuations of the signal in the channel, think of these meters and indicators as your early warning system. They flash their warning when a runaway transient or other high-level signal threatens your mix. A *transient* is a burst of sound/signal that often comes with the instrumental *attack*—the moment a drum is struck, a guitar strummed, or when a vocalist hits a word with a hard consonant ("p" is particularly potent in this panorama).

What's better to have—a meter or an LED? A combination of the two is ideal: a meter with a peak-indicating LED. LEDs are set to flash whenever the signal crosses a certain level. They are quick to respond and the flashing light draws attention. But LEDs don't give you any measurement of what the signal in the channel is doing the rest of the time. Meters give you constant feedback on what the signal is doing. The needle of the meter bounces along, showing you an average picture of what's happening. But meters are slow. Those

---

*When we say "after the EQ," we mean following it in the signal flow sequence. The LED or meter may be located at the very top of the channel strip on the mixer top panel, but it is wired into the strip at a point somewhere between the input selector and the buss assignment switches.

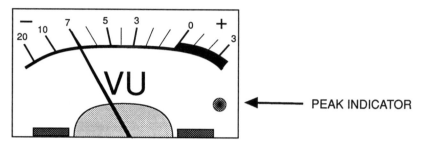

FIGURE 2-8.   A VU meter with a peak-indicating LED.

needles just can't bounce fast enough to catch and show those speeding-bullet transients that may be passing through your channel. Meters with peak LEDs are perfect (Figure 2-8).

Insert and Direct Out

Insert is a double-swinging electronic door that allows you to send a signal from a specific channel to a signal processor—for example, a guitar part that you want to spice up with some digital delay—and then readmit the signal back from the processor into the channel. Using an insert point makes it possible to add effects such as reverb or flanging to a single channel without affecting the signal in other channels.

Similar features are often labeled *access* and *direct out* by various manufacturers. Access works the same way insert does, but it uses two connectors instead of one. Its doors only swing one way, so there is a connector for *access out* and one for *access in*. Access has separate entrance and exit doors. *Direct out* is similar to the access out function, only it allows you to use some of the signal in the channel for uses outside the mixer, while the same signal also progresses along in the channel. Direct outs can be used for signal processing or to create special monitor mixes.

Aux and Effects

These controls, shown as dials in Figure 2-7, are the input level controls for the aux and effects submixer systems. The signal in your channel can be duplicated, amplified, and sent to one of the submixer systems we talked about earlier.

The primary purposes of aux and effects submixers are for the controlled use of signal processing on multiple channels simultaneously, or to provide special *cue* or *monitor* mixes for the performer during recording.

For example, a special cue mix might be needed for a vocalist who wants to hear the piano part prominently without having to listen to the distracting drums. As engineer, however, you will need to hear the mix as it's going to tape in its entirety—both piano *and* drums. You can use the aux system to create a special cue mix for the vocalist while listening to the main mix yourself.

Just as insert gives you an output and a returning input to the channel strip, effects submixers come with output(s) and returning input(s). You may be sending four channels of your mix to a digital reverb using an effects or aux control in each channel. These *sends* from the individual channels are joined together and sent to outputs on the back panel of your mixer. Cables connect these mixer outputs to the inputs of your digital reverb. The reverb does its thing to the signals and sends its results to the outputs on its back panel. These outputs from the reverb must get back into the mixer in a usable way so that they may be combined with other signals in the mixer.

When the reverb signals come back into the mixer, they are routed to a set of *faders* (sliding level-control knobs) that allow you to match the level of the returning signals to those of other signals in the mixer. The reverb signals are then combined with other signals and sent to the *mixer busses* (see page 35), where they join the signals from the other mixer channels.

The Channel Fader

Each mixer channel has a control near the end of its electronic pathway that determines the final level of the signal before it is sent to the various busses of the mixer. Most often, this control is a sliding knob called a *fader*. (It is shown at the bottom of Figure 2-7.) Working in much the same way as the volume control on your stereo or television, the fader offers very precise control of the final level in the channel. Also, because faders for the channels are generally set up relatively close to each other, you can get a visual "sense" of the mix because you can see the level positions of the different channels in relation to the others—very helpful in a mixer with many channels.

Pan Control

No, this is *not* a thermostat for your stove, though it is often called the *pan pot.*

Pan is short for *panorama* and is a by-product of stereo and stereo imaging in audio. In the early days, there was a single sound

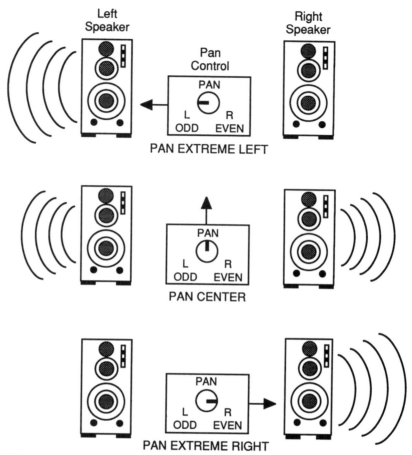

FIGURE 2-9. The pan control permits placement of a sound anywhere in the stereo panorama.

source and a single speaker cabinet in audio systems. This is now called *monophonic, mono,* or, more accurately, *monaural.* Mono merely refers to the single signal. And no matter how many instruments were playing, they all emitted from that one spot.

This is, of course, different from stereo, where we have sound coming not from one but two sources. Stereo was developed to reproduce sound more accurately as it happens in a live environment. For example, an orchestra or band emits sound from many sources. The sound waves from these sources bounce around rooms and concert halls in a myriad of ways. Stereo was designed to help the listener experience the ambience of the concert in his or her own home.

Which is exactly what happens with live stereo recordings. Though you can distinguish, say, the left side of the orchestra from the right, there is some blending between the two sides.

In the early days of stereo multitrack recording, however—right up to late 1967, in fact—the individual tracks appeared on either the left side or the right. Nothing occupied the middle ground. At the very best, it was an unnatural sound.

The *pan pot* was the solution, first experienced by listeners with the passing bus in "Magical Mystery Tour," because what it does is locate your channel signals in the panorama of sound. It does so by sending signals to the left (odd-numbered) busses and right (even-numbered) busses in a balance set and controlled by the pan knob. Rotate the knob fully left, counterclockwise, and the sound appears to be coming from the extreme left side of the mix. Place the pan in the middle, sending signal equally to both left and right busses, and you will sense the sound coming from center stage, and so on (Figure 2-9).

In order for panning to work properly, however, you must send the signal in your mixer channel—your guitar, for example—to at least one left-side buss and one right-side buss. If you have a mixer that has a *stereo buss* system, the odd-numbered program busses will be sent to the left-side buss and the even-numbered program busses will be sent to the right-side buss.

BUSSES

Like the Magical Mystery Tour bus, a *buss* is able to pick up many passenger channels and transport them along as a single unit down its electronic thoroughfare. Unlike the bus passenger, the signal from a channel may be duplicated and put on board several busses at the same time. The channel assignment switches located in the channel strip (see Figure 2-7, page 24) place that channel's signal on the appropriate busses.

This is the basic mixer function: taking the many channels and mixing them together in fewer busses. The busses that *sum* (combine) the signals from the channel strips are usually called *program busses*. They lead to *program outputs* on the back panel of your mixer. These outputs are connected to the inputs of your multitrack recorder. In an ideal mixer/recorder setup, you will have the same number of program busses in your mixer as your recorder has tracks.

Each multitrack recorder will have an input connector that corresponds to each track of tape. By hooking up program buss number one to recorder track number one input and so on, the channel assignment switches in your mixer channels will correspond directly to the tracks on the recorder.

The program busses are the natural ending points of the main mixer we discussed earlier. There is a fader for each buss to control the level of the composite signal before it is sent to the output. Program busses also receive the returning signals from the aux and effects subsystems. These returns are brought back into the mixer and then routed through a level control knob or fader before they are sent to the busses by a pan control and/or assignment switches. Effect returns are often routed to a separate stereo buss system.

The Stereo Buss

Many mixers have an additional program buss system labeled "stereo." This two-buss system has a left and right buss each with its own output and fader. A simple implementation of a stereo buss in a recording mixer routes all of the signals in the odd-numbered program busses to the left stereo buss and the even-numbered program busses to the right stereo buss. This routing left and right happens either at the pan control in the individual channels, or at the program buss itself.

In recording systems, a stereo buss is primarily used to listen to the recording in progress over a pair of speakers, or to mix down the multitrack master tape. As we mentioned before, signals that are returning from effects are often sent to the stereo buss system instead of to the program busses. The composite signals from a monitor subsystem often also end up in the stereo buss.

A mixer that has only a stereo buss, without a group of program busses, is a mixer designed for live sound reinforcement. An ideal recording mixer will have both program busses and stereo busses to make the recording of our multitrack master and the mixdown to two-track, stereo master possible without a lot of cable connecting and reconnecting.

THE PA MIXER VERSUS THE RECORDING MIXER

Many of you who are delving into home recording will probably have some background playing music for others. You may also have some equipment designed for live music performance, including a PA (public address) mixer, amplifier, and speakers. These pieces aren't completely useless in your new studio system, but you should take a hard look at them—they may be lacking in some important ways.

You should give the PA mixer a particularly hard look. One problem is that PA mixers tend to have a lot of input channels and few busses. The movement in live performance toward putting microphones on just about everything, along with the evolution of stereo keyboards, means that input channels are being eaten at a voracious pace. Yet it is common to see 16- or even 24-channel mixers with only a stereo buss. Most PA systems require only a stereo two-buss, or even a single buss for the "mains"—the speakers for the audience. Thus the configuration for PA always works out to very many combined into very few.

The limited number of busses available in a PA mixer makes multitracking difficult because even a four-track machine demands twice the bussing capability of a stereo mixer. Assuming that the first recordings are done on Tracks 1 and 2 of the recorder, using the left buss output for Track 1 and the right buss output for Track 2, when it comes time to record on Tracks 3 and 4, you must disconnect the outputs of 1 and 2 and reconnect them to 3 and 4.

For the mixer to be as effective as possible, it should have the same number of program busses as your multitrack has tracks. If you're making the leap directly into a 16-track recorder, you may be able to effectively use a mixer with eight busses that have parallel outputs. If you're in the four- or eight-track market, look for a four- or eight-buss mixer. If your mixer has to do double duty as a live performance mixer, it is easier to use a recording multiple-buss mixer by assigning your channels to one or two busses than it is to create busses that don't exist when trying to use a PA mixer in a recording setting.

Another problem is that the inputs of PA mixers are designed to perform best with microphones or instruments as sources. They don't usually have any specialized tape inputs. The lack of specialized tape inputs makes it difficult to effectively use a PA mixer in the multitracking process.

Earlier on, we mentioned the importance of a good monitor subsystem for your recording mixer. This feature is essential to your ability to perform overdubbing and *track bouncing* (explained later). And it is the ability to overdub and track bounce that defines multitrack recording. It is absolutely vital for you to be able to hear your previously recorded tracks along with new signals without a lot of repatching of cables and connectors. Although there is often a subsystem labeled "monitor" on a PA mixer, this subsystem is really an aux mixer under an alias. It is called "monitor" because it feeds the stage "monitor" speakers. These speakers help the people on stage hear the overall mix that the audience is hearing through the main speakers.

Another difference: recording mixers tend to have as many aux/effects subsystems as possible, while PA mixers tend to have limited effects mixers and aux mixers designed primarily for stage monitoring. The flexible aux systems found in recording mixers are used not only for reverb and other signal processing effects, but also for special submixes for cueing the player.

Today's recordings use effects (digital reverb, chorus, delay, flanging, etc.) very extensively. As a result, you most certainly will want to use some of these effects to make your own recordings sound as professional as possible. Effects subsystems are simply aux subsystems that are optimized (designed specifically for) use as effects subsystems.

In the ideal situation, your mixer should give you several aux mixes that originate before the EQ in your channel strip as well as several that originate after the EQ. The terms "pre" and "post" mean that the signal used by the aux mixer comes from a point in the channel signal flow sequence either before (pre) or after (post) the EQ. Sometimes, aux mixes can be switched to originate pre- or post-EQ.

Mixers designed for recording often have these flexible aux systems that originate from various points in the signal path. PA mixers tend to have fewer aux/effects systems, and their points of origin are not as flexible or, therefore, as useful in the recording environment.

THE STUDIO-IN-A-BOX MIXER/RECORDERS

The portable studios that have a mixer, a multitrack recorder, and noise reduction in a single box are the units that have really stimulated the rush to record at home (Figures 2-10, 2-11). Many offer high performance for a very modest investment. They are compact and, in most cases, contain well-matched components.

On the whole, portable studios offer many advantages. They are usually easier to use than separate components. Most connections between the components are "hard-wired" so that patching cables are not necessary. In some cases, the most commonly used functions are set so that switching happens automatically. For example, the monitor subsystem may automatically get signals from

FIGURE 2-10. TASCAM 424 MKII Portastudio (Courtesy of TASCAM, Teac Professional Division)

FIGURE 2-11. Roland VS880, a hard disk based recorder and workstation (Courtesy of Roland Corp. US)

the tape tracks when the transport is put into the play mode. This automatic patching often makes complex recording operations much easier to perform and understand.

Often, the recorder section and the mixer section of the portable studio are "matched." Ideally, the two sections are designed to help each other perform to their maximum capability. The nominal operating levels of the mixer and recorder will be the same—usually, −10 dB. The mixer's buss assignment switches will often have labels that correspond to tracks on the recorder, rather than generic buss labels.

The packaged portable studio will also have some kind of noise reduction system. Noise reduction is vital to any cassette-based multitrack system.

It's obvious that a portable studio is a great way to get started if you haven't already invested in a recorder or mixer.

What kinds of features should you look for in a portable studio? As we mentioned in the Introduction, features must be consistent with wishes and goals; and goals must be consistent with finances and abilities. If your goal is to have an "electronic sketch pad" in order to work out song ideas, then almost anything that records will do. The following list of features is more consistent with the ability to record something that you will share with other people. Those other people may be members of your band, your family, or someone you're trying to impress with your songwriting or performing ability. Here's the wish list for portable studios:

- The ability to record on all four tracks simultaneously, which is very useful when recording sync-tones and music tracks, and in bouncing tracks.
- The ability to assign any mixer channel to any track, or all tracks, of the recorder.
- A separate monitor subsystem.
- A meter system for the busses as well as overload indicators for the mixer channels.
- At least two aux/effects subsystems.
- Two-speed transport—3¾ ips and standard 1⅞ ips—on a cassette-based multitrack. This improves audio quality.
- Flexible noise reduction that can be turned "off" when necessary, or can be turned off for at least one separate track. This makes it easier to record some sync-tones and very percussive material.
- A couple of balanced low-impedance microphone inputs.

EVALUATING A RECORDING MIXER

When checking out a mixer for your home studio, you will be using several criteria. One of these is adaptability. As a command center, a recording mixer must handle signals going in many directions, at many levels, and in varying mixes for specific purposes. As you progress through the tasks of making a recording, your mixer must perform a wide variety of jobs.

Another criterion is the quality of quiet. A recorder is ruthless in that it will record noise and bad signals just as well as it does high-quality signals. A slightly noisy mixer with a lot of inputs may work well in the nightclub, but it just won't cut it in the studio.

Another crucial issue is that of reliability. All of us want our investment in a mixer to last. You need the mixer to be well-built and *reliable*.

Adaptable, quiet, and reliable—these are primary qualities of a good mixer.

Adaptability

While the individual features and components of your mixer must be adaptable, the systems and subsystems within the mixer themselves must also be adaptable. Their capabilities must be easy to access—you want to spend your time recording and listening, not plugging and unplugging. The mixer must have input stages that accept all the different source signal levels that you will throw at it. The input stages must make it easy to select input sources. A switching system which allows you to leave several sources connected to the channel without repatching is ideal.

After the signal you want is *in* the channel, you must be able to get it *out* in a variety of ways. A good recording mixer should have the insert/access feature we talked about before. These "patch points" can be used to create submixes or bring external effects devices into the channel. They help make the channel strip adaptable.

Your mixer must give you a sufficient number of aux/effects subsystems. How many is enough? It seems that there are never enough aux mixes available. But your recording mixer should have at least two aux/effects systems. Three or four is better. Eight is, as they say, "just about happening." Sixteen and this writer, at least, is one happy camper. Direct outs and insert/access can be used to create additional aux mixes, so you can use the presence of these to offset a shortage of an aux subsystem or two.

The aux subsystems must be adaptable, too. One or two of them should be able to be switched pre- or post-channel fader. It would also be nice if they were able to be switched pre- or post-EQ. Some companies give you a semblance of this flexibility by permanently routing one aux system post-fader and post-EQ, and another pre-EQ and pre-fader. Other companies route one aux pre-fader and the other post-fader; they will then make one of these switchable to pre- or post-EQ. Check to see where the mixer's aux systems originate in the channel strip. A good selection of origination points and switching is ideal.

There should be a good system of meters and overload indicators on your mixer—ideally, a combination of meters and LED peak indicators. The point is to prevent a raging audio signal from getting through your mixer and onto tape without your detecting it.

Each channel should have an indicator just after the input trim/pad controls to help in your basic adjustment of the input level. Another spot that needs some level watching is just after the EQ system in the channel strip. It is very easy to boost a signal too much using EQ controls. (We'll look at ways to use EQ properly later on.) The busses need some type of meter or LED system to let you know whether you have created a monster signal by summing, combining, several channel signals together in a buss. A buss "warning" system will be helpful with even one channel's signal going to a buss because it is possible with some mixers to boost the channel signal too much with the channel fader.

The mixer's warning system, if it is thorough, will give you the assurance you need to experiment with your signal routings. It will also give you the flexibility to be creative while you maintain the integrity of the signal.

The Quality of Quiet

Maintaining the integrity of the signals you are going to record is probably the most important job your mixer does for you. The integrity and quality of what goes to tape will be the result of the quality of the engineering, the quality of the electronic components, and the quality of the manufacturing techniques used to make the mixer.

Even for trained engineers, it is getting tougher to appraise the quality of a mixer by popping the hood and taking a look at the components. To understand how an integrated circuit is working, you have to know how it is "mapped," but this is impossible to determine just by looking at the circuit. Indeed, forget about specs—noise-to-signal ratios and the like—the fact that Johnny

Dooduh plugged it in the last issue of *Dishpan Audio* magazine, or that you like the color of the finish (black).

You must use your ears.

An audio component will only sound as good as the weakest link in the entire audio system. If you are shopping for mixers, you may find it difficult to get a reliable test-listen to the various choices. Try to use the same sound source to evaluate mixers. A CD player with a disk that you are really familiar with would be perfect—particularly if the disk has material that has wide dynamic range (lots of soft and loud passages). Insist that speakers used are either identical for each mixer, or use your own high-quality headphones. Power amps should be of similar wattage if you can't use the exact model for each test.

Computer hackers have a saying: "Garbage in; garbage out." By controlling the source material—your CD player—you will be sure that garbage is not going in. If garbage comes out, pass on the mixer. Here's a list of things to try:

1. Run your CD through two of the mixer channels. Set the channel faders to their "nominal" setting, which will either be at about 7 or all the way open at 10. Leave the EQ at its flat settings. Set the program buss and/or stereo buss faders to nominal. Now listen for a bit. Listen carefully when the music changes from soft to loud. This will give you an idea of the mixer's "headroom."

2. Now begin using the various controls while the music is playing. Open up the trim or input level control. Hear at what point it overloads and see how the warning system works.

3. Press the various buttons and switches, listening for pops and buzzes when you do.

4. Move the channel faders and then the buss faders up and down slowly. The music levels should change slowly and evenly.

5. Move the channel faders to their "off" position. At this point, there should be no signal leaking into the busses.

6. After returning the channel faders and buss faders to nominal, you should begin checking the EQ. Move the various controls throughout their complete ranges of motion very slowly and one at a time. The sound will begin to change, but the changes should be smooth and even. There shouldn't be a lot of buzzing or other noises present. If the EQ section has an on/off function, check that too. In its "flat" position, turn the EQ on and off. There should be no pops or noises; and the flat EQ position should sound as if it were off.

The important thing to remember about mixers is this: Though they do a great deal for you in the recording process, they should be seen, and not heard.

Reliability

Regardless of the piece of equipment you're looking at—recorder, mixer, or a portable studio—there are some things that are difficult to check in a superficial examination. At some point in your search, you must get some deep and positive response for the pieces you are examining.

Often, people develop this by traveling the "name brand" route. They've heard a lot about Brand X and some of their favorite artists use it, so they just naturally gravitate toward that brand. The problem is that you're going to develop a personal relationship with this equipment, and buying it just on someone's say-so—or worse, merely on the basis of an ad—is asking for trouble.

My advice is this: *Check things out.* Regardless of the equipment, you want to get your hands on a complete and understandable manual and documentation—no small task in and of itself. It's a good way of finding a good dealer: if your local store doesn't deliver the proverbial goods even on this level, then the chances are very good that they won't be there for you later.

As for the manual and the documentation, if you can't understand what they're talking about, then they aren't going to be much help when it comes to running the equipment. This book will help you a good part of the way, but the manual is important for the particulars of the machine.

You will also want a reasonable level of expertise from your dealer, local and national service, and the highest quality components and construction.

Find out who does the local service on the brand. Call the service center and talk to them about incidence of repair and quality of construction. Most service technicians love to talk shop. They will also tell you a lot more about the product than you may want to know—but it's worth the effort if you learn how well the product works, how quirky it is, and how it stands up to good, hard use.

Find out if there is a national service center that is staffed with consumer service representatives. Call the company and talk to one of these people. Get a feeling for the kind of support you'll get if the product breaks down.

Before you go into the store, write down all the things that you want to ask. Then, when you get to the store, make sure that you get reasonable answers to *all* your questions. Never let any specs-wielding salesperson make you feel foolish or uninformed for asking. If you feel like an idiot asking what you think are basic questions, imagine how much dumber you'll feel when you get your expensive mixer or recorder home and find out it doesn't do the job you want. Don't let yourself be intimidated.

What about quality of construction? Performance tests like that we suggested for the mixer should tell you a great deal about the quality of the product. Talking with service technicians will help, too.

While you want to trust one of your senses—hearing—you should try to ignore another one of your senses: sight. Some companies spend a disproportionate amount of money on cosmetics. These pieces look sleek and sexy, but they've got no guts. They're all show and no-go. On the other hand, something that looks like a lost dashboard from an army jeep won't fill the bill either. A product should show a reasonable balance between function and good looks.

One word of warning: beware of sleek black mixers with LED "ladder" metering systems. You've seen 'em: those tall skinny stacks of LED lights that create dazzling displays of color when signal is going through the mixer. They look great just sitting there, but when you try to work with them, you can't see anything. When your ears are in charge, your eyes take the opportunity to rest up a bit. Those sleek black consoles get hard to decipher in a hurry. "Where's Aux 1?" "Which channel's LED is flashing?" These types of questions drive you crazy when you're working.

In other words, make sure that you will be able to develop a feel for the layout of the controls, the read-outs, the placement of the connectors, and so on. Some gaudy carnival piece may go nicely with the white walls of your workspace, but if you can't read the basics at a glance, go for a piece that looks a bit more mundane.

CHAPTER 3

Microphones

The microphone and speaker are the entrance and exit of natural sound into and out of the world of electronics and recording.

The species *microphonus* comes from the family of *transducer*. "Transduce" means to translate from one form of energy to another. The microphone's job is to translate the moving air waves and pressures created by sound into fluctuating signal levels used by electronics (Figure 3-1). A speaker's job, on the other hand, is to take fluctuating signal levels and translate them *back* into the moving air waves and pressures that we hear as sounds.

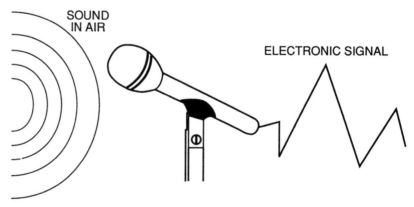

FIGURE 3-1. The microphone translates the energy of moving air waves into electrical energy.

Music as sound involves a wide dynamic range that microphones must be able to handle if they are going to contribute to the quality of your recording. When a drum stick strikes a snare drum, for example, the contrast in volume between the moment before the stick strikes the drum and the moment of the attack itself—BAM!—is extreme. A microphone should handle these startling contrasts of quiet and loudness.

Even the human voice is capable of creating a wide range of sound levels—what we call the "dynamic range." Microphones used for music recording must accurately translate whispers and shouts into electrical energy that will pass through our mixers and processors before reaching tape.

Most of the microphones you will come across in your musical recording will be of two broad types: *dynamic* and *condenser* mics. The dynamic microphone works much like a speaker in reverse. There is a diaphragm made of some type of fabric that responds to the moving air waves by vibrating (Figure 3-2). This diaphragm is connected to a voice coil that has several turns of wire around it. The moving voice coil alters the magnetic flux of a magnet. The alterations in the fluxivity of the microphone's magnet causes electrical current to flow in patterns consistent with the vibrations of the diaphragm. It is this current that serves as the signal.

Although there are various kinds of dynamic microphone, most notably the ribbon microphone that replaces both diaphragm and coil with a single metal ribbon, the "moving coil" dynamic mic has become so popular that the terms dynamic and moving coil

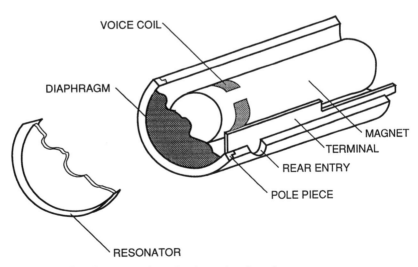

FIGURE 3-2. Cross section of a dynamic microphone.

have become nearly synonymous. Dynamic microphones are dependable, simple to use, and produce a very smooth and extended frequency response. They are widely used in both live performance and in recording studios.

Not all dynamic microphones are created equally, though. The quality and consistency of the microphone manufacturer are very important.

Condenser microphones translate sound waves to electrical energy differently. In a condenser mic, there are two plates set closely together, but they do not touch. The plates are charged; they are hooked to a battery or another electrical source. One of these plates is made so that it will move in response to sound pressure, while the other does not. As the movable plate approaches and recedes from the static plate in response to fluctuations of sound pressure, the two plates together generate an amount of voltage consistent with the increases and decreases of sound pressure. The resulting charge becomes the signal that passes through the mixer (Figure 3-3).

Some of the finest studio microphones produced are condenser mics, but they are notoriously expensive, sometimes costing thousands of dollars. Not quite the stuff of home studios, eh? There are several variations on the condenser theme, however, that are more practical for the home studio.

The *electret condenser* is a very cost-effective condenser. Rather than having two plates that each require a charging source, an electret condenser uses a capacitor (condenser) that retains,

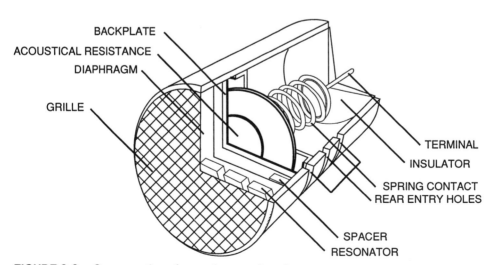

FIGURE 3-3. Cross section of a condenser microphone.

almost indefinitely, a charge given it during manufacture. An electret condenser requires an amplifier/impedance converter, which in turn requires a small voltage battery.

Though some condensers might be considered the perfect mics, they are fragile, expensive, and not very versatile. As a rule, condenser microphones are more sensitive than dynamics, particularly to high frequencies and *transients*—bursts of sound that occur suddenly and go away just as suddenly. Though condensers respond well to transients, they can be overwhelmed by them. Thus condensers are not usually used for drums, explosions, or rock guitar.

A new kind of microphone called a PZM (*pressure zone microphone*) has been developed (Figure 3-4). The PZM has already earned quite a good reputation. This is a condenser microphone that utilizes a flat surface as an exterior pickup device. The microphone registers the acoustic pressure of sound waves that build up on the surface of the plate. PZMs are great for picking up room ambience and instruments with wide frequency ranges. They work well with pianos or with small ensembles (using just a couple of microphones).

A PZM's bass response can be enhanced, to a point, by a larger surface plate area, and for this reason they are often taped to walls, music stands, piano lids, or other flat surfaces. Though PZMs work well in many applications, they are no great shakes at vocals. Later on, when we discuss specific recording techniques, we will talk more about the qualities that make certain types of mics well-suited to particular instruments.

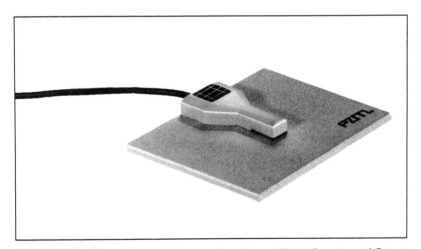

FIGURE 3-4. Crown pressure zone microphone (PZM). (Courtesy of Crown International Inc.)

RESPONSE PATTERNS OF MICROPHONES

The ways that microphones pick up sounds are called *response patterns*. There are two types of response patterns: *polar response*, pertaining to the physical position of the sounds that the mic picks up (in front, in back, or surrounding); and *frequency response*, which relates to the mic's sensitivity to pitches (high and low sounds).

Polar Response

Because of their various designs, microphones pick up sounds with varying degrees of sensitivity; they do not pick up every sound going on around them. They are limited by distance, for example; sounds too far away cannot be heard. Also, you may have noticed that you do not hear sounds originating behind you as well as you hear those that come from in front of you. Your mic may be more receptive to sounds arriving from directly in front or behind, but not so receptive to those arriving from either side.

These patterns of performance for microphones can be charted (Figure 3-5). Looking very much like maps, these diagrams are usually two-dimensional, although several companies attempt to give you a three-dimensional view of the response patterns of their mics. These patterns are categorized with such very scientific-sounding terms as *cardioid, hypercardioid, supercardioid, omnidirectional, bidirectional,* and *hemispheric.* When you are shopping for microphones, you will most often hear them referred

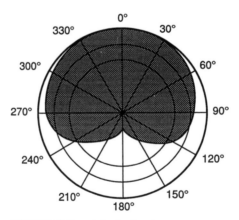

FIGURE 3-5.   A typical polar response pattern for a cardioid microphone.

to by their construction type (condenser or dynamic) and their polar response pattern—cardioid, for example. ("Looking for a dynamic cardioid, eh?")

The *cardioid* pattern, which is sometimes called *unidirectional* because of its bias for straight-ahead sounds, looks a little like an upside-down heart (Figure 3-6). You point these mics directly at what you want to pick up. They are great for vocals and other close microphone placements. Because they don't pick up sounds to the rear, cardioids are the pattern of choice for PA and sound reinforcement use. Microphones that do pick up to the rear cannot be used well by performers on stage because they will pick up the sound of the loudspeakers, thereby causing feedback or something equally unattractive.

A *hypercardioid* pattern retains its bias for the sounds directly in front of it, but adds sensitivity to the rear. The response pattern looks a little like a double-decker snowman upside-down. Hypercardioids are useful for picking up an instrument and some room ambience through the reflected sound waves that will be picked up to the rear.

The *supercardioid* has a pattern that looks like the last scene in the movie *Dr. Strangelove*: it looks decidedly like a mushroom cloud. This pattern picks up very broadly in front of the mic—a full 180 degrees and slightly beyond. To the rear, the supercardioid

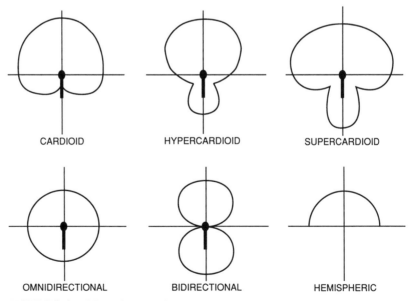

CARDIOID   HYPERCARDIOID   SUPERCARDIOID

OMNIDIRECTIONAL   BIDIRECTIONAL   HEMISPHERIC

FIGURE 3-6. Microphone polar response patterns.

picks up a narrow beam of sound waves. Supercardioids are nice for picking up horn sections or a group of vocalists using a single mic.

The *omnidirectional* microphone picks up sound pressures more-or-less equally from all directions. Its response pattern looks like a circle in two dimensions and a sphere in three dimensions. These mics are good for picking up large ensembles along with the audience and room sound for that "live-at-Carnegie Hall" feel.

A *bidirectional* microphone picks up well to the front and to the rear, but does not pick up to the sides. As a result, its pattern looks like a figure 8. Panel discussions with speakers sitting directly opposite one another, or backing vocalists who want to see each other while they sing, are ideal candidates for bidirectional microphones.

PZM microphones, because of their design, pick up sound pressures almost equally in a complete half-sphere that is bounded by the base plate or other surface base of the mic—hence the term *hemispheric* to describe its response pattern. If you were to see this pattern in three dimensions, it would look like half of a globe.

Frequency Response

Your ear hears certain frequencies (pitches) and types of sounds (waveforms) better than others. Most people hear midrange frequencies much better than they do very low frequencies or very high frequencies.

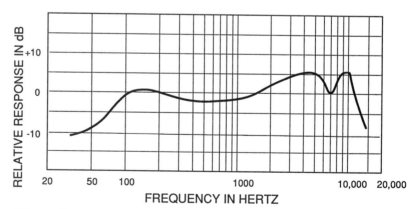

FIGURE 3-7. A microphone frequency response pattern. The horizontal axis shows the frequencies that the mic can "hear." The vertical axis shows how well the mic hears those pitches. For example, this mic has better response at 1,000 Hz than it does at 50 Hz. (Courtesy of Shure Brothers, Inc.)

Microphones likewise operate better at certain frequencies than at others. For this reason, you may sometimes see multiple response patterns for the same mic. More often, if patterns for several test frequencies are given, you will see a single graph with different types of lines (dotted, solid, dot-dash) representing the various frequencies. Though these multiple patterns may look like "too much information," they are an honest attempt to show the performance characteristics of the mic. A simpler depiction of a pattern is shown in Figure 3-7.

EVALUATING MICROPHONES

Learning the type of construction (dynamic, condenser) and the pattern (cardioid, omni, and so on) can tell us a lot about a microphone's adaptability to our intended use. It doesn't tell us much about the quality of the mic's performance, however.

As we mentioned earlier, your audio quality will only be as good as its weakest component. You can't put high-quality vocals or acoustic instruments on tape if you don't have microphones capable of picking them up accurately. High-quality microphones can help get maximum performance from some of your other audio pieces.

A microphone's sensitivity and frequency response are two vital areas to consider when evaluating performance. The sensitivity of a microphone is determined by how much signal voltage the mic will generate for a given signal. (To a point, the more signal the better. By generating higher signal output, a microphone will have a better signal-to-noise ratio. In any energy conversion, there will be a certain amount of wasted energy that will produce noise. Higher output for a similar sound source will usually mean less noise.)

There are a number of relatively confusing specifications that tell us a microphone's sensitivity. If you need to focus on a single specification, *sound pressure level* (SPL) is the place to start. Low-impedance microphones have output signals that are less than the input sound level. The SPL specification will tell you how much less. It is given as a negative decibel number, i.e., −50 dB (in this scheme, −50 dB is more than −60 dB).

We must warn you that not every maker references the SPL levels to the same input signal. When comparing mics made by different companies, you must make sure that the reference level used is the same, or you must know how to do the sophisticated math involved in finding equivalent references. Reference signals will usually be listed after the SPL, i.e., −74 dB (0 dB = 1 volt/microbar,

1 kHz). Refer to the Appendix, "Specifications," if you want to know more about the hows and whys of numbers and abbreviations.

The *frequency response* of a microphone is a measure of how well the microphone "hears" pitches from low to high. The absolute range of human hearing is said to be from 20 Hz to 20 kHz. An ideal microphone would then respond evenly to frequencies from 20 Hz to 20 kHz. A reasonable expectation for a microphone's frequency response would be 50 Hz to 15 kHz. You would be best off matching the frequency ranges of the instruments you intend to pick up with microphones that work best for those frequencies.

Most pianos, for example, have a lowest note of about 27 Hz and a highest note of about 4.2 kHz. Human singing voices range from just about 100 Hz to 1.2 kHz. You can see that microphones intended to be used for picking up piano and those intended for use with vocalists require different levels of frequency response. So we must look for "useful" frequency response. A vocal mic doesn't need to perform much below 100 Hz, while a piano microphone must be very broad-ranged. Cymbals generate pitches in the 7.5 kHz to 10 kHz range, so microphones for cymbals need good, high frequency response.

While the range of notes (frequencies) covered by the microphone is important, it is also important that it cover those frequencies equally well. Due to the physical limitations of microphones, some frequencies within its range will be more difficult for the mic to pick up. There will be peaks and valleys on its frequency response chart. An ideal frequency response chart would be flat as a table top with sharp roll offs at the extreme ends of its range.

But why is it that many vocalists and recording engineers prefer a mic with a response peak in the 1 kHz to 5 kHz range? A slight peak in this range adds some clarity and brightness to vocals, so flat is not always best. Just as there is no ideal red that the artist uses whenever scarlet is called for, or no ideal lighting used by a photographer in every setting, there is no ideal microphone response for every situation. In some instances, flat response is what you'll need, but a peaked response may be perfect for another application. However, these peaks should not be a manufacturer's excuse for making a sub-par mic.

Matching Microphones to Other Equipment

We talked a bit about impedance during our discussion of the input stage of the mixer. *Impedance* is the traction and resistance element in transmitting the electrical energy or signal. It is a law of nature that any movement, even that of an electrical current, will experience a certain amount of friction/resistance/traction. Every device that generates or receives electrical current has an impedance value.

You probably know that microphones are referred to as "low impedance" and "high impedance"—sometimes even the more confusing "low-Z" and "high-Z." As generators of electrical current, microphones have not only internal resistance, but also output impedance. For the signal to move effectively from the mic to your other components, like your mixer, the impedance of the mic and the mixer input must "match." Makers of both microphones and mixers classify their respective outputs and inputs as either *high impedance* or *low impedance*. The only thing that you need to remember is that high impedance goes to high impedance and low impedance goes to low impedance.

Low-impedance microphones are able to send their signal through longer cables with less noise, hum, or loss of high frequencies than are high-impedance mics. High-impedance microphones generally produce more output signal and drive inexpensive *input preamps* (mixer inputs) better.

Which mic should you choose? If your other equipment uses low impedance, then buy low-impedance microphones. If your other equipment uses only high impedance, then consider high-impedance microphones. If your equipment offers both low *and* high impedance, then choose low-impedance mics. If your current equipment offers only high-impedance connectors, but you may someday want to upgrade, then consider low-impedance mics and use line-matching transformers at the mixer inputs. *Line-matching transformers* not only provide a three-prong (XLR) to quarter-inch phone jack adaptor, they also change (transform) the impedance level of the mic from low to high.

Evaluation Summary

Here are some basic points to keep in mind when considering microphones:

- While a high-quality condenser may be the closest thing there is to a perfect mic, they tend to be more fragile and expensive than dynamics.
- Condensers are not particularly well-suited for high-sound-pressure sources such as bass drums, raging electric guitars, or screaming rock vocals. Dynamic mics are better suited to these applications.

- Flatter is better when it comes to frequency response, but a little "presence peak" is often found in mics that are very popular for vocals.
- Low impedance is preferable to high impedance for most applications, but the key to working well with your other components is having matching impedances.
- You will probably need at least two microphones in your arsenal to capture the wide range of frequencies you generate with your acoustic instrument(s).

But most of all, remember that saving a few bucks by buying a second-rate microphone won't do you any good at all. The computer hacker's line holds true for mics as well: garbage in, garbage out.

CHAPTER 4

Effects and Signal Processors

In the strictest sense, anything that changes the characteristics of a signal in any way is a *signal processor*. This includes amplifiers, equalizers, compressors, limiters, delays, echoes, reverbs, flangers, chorus, and distortion boxes—all in all, quite a respectable list of items when you tally them up. Vastly different in how they affect signals, these all serve the same general purpose of manipulating the signal's timbre, its *decay* (the length of time for which a note or chord endures), its dynamics, and/or its imaging.

In modern recording practice, effects and processors are so pervasive that mixing boards, as we've already seen, come from the manufacturer with a great deal of circuitry already devoted simply to sending and receiving these devices. The problem is knowing what you need for your work. It's easy to go processor crazy—using the processors often becomes an end in itself rather than a means of helping you accomplish your recording goals.

I'm not saying that processors and effects aren't good things to have, but it is all too possible to go too far with them. Their purpose is to enhance your signals; your signals are not there just to display your special effects.

Some processors, however, are all but essential to home recording—just as they are in those pricy commercial studios. The purpose here is to introduce you to what these toys can do for you.

EQUALIZERS

As we noted in the chapter on mixers, equalizers are so important in modern recording practice that they generally come with the mixing boards. Even so, you'll often see separate equalizer units in all shapes and sizes which in the main are more powerful and versatile than those found in the typical mixer channel. But they work the same way: they change a signal by amplifying (increasing) or attenuating (decreasing) levels at very specific frequency ranges—high, low, and in the middle.

While EQs are not intended to make your guitar sound like a saxophone, these circuits are first cousins to the filters and envelope systems found in synthesizers. The EQ, even the one in your mixer, is powerful enough to alter your sound for the better or very definitely for the worse.

Professionals use EQ very carefully. The very first EQ systems were designed to compensate for the poor quality of early recorders—to "fix" frequencies that were not recorded properly. Amateurs tend to overuse EQ. Recording your 1939 Martin guitar or your genuine Stradivarius violin should not require the use of much EQ. You're not going to improve the sound of these instruments much. At best, you will use EQ to compensate for your recorder's inability to capture their beauty.

Equalizers work within the consensus frequency range of human hearing—20 Hz to 20 kHz—by divvying up frequencies into "bands" not unlike slices cut from a loaf of bread. The width of the band—*bandwidth*—is the thickness of the individual slice of bread. The thickness of the slice is sometimes referred to as "Q"—Q being the result of dividing the center frequency of the band (10 kHz, for example) by the bandwidth (also measured in Hz). A center frequency of 10 kHz with a bandwidth of 50 Hz will have a Q of 200.

Raising the level of a high frequency area will brighten the sound, and lowering the level of a low frequency sound will also brighten the sound. We will cover the specific use of EQ in later chapters, but remember two things now: EQ is more often over-used than under-used; and cutting the opposite end of the frequency range may bring the same benefit as boosting the desired area.

Types of Equalizers

EQs are usually identified by the number of bands they work in and the types of individual components. A *sweep EQ* can be adjusted up and down the frequency range. You can dial in the frequency you want to cut or boost. A sweep EQ usually has a pre-set bandwidth that is not adjustable. These are very handy in mixer channels where they are used in the mid-ranges and are combined with shelving-type EQs.

A *shelving EQ* circuit is often used at the extreme upper or lower frequency ranges. They affect all frequencies above or below their assigned spot. As a result, a shelving-type usually just has a control for cut and boost, and is labeled simply "high" or "low."

Add-on, rack-mountable equalizers are usually of two types: *parametric* or *graphic*. A fully parametric EQ gives complete control over frequency and bandwidth (Figure 4-1). These are very precise, pretty complicated, wonderful, but a little too expensive for most of us. Graphic equalizers divide the loaf into many small slices

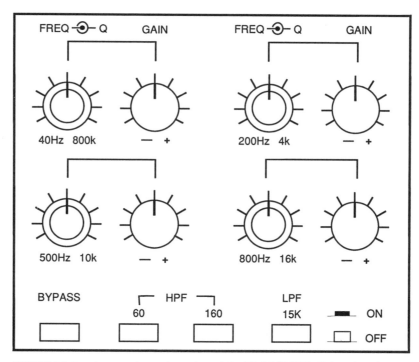

FIGURE 4-1. A control panel section of the TASCAM PE-40 four-band parametric equalizer. Each frequency control sweeps the range of its respective band and permits selection of a center frequency to be equalized. The Q control permits variation of the width of the frequency band that is to be equalized. The gain control permits boost or attenuation of the selected frequency at the selected Q.

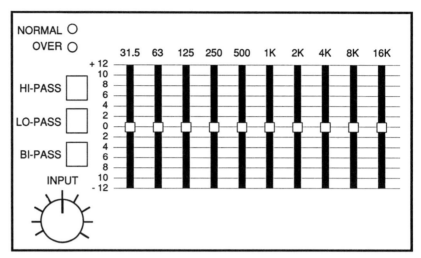

FIGURE 4-2. A control panel section of the TASCAM GE-20B 10-band graphic equalizer. Slider controls permit adjustment of the cut or boost of the selected frequency.

(Figure 4-2). A slider control adjusts the cut or boost of the specific frequency. The bandwidths of the individual adjacent sliders cross over each other. A well-made graphic can be very useful, but unfortunately this type of EQ has enough flash in its looks to appeal to some of the low-budget gadget-oriented manufacturers. A cheap graphic may have pretty lights and lots of sliders, but may be worse than having no EQ at all.

There are some equalizers that combine various systems. They are called *composite EQs*. EQs may also come with added *filters*, which can be used to block the passage of the sound within specific realms of frequency. Filters are very useful because there is a lot of noise and rumble at the extremes of our audible frequency range. A filter can eliminate just these areas and their unfortunate baggage of noise. A *low-pass filter*, for example, lets anything below its assigned frequency pass while it stops anything above. A *high-pass filter*, on the other hand, stops anything below its frequency assignment.

DYNAMIC EFFECTS

Dynamic effects work by manipulating the relative signal level—the loudness and softness of sound. Although much of this work could be done by someone with very fast hands on the mixer faders, dynamic effects work automatically to facilitate the recording of difficult signals such as transients.

A *compressor,* which does exactly as its name implies, is a dynamic effect. It squeezes the signal into a smaller dynamic space. Working on a ratio basis—that is, applying more of its squeezing effect as the signal level gets bigger—the compressor will make signals with wide dynamic swings easier to handle by bringing down the levels of the transient peaks. When these peaks of signal are leveled out, the valleys or soft signals also benefit by comparison. They will seem louder and more present. This is the reason why television commercials seem so much louder than the programs they persistently interrupt. They have been compressed to the Nth degree. The peaks have been eliminated while the valleys have risen in comparison, and the whole thing is recorded at a high signal level. Kind of annoying, isn't it?

Compression, like EQ and all other effects, must be used sparingly. An overly compressed track can sound lifeless and "far away," particularly if it is recorded at a low overall level on tape. Later on, we'll look more closely at how to use compression. This is just a brief warning that compression is not necessarily the cure-all for transients on the rampage.

Other dynamic effects include *limiters* and *de-essers.* A *limiter* puts a brick-wall limit on the amount of signal it will let pass. It is the dynamic equivalent of filters. While a filter blocks the passage of certain frequency levels, a limiter blocks the signal at a certain dynamic level. A good limiter can sound more natural than a compressor on some signals.

A *de-esser* works on cleaning up some of the horrible sounds that humans can make, particularly the sibilance of the "s" sound. Classically trained vocalists and professional on-air television and radio personalities spend many hours cleaning up their enunciations of sounds such as "s" and "t" and "th." These consonants and consonant blends can explode through your audio system, letting loose basketfuls of hissing cobra sounds on your tape. Cleaning up these splashes of sound is a de-esser's primary task. Some compressors and limiters have de-essers built into them.

NOISE REDUCTION

The two predominant noise reduction schemes on the market are also dynamic devices. Both Dolby and dbx systems operate by compressing and later expanding the audio signal. This process is often called "companding." By compressing the signal before it hits the tape and expanding the signal after it is picked up by the playback head, the resultant noise from the tape rubbing across the heads is reduced in terms of the compression/expansion ratios.

You will run across gadgets known as *noise gates* as you poke around in the music or audio store. These are well-named devices designed to open and close at user-determined levels. The threshold determines where the gate opens to let the sound pass, and the release control determines how quickly the gate will close again. The idea behind a noise gate is that a loud sound will cover, or mask, the noise that may be present in the material. When the sound stops completely or gets soft as it decays, then the noise becomes more noticeable. As the gate closes, it stops all sound from coming through, including ambient noise.

Noise gates, like all effects, must be used carefully. They can sound very artificial as they chop off the front and end of your beautiful notes too soon. Professionals sometimes use this artificial gate effect to create spectacular sounds. The gated snare drum sounds on many Phil Collins records produced by Hugh Padgham are an example of this.

Finally, you may run across some units called *single-ended noise-reduction systems*. These units are not a two-step process of compression and expansion like the Dolby and dbx systems. They use a single step, similar in function to the noise gate. In some systems of this type, a dynamically controlled filter is used. As the level of the signal increases, the action of the filter (a low-pass filter) is decreased. As the level of the signal decreases, the filter action increases. The idea here is that higher signal levels mask any ambient noise in the music so noise reduction per se isn't needed. But as your music gets softer, noise becomes more apparent, thus requiring more noise reduction. The effect is like an automatically self-adjusting gate.

Other single-ended systems act like little fingers riding the faders. As the input signal goes down, the output signal is brought down even more, proportionally. So, as the noise floor rises to prominence with the drop of the music signal, the noise reduction device closes the noise frequency down at an ever-increasing rate. This effectively pushes the noise down below the level of hearing.

We'll talk more about using some of these noise-reduction systems in the applications sections to follow.

TIME DELAY EFFECTS AND REVERBERATION

Sound waves bounce around the natural world like ping-pong balls on steroids (Figure 4-3). As they move, they create an audio landscape that is very difficult to reproduce in the recording studio world of electronic signals and magnetic particles on tape.

It's a little like the two-dimensionality that plagues the visual arts of painting, video, and film. No matter how well the artist details the perspective, or how well the camera deals with the depth of field, we still see that the image is on a flat surface. It's just as easy for us to hear the two-dimensionality of audio.

The 3-D glasses for our ears are the various systems intended to recreate the natural audio landscape. They're called *reverberation* and *delay effects*. *Reverb* is the most important signal processor you can have. It puts back the sense of physical space that recording sound tends to take out and can add it to electronic instruments that never had it to lose.

Reverb works by first delaying signals in a random or complex scheme and then recombining them with the original, unaffected signal. We do not hear these delayed signals as separate echoes; rather, they give the impression of sound waves as they would bounce off nearby walls and other surfaces. While we tend

FIGURE 4-3. Controlling bouncing sound waves is crucial to effective recording.

to hear delays of more than 45 or 50 milliseconds as echo, reverb delays are so short that we just can't separate them from the original signal.

There are a variety of ways to make reverb devices. Capitol Records has some special concrete rooms that were built to provide various reverb types. Many people, realizing how good they sound in the shower, have used the old faithful tiled bathroom to get just the right warmth for their vocals.

Most of the reverbs used today are effects devices that operate on either an *electro-mechanical* or a *digital* principle. An *electro-mechanical reverb* uses a spring or a metal plate of some kind to create the random signal delays. The springs and plates have inconsistent patterns of carrying the signal, so it arrives at various pickup points haphazardly. These pickup points then send the various delays which are combined with the pure original signal. Though they seem archaic in today's digital age, these reverbs have been responsible for some beautiful ambience on tape over the decades.

Microprocessors do the signal manipulating now in *digital reverbs.* With these devices, you choose reverb in terms of a wide variety of room sizes. If you want to recreate singing in the shower, you choose a small room with fast reflections. If you want to sing at Carnegie Hall, you want a pretty big room with slow reflections. These are the "rooms" that are referred to in the literature for reverbs.

Some of these reverbs combine other time-delay effects such as chorus, flanging, echo, and more—which is why these devices are often called *multiple effects processors.*

Other Time Delay Devices

Reverbs use many random delays simultaneously. A *delay* is a similar type of device in which a signal is held up for a period of time before it is recombined with the original signal. A delay uses a very precise number of delays that you select in terms of time or amount of delay.

Many of the effects you hear on record are created through the use of delay. *Echo* and *slapback* are two commonly used delay effects. *Echo,* as its name implies, is a discrete delay of an original sound, like the one you get shouting up a box canyon or in a big gymnasium. *Slapback* is a very short delay. When combined with the original signal, it fattens up the sound, making it sound as if there were two instruments playing the same note.

Delays can also be used for multiple repeats, often triggered rhythmically by a drum machine, or to create a stereo image from a single sound source, or to create more elaborate reverb effects in conjunction with an actual reverb. When working with a reverb, a delay can be used to create some of the "early reflections"—called "pre-delay" in the electronic gizmo world—found in natural reverberation.

A delay can help create a stereo image from a mono source by using very short delay times and then panning the original signal hard left and the delayed signal hard right, or vice versa. Pretty useful gadgets, these delays.

Combining time delays with filters and modulators such as low-frequency oscillators, you can create such effects as flanging and phasing. A *flanger* combines a signal delayed by varying lengths of time with the original signal in such a way that it creates a "comb filter," boosting some frequency ranges while totally canceling others. The altered signal gives the effect of altering the pitch. The delay times are controlled by a low-frequency oscillator.

Flangers can produce effects that are similar to both the *chorus* effect and the *phaser,* but the flanger has greater impact on the harmonics of the original signal. Flangers have often been used often with bass, especially popping bass tracks. Some heavy metal guitarists have also used flangers successfully. A flanger can make a traditional sound such as a piano or voice sound oddly appealing. It can make a voice sound like it's emanating from a box or radio somewhere, while a nice grand piano can be made to sound like an old, slightly out-of-tune upright.

A *phaser (phase shifter)* changes the electronic phase relationship of the affected signal in relation to the original by using a low-frequency oscillator. It is not technically a time delay device, but its similarity to flangers and chorus effects cause us to include it here. A sweeping, ringing sound combined with what seems to be a bit of high frequency noise, this effect has often be compared to a jet plane taking off. Jimi Hendrix and the Doobie Brothers are performers who used phasers with great success.

A *chorus* effect uses a delay time that is longer than those typically used by flangers. By using a longer delay time, a chorus doesn't have the high-frequency "sweeping" effect of the flanger; instead, it produces a shimmering, thick sound.

When you first get a chorus effect, you will use it on everything. You'll put jam and chorus on your toast in the morning. It's very seductive because it makes everything sound good, but after a while, you will acquire some sense of moderation. Don't worry, though; chorus had a similar affect on the recording industry of the late '70s and early '80s. You can hear chorus on almost every arpeggiated guitar part recorded during that time. (Think of the little guitar fills in Cyndi Lauper's "Time After Time," an early example of what was to become a signature sound of the MOR ballad on the radio.) Even Chet Atkins used a chorus effect.

But chorus is not just a guitar effect. Chorus has been used successfully on vocals, synthesizer parts (particularly strings), and even drums.

SOME ODDS AND ENDS

A couple of other effects that you may run into when confronted with an over-zealous salesman at the pro audio store are *pitch shifters, exciters,* and *auto-panning.*

If you have ever wanted to sing upper harmony parts, but you just couldn't reach the high notes, then a *pitch shifter* might be worth a look. Pitch shifters digitally record—"sample"—the incoming signal and then transpose it to an interval above or below the original. Unlike sampling keyboards, pitch shifters don't lengthen a sound when transposing down, nor do they shorten a sound when transposing up. They avoid this by editing out samples when transposing down and adding samples when transposing up. It is a pretty complex procedure, and the price of pitch shifters reflects this complexity. Laurie Anderson and Alvin and the Chipmunks are famous examples of pitch shifting in action.

Exciters add brilliance or presence to audio signals. Two of the most common methods of exciting signals are by adding either some phase shifting (which is dependent upon the pitches of the signal) or some varying amounts of second-harmonic distortion. For home recordists, exciters will be used to prepare tracks for "bouncing," or to add some life to older recordings that have lost their brilliance.

At this time, there are a few panning devices on the market. *Auto-panners* move the signal around in the stereo field: left, right, center, and places in between. This can be a very pleasant audio sensation. If you've had the pleasure of seeing and hearing an IMAX film with its six-channel audio, you have been put through the auto-panning mill. Some more familiar, but classic panning sounds are those created by the Fender Rhodes Suitcase Piano and the Roland Jazz Chorus amplifier. The sound in the Rhodes and Jazz Chorus bounces from speaker to speaker, effectively panning the image from side-to-side or front-to-back.

A WARNING ABOUT EFFECTS DEVICES

Other than the artistic warnings about over-use that we've sprinkled throughout this section, you should also take note that effects devices vary radically in their design and construction. Input and output levels and impedances have no standardization whatsoever. Some effects are designed to work with guitars and amplifiers. By design, they may want to drive their output so high that anything accepting it as an input will distort madly. On the other hand, some are designed for work in the professional film, video, or broadcast audio business.

So, remember one thing: match levels and impedances whenever possible. The output of a device should match the input of your mixer, aux return, and so on for impedance and levels. We will deal further with the sticky issue of levels and impedances in our section on specifications and the infamous dB.

CHAPTER **5**

Connectors

If you are the kind of person who likes to build models or put puzzles together, one the great joys of the average studio is its myriad of plugs, connectors, and wires. But one person's fun is another's woe. To some, the jungle of wires and plugs necessary to get everything hooked up and running can be a bit confusing.

There are three basic types of connectors/plugs that you will be using for your audio signals: the quarter-inch phone (mono or stereo), the RCA, and the XLR three-pin (Figure 5-1). In your reading, or in a professional studio, you may run into a connector called either a Bantam or TT (Tiny Telephone). This is a smaller version of the quarter-inch plug, but is seldom used in the type of equipment we will consider.

The quarter-inch phone plug is the kind found on the end of a guitar cord. Indeed, most electronic musical instruments use this type of connection. Your headphones come with a slight variation on this theme, because the headphone cord has a stereo connector. You will notice a second black band around the stereo connector on the headphones. The space between the two black bands offers another connection point so that the Ring Tip Sleeve connector has three "pins" instead of just two.

Most of the connectors on a home stereo system—and many of those found on the cassette-based multitrack we've been talking about—are the RCA type. They give a good snug connection, a decent amount of surface area, and, happily, they are inexpensive. You'll be using a good many RCA cables and connectors.

Low-impedance microphones use three-pin connectors that are often called "XLRs." Microphone inputs on many mixers, for

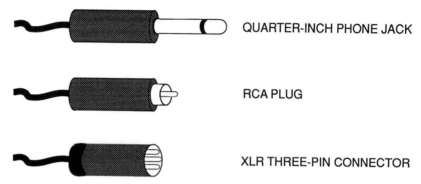

QUARTER-INCH PHONE JACK

RCA PLUG

XLR THREE-PIN CONNECTOR

FIGURE 5-1. Three basic types of connectors.

example, use XLR input connectors. You will also see XLR connectors used as the outputs of many mixers and signal processors, as well as the inputs of some recorders and processors. These inputs and outputs are balanced with an output level that is higher than those using RCA or phone connectors.

CABLES

Primarily due to the length and great numbers of cables used in professional recording and broadcast facilities, the signal level used there is significantly higher than the signal used by most of the equipment we will be using. If you acquire a piece of gear using these ins and outs, realize that its standard level is +4 dBm and not the -10 dBV you generally know and love.

How many cables will you need? Starting with a dozen RCA cables, two or three XLR (mic) cables, five or six guitar-type phone cables, and 100 feet of good speaker cable should get you started. Cables are a more significant investment than most people consider.

Keeping track of cables and what they connect is important, so get cables of different colors. They really help you find the one you're looking for when *repatching* your system. It's also wise to label your cables—at both ends—using either premade labels or masking tape and a permanent felt marker. It's also a good idea to keep a notebook with a diagram of your cable routings.

ADAPTERS

What happens when slot B isn't big enough to accept tab A? How do we plug our XLR mic cable into our phone connector mixer input? Do we run to the nearest audio store and pick up some adaptors? Clip the plug off the end of the cable and strap on a phone plug? Both of these options will get you the kind of result you would expect connecting your $2,000 speakers to your audiophile 10-star-rated receiver using the mechanic's wire from your tool box: very unsatisfactory.

Mismatched cable connectors will occur in a few places: connecting your microphone's XLR to your portable studio's phone inputs, or connecting instrument phone jacks to various RCA inputs. Do you remember what we said about matching levels and impedances? Although the input section of the portable studio's mixer is designed to handle a pretty wide range of signal levels, there is an impedance mismatch from a low "Z" mic to the high-impedance phone jack input. You'll need an Impedance Transformer or a Direct Box to connect mic to mixer input on the portable studio successfully.

A basic transformer is available from most microphone manufacturers. All of them work, but you generally get what you pay for. A quality name and better construction will ensure that your transformer is not too weak a link in the audio chain. For the really quality-conscious, a direct box will provide the best link between two audio components with very different levels and impedances. Direct boxes have the highest-quality circuitry, which means they'll do the job with less noise and signal loss created in the process. Many also have extra handy circuits for lifting ground wires and so on. Later chapters will discuss the ways direct boxes can help the sound of effects and help reduce noise.

PATCH BAYS

Patch Bays are those banks of plugs that you see sitting beside the console/mixer in pictures of recording studio control rooms. With their millipede legs of cables hanging from them they can look pretty intimidating, but the purpose of a patch bay job is really to make things easier on you.

Each component in your system has a variety of connection points, usually located on the back panel. While this is aesthetically pleasing, it's a pain in the neck when it comes time to rearrange your connections for a particular use. A patch bay brings all your connection points to a single panel that can be placed right next to your mixer for easy access.

In some cases, when you are looking for a patch bay, a salesman will start babbling about "normalling." All this means is that the connection points on the patch bay can be hooked together in your "normal" configurations. For example, the top connection point may be the signal coming from one of the buses of your mixer and the bottom connection point could be sending that signal to one of the inputs of your multitrack.

Most of the time, then, the mixer signal would be going uninterrupted to the multitrack. The jacks on the front panel come into play only if you want to send the mixer signal somewhere else or plug another signal into the recorder input.

However you cut it, the beauty of a patch bay is that these connections can be made on a panel within easy reach. If you don't know what I'm talking about, try spending some quiet time squeezing your head between your equipment and the wall. Then you'll understand just how beautiful a patch bay can be.

DIGITAL CONNECTIONS

Digital recorders, samplers, and so on usually offer analog connections using the three types of cables and connectors already mentioned. But they also offer some connections only found on digital devices.

Binary data transfers can happen at amazingly high speeds. To facilitate this, digital machines often have optical connectors, or multipin computerlike connectors. These are pretty common in the computer world and, therefore, are available at computer stores. There is no way to "transform" these signals though. Be sure you send "outs" to compatible "ins."

Some companies have developed their own data-transfer systems that cannot be shared easily with other equipment. Read your manuals and get the necessary connectors or devices to interface your gear. Get explanations on what you're buying: before you leave the store, make sure you know whether your new toy will hook up to and work with your gear at home.

On many digital units you will see the familiar RCA connector that may be labeled "digital" or "coax." This is a digital transfer port that sends data screaming down the cable at awesome speeds. Your usual RCA cables won't work too well on these connections. You will need to purchase specific coax digital cables.

Standardization is coming to the digital field but it is coming slowly. So make doubly sure you have the right cables and gizmos on hand.

CHAPTER 6

The Monitor System

Up to this point, we have been concerned with the equipment you'll need to get your material on tape: the recorders (don't forget—you will need at least two), the mixer, the mics (again, think in terms of twos), signal processors, and the various connector cables to link your recording equipment together and link it up with your instruments.

Still, without headphones, speakers, and an amplifier to drive them, you wouldn't be able to hear a single note of the recording. The last link in your chain, then, is the means to monitor your material so that you can mix it and hear your final product. And though the monitor system is the last link, it is every bit as important as the other elements in your recording system.

Speakers and headphones are microphones in reverse. Like microphones, they are transducers in the sense that they take one form of energy and convert it to another. Mics take sound waves and translate them into electrical signals; speakers take electrical signals and convert them into sound waves (Figure 6-1). And because speakers and headphones require power in order to sound, you need an amplifier to send the signals from your recorder and mixer.

In most cases, you should use your stereo receiver and speakers as your monitor (assuming, of course, that your significant other doesn't mind losing them from the family room). Why the old warhorses when you're having fantastic visions of monstrous studio speakers as big as a house?

One of the key attributes of *your* speakers will be familiarity. The speakers you are most familiar with will be those you have

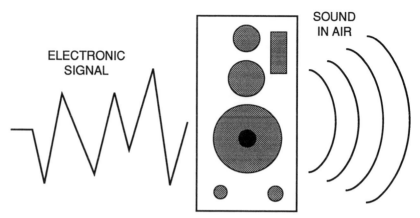

ELECTRONIC
SIGNAL

SOUND
IN AIR

FIGURE 6-1. Speakers convert electronic signals into air pressure fluctuations that we hear as sound.

listened to the most. You know what high-quality mixes sound like on your stereo speakers because you have listened to Michael Jackson, Bruce Springsteen, or George Winston records and CDs through them for years. If your own mixes sound good to you on these speakers, they probably *are* good mixes. So if you must buy another set of speakers to set up your studio, you may be better off getting new speakers for the family room and stealing away the "old faithfuls" for the studio.

If you're determined to have "real" studio monitors for your recording, use the evaluation criterion of *flat frequency response*. Any speakers you consider for studio use should come with a chart showing performance characteristics across the frequency range. It is much more important that the speaker have a flat response than it is that the speaker reproduce signals at 30 Hz or 20 kHz.

There is one warning concerning using your old faithful speakers for monitors. You are likely to record music that has very loud and very soft passages. You may be recording drum machines and other instruments that generate a lot of transients. The very first milliseconds of a drum or crunch guitar, even loudly sung vocals, particularly those with popping "p's," are very difficult sounds to reproduce and record. Commercial recordings tend to compress these transient peaks of sound so they don't sound abrasive and don't wreak havoc with home stereos.

In other words, your stereo speakers may not be ready for the high-intensity workout that home recording will put them through. You really should consult your speaker doctor before beginning this exercise program.

This warning also applies to your receiver/amplifier. The amp must be able to respond to transients as they come exploding through the signal chain. Each one of these sounds generates more power and wattage, and many amplifiers do not have the resilience either to respond quickly enough or protect themselves from these particular shocks to the system.

HEADPHONES

Your final mixes must sound good on your studio speakers, but most of the multitrack techniques you'll be using will require you to use headphones. Overdubbing, bouncing tracks, and punch-ins will all be done with a set of "cans" (headphones) firmly in place on your cranium.

There are two basic types of headphones: open and closed. Open phones allow the sound to emanate slightly from the back side of the transducer, or speaker element; this inexpensive, relatively high-performance headphone is light-weight.

Open phones are a good buy, but present a serious problem in the multitrack situation: they leak sound. The sound coming out of the back of the speaker element is easily picked up by your microphones and sent to your recorder again. Such leakage and recycling can all add up to poor recordings of your music.

Closed headphones seal off the outside world so that none of the sound going to your ears gets away to be picked up by microphones. They also keep outside noises and voices away, allowing you to concentrate on your mix. Of course, closed phones can drive spouses or roommates crazy. "You're oblivious to the outside world whenever you go in that studio room!"

You may need two or three sets of headphones if you typically record with other musicians. And if you do use headphones for other musicians, you will probably need some kind of specialized headphone amplifier. Connecting multiple sets of headphones to Y cords or other jerry-rigged arrangements will end up damaging your receiver or mixer headphone circuits.

CHAPTER 7

Putting the Studio Together

We've asked this before; we're asking it now; we'll be asking it again before too long: What do you want to do with your recording?

1. Develop an opera idea about your neighborhood postman (it doesn't matter that it's been done before).

2. Impress that cute teller (ATM?) at your local bank.

3. Impress your song publisher by interpreting your material as if you were both Garth Brooks and Mary-Chapin Carpenter (publishers like to know where they can sell things).

4. Master compact disks. (Why stop there? Why not master the universe?)

5. Have fun (musicians play at their jobs, other people work).

For our purposes, we're going to assume that you want to do some variant of 1, 3, and 5. (If you impress your song publisher enough and he sells lots of your songs, you may very well impress that cute bank teller—not to mention the branch manager).

Our model studio is designed to work out your song ideas in a fun and easy format. It should also allow you to create song demo tapes that are just above the minimum standards of professionalism for submission to a music publisher. If you're already working with a publisher, seek the publisher's advice on the format and style required for submissions.

THE MULTITRACK RECORDER AND MIXER

We are going to be working with a cassette-based portable setup. The unit specified here is not the least expensive type available, but it is also not the most expensive way to go.

Several brands all do a good job, but whichever brand you choose could have a number of important features, including high-speed operation; switchable noise reduction; the ability to record all tracks at once; the ability to assign any channel to any track; aux or effects submixes; more than one headphone jack; and possibly eight tracks instead of four.

High-Speed Operation

One of the best ways to wring more audio quality from a cassette machine is to double the speed at which the tape passes by the heads. A normal cassette runs at $1^7/_8$ inches-per-second (ips) while high-speed machines run at $3^3/_4$ ips. This provides more physical tape space for the given sounds. The results may not match digital recorders or open-reel recorders that run at 15 ips, 30 ips, or even 60 ips with quarter-inch or half-inch tape, but cassettes at $3^3/_4$ ips definitely give you your money's worth.

Switchable Noise Reduction

You'll need noise reduction, but you also want to be able to turn it off and on for individual tracks. Why? When you read about MIDI systems in a later section, you will see that noise reduction can interfere with the recording of some synchronizing signals used by sequencers and drum machines. Noise reduction may often be poorly suited to the audio material that you are recording, particularly loud bass or drum sounds.

Which type of noise reduction? The major companies that make these systems, Dolby and dbx, both produce systems that work well. A broad-band noise reducer, dbx boasts better numbers for overall reduction. But it is more finicky; even if it's slightly out of adjustment, dbx can "pump and breathe" a little on the low and percussive material (your bass and drum parts, in other words). Dolby systems, on the other hand, work only on specific frequency bands where the really obnoxious noises exist. But noise exists in all frequency ranges, and Dolby doesn't work at all on some of the noise present. So the type of noise reducer you choose is a matter of personal preference.

Ability to Record All Tracks at Once

Although you will seldom want to record all four tracks at once, the inability to do so can be frustrating. Should you have a couple of musician friends over to play, you might want to record something that's happening rather spontaneously. To do so on only two tracks severely limits what you might be able to do later with the material, such as adjust the levels of individual instruments. Spreading the same material out over four tracks lets you change or delete parts later. It keeps the individual performances as separate as possible for later use.

Many of the machines that restrict you to two-track recording also limit you to the combinations of tracks and mixer channels. This can require additional cable patching and time.

Ability to Assign Any Channel to Any Track

When you've worked to get the EQ set just right on your vocal mic, you don't want to reset the controls just so you can record your voice on a different track. You will want the ability to set the EQ one time and then assign that setting to any track. Any channel of the mixer on the portable studio you own should be able to be sent to any track of the recorder by means of the assign buttons.

Channel assignment flexibility will also help you perform the multitrack techniques of bouncing and overdubbing.

Aux or Effects Submixes

You will need at least one good aux submix system with sends in your mixer channels in order to use your effects properly. This system should have a stereo (left and right) set of return jacks, if possible. Our reverb, delay, and chorus effects, even those that only have a single, mono, input, often have stereo outputs that can help create wonderful sounds.

More than One Headphone Jack

Don't even think you can just use some kind of "Y" cord on a single headphone jack. This will usually blow up the little amps used in headphone systems. If you usually record with more than two people, or you already own a portable studio or mixer with a single headphone jack, you should consider a separate headphone amplifier for your system.

Eight-Track Cassette Options

Some machines put even more tracks on the narrow, thin cassette. Surprisingly, the units we've tried perform very well. However, the margin for error is smaller with this small format. Although cassette tape itself is very convenient and inexpensive, these 8-track machines are fairly expensive. Open-reel or digital machines become a viable option if you're shopping at these price points.

Digital Multitracks

Since the cost of digital storage (hard disks and digital tape) has come down, these machines have become a more viable option. But be wary of the idea of turning your personal computer into a digital recorder. These options usually compromise the performance of both the computer and recorder too much. If digital is your way to go, shop for a dedicated recorder.

Dedicated digital recorders come as tape-based or hard-disk-based systems. The Alesis ADAT and TASCAM DA88 are examples of tape-based digital multitrack recorders. They use video-type tape transports and tape to record and store the data that is your music. With the exception of razor-blade editing, which is really only done on open-reel machines anyway, the ADAT and DA88 machines function just like cassette multitracks. They just provide better audio and come at a higher price. In terms of our recording tips and techniques sections, they function in the same way as our portable studio.

Hard-disk-based recorders substitute a computer hard drive for the tape and its transport. They are, essentially, computers dedicated to the job of recording audio. Many of these units offer some of the editing tricks formerly reserved for sequencers, such as cut-and-paste editing, quick search, undo, and pitch shifting.

Despite their zoomy repertoire of tricks, these machines have been made to function very much like analog tape machines of the past. You will find, therefore, that our recording tips and techniques will also translate well to these machines

In sum, we have selected for our model studio a four-track cassette portable studio that: (1) will operate at high-speed, (2) has defeatable noise reduction, (3) will record all tracks simultaneously, and (4) will assign any mixer channel to any track. The mixer section will have a decent aux subsystem for use with our effects. And it will have two headphone jacks for monitoring.

THE MIXDOWN RECORDER

The recorder you will use to make your stereo mixes is the standard consumer variety. Since we have selected a cassette-based multitrack, it makes sense that we also select a cassette-based mixdown recorder.

Don't skimp here. The mixdown recorder must perform at least as well, in the audio sense, as your multitrack (remember our earlier discussion about the weakest link of the audio chain?).

Does this mean you'll need a cassette deck designed for music or broadcast applications? Not necessarily. Consumer cassette decks can be used as your mixdown machine, but they should certainly be at the higher end of the consumer market. You don't need a lot of frills—timers, music search, auto-reverse, remote control, and so on. What you do need is a solid transport that uses as much metal in its construction as possible. Solinoid transport controls and three motors are considerations. Three heads wouldn't hurt; and a noise reduction system compatible with your multitrack is nice.

Expect to spend about 60 to 70 percent as much as you did on your multitrack for your mixdown recorder. In the context of our model studio, you should probably avoid expensive DAT machines unless it is your intention to upgrade to a digital multitrack in the near future.

MICROPHONES

We suggest two microphones for your studio: a dynamic cardiod and a PZM. The dynamic can be used for vocals and for bass drums and other instruments with high sound pressure. The PZM—and there's one available from a national electronic supply chain for about $50—is great for acoustic instruments, ensembles, and room ambience. While we would like to think that these two mics are the minimum requirements for the home studio, we realize that some of you won't be able to afford two mics.

If two is one too many, then the single best mic for every application in home recording is a good-quality electret condenser. If your one and only mic must double as an on-stage mic, then you should consider the dynamic cardiod as your main axe. As we discussed in earlier chapters, the electret condenser will provide better clarity when recording very low- or very high-pitched sounds. But the electret condenser doesn't deal very well with the high sound pressure levels of live performance.

THE MONITOR SYSTEM

Your basic stereo receiver will probably power your monitor speakers in your studio. The receiver should have about 50 watts or more per stereo channel to be most effective. You don't need a lot of doodads like remote, surround sound, or subsonic filters. You don't want your receiver to cover up imperfections in your mix, you want it to help you find them. Good, clean power in a no-nonsense package is the ticket for your monitor system amplifier.

A decent set of home stereo speakers can be the "main monitor" speakers in your studio. Some speakers are designed to make anything sound good. But you really don't want that—you want to find your mistakes before you commit them to the master tape. A basic set of two-way or three-way speakers from a reputable manufacturer should do the job.

You may want to supplement these with a small set of speakers or a "boom box." These small speakers will let you hear what your tape will sound like on the radio or a smaller audio system (perhaps like the one your publisher might use in his or her office).

You should use closed headphones for recording. They don't let the music out into the air the way "open-air" 'phones do. If you are performing a vocal track while listening to previous tracks through heaphones, you don't want the previously recorded tracks leaking from your 'phones back through your vocal mic.

Since you'll be using them so much, your headphones should be comfortable and they should be of the highest audio quality you can afford. You will probably need a backup set of 'phones for anyone you usually record with. If you do this regularly and you already own a portable studio or mixer with a single headphone jack, you may find that you'll need a special headphone amp.

EFFECTS AND SIGNAL PROCESSORS

The only truly indispensible effects for the home studio are reverb and EQ. You'll probably have sufficient EQ controls in the mixer section of your portable studio. So the effect that tops our most wanted list is reverb. And the reverb for our suggested studio must be stereo.

Some reverb devices offer mono inputs and stereo outputs. This won't do. There are some fine values these days in digital reverbs that offer some of the most used reverb effects (such as Rooms or Halls) that sell for around $200.

Depending upon your budget, there are also some multiple-effects processors on the market that may be worth your consideration. For about double the investment of your basic reverb, you could snare one of these Disneyland effects boxes. They usually offer reverb, delay, chorus, flanging, and equalization in a single rack-mountable package.

Almost as vital on the effects hit list is a piece that's not really an effect at all, the direct box. A good direct box can solve so many problems that it is almost, but not quite, essential for Studio 1. Most of you will plug your low-impedance microphones into a transformer, and then into the mixer of your portable studio. You'll plug your instruments, from electric bass and guitar to drum machines and synthesizers, directly into the mixer of your portable studio. If you had a direct box, you'd find it helpful in all these applications because direct boxes treat the "transforming" process more carefully and more thoroughly. They are quieter and more efficient than simple transformers. A direct box can also be used to help quiet noisy effects devices, particularly those "stomp box" guitar effects. Running the output of these effects into a good direct box, and then using the low-impedance mic input of your mixer, can really help increase the signal-to-noise ratio (that's shop talk for the relationship between the strength of the signal and that of the noise) of these guitar effects.

CABLES AND CONNECTORS

Obviously, you know you need some cables and wire to hook your studio together, but these things deserve a little more attention than most of you will want to give them. Use the highest-quality cables and speaker wire that you can find and afford. This does not necessarily mean the kind with gold connectors, but bad cables will create all kinds of buzzes, pops, crackles, and other Rice Krispie effects when you least need them—which is often. Mediocre cables simply won't get all the signal down the line, and will lose high frequencies in the process, opening the door for some buzzes too. You can very easily use more than a dozen RCA audio cables in setting up your studio. If one bad cable causes noise, imagine what twelve or fourteen bad cables can do.

These suggestions apply to instrument cables as well. More tracks may have been ruined by crackling cables than bumbling fingers. Keep a good number of extra cables around for emergencies.

Since capacitance—a buildup of energy—can start to affect the quality of the signal transmitted down the cable, look for cables labeled "low capacitance." These cables help prevent the energy buildup in the shield and wire elements.

When you are setting up the studio, don't attempt to be overly neat about bundling your cables. Tightly bundled and bound cables have a tendancy to start acting like radio antennae in the studio. Leave cables a little loose.

A surge-protected power supply is another good idea. This will help protect your equipment and your music from any surprises generated by the power company. Having a few AC ground lifts (three-to-two power adapters) around the studio is also a good idea. These can reverse the polarity of some of the two-prong electronic devices on the market when needed (those with the large prong on one side). The surge protector and ground lifts will help keep buzzes from the refrigrerator and air conditioner from ending up in the middle of your ballad.

OTHER ESSENTIALS

There are several additional items you might find helpful. Among these are:

- Labels
- Track sheets
- Head cleaner
- Swabs
- Degausser
- A small tool set
- An electronic tuner
- A metronome or drum machine

Those little labels you get from the stationary store can be life savers. Label everything you can: cables (both ends), channels in the mixer, tapes, boxes—everything. Track sheets help you plan and keep track of the recording process: "Voice, track 1; guitar, track 2;" and so on. This may seem unnecessary, but once you begin bouncing tracks together or doing several solos, you'll find it very easy to forget where things are. By using track sheets to help plan the sessions, you'll also avoid painting yourself into some audio corner.

Unless you really enjoy burning dollar bills or wasting your time, don't forget the cleaning and maintenance goodies. Head-cleaning fluid, rubber cleaner for the pinch roller, swabs, and a degausser (demagnetizer) are absolutely vital. The author has seen machines totally ruined simply by being used too long without cleaning and degaussing. The tapes made on these machines for a long time before they went belly-up must have sounded terrible.

This isn't school, or your mother telling you to clean your room; this is real life. It's your music—keep it clean. We'll talk more later about maintenance routines and schedules.

Got a good ear? Well, save it. An electronic tuner will consistently deliver good pitch, and pitch can become a problem in multitracking—particularly when a guitarist tries to tune a bass. Nothing's worse than laying down some tracks, doing a bounce, and discovering that one of the original takes now buried and out of reach is out of tune.

And you say you have a good sense of time? You can save that too. Particularly if you are going to record with other musicians, you really need a "click track" metronome or drum machine. If out of tune is bad, ragged time isn't better. And you can waste a lot of time trying to sync up to a sloppy off-beat strum. Recording a metronome click track or a basic drum part before you begin recording your guitar, keyboard, and other parts will help keep everything "in time."

WHERE TO PUT THE EQUIPMENT

Some people are fortunate enough to have an extra room, or a large portion of a room, that can be set aside specifically for the studio. Others may have to set it up on the kitchen table every time they want to record. A permanent—or at least semipermanent—place is best. Inspiration fades rapidly in the flood of perspiration. Even if your studio is simply a portion of the guest room closet, it's great to have it permanently set up.

There are many garage bands and a few garage studios. If you go the garage route, make sure the area is clean and dry; dust and moisture can kill machines. You may want to get a tarp or plastic cover that can be put over the studio between sessions.

Some people get very creative when finding the perfect location for their studio. A songwriter friend of the author had his studio set up on one of the shelves in his linen closet. He claimed he loved the natural reverb in the hallway. Another friend, a traveling musician, had his studio set up in two briefcases that could be pulled out and set up in just a few minutes.

The recording tips sections will give you some ideas of things you can do at home to help create a better recording environment.

PART TWO

RECORDING
TECHNIQUES

Tom Petty may have been right. The waiting is the hardest part.

You've got your equipment (hopefully, in your unbridled enthusiasm, you managed not to destroy the box your machine came in as you opened it up). You've made some space for your studio. And you've got all this material you can't wait to get to work on. Finally, you can begin to think of these songs in terms of more than just voice and another instrument.

The only thing stopping you is this: How do I turn this darned machine on? Once you figure that out, we will run through the various steps and processes you'll need to know to get the best sound out of your equipment, from miking your acoustic guitar to using MIDI to mixing down. But first things first: getting to know the layout of your equipment is probably the best place to start—you know, like finding the On/Off switch.

Every effort has been made to make the following instructions generic and thorough. You will find that no matter what brand name rides on the grill work of your particular equipment, you should be able to utilize the following instructions almost to the letter.

Even assuming you jumped immediately into the deeper end of the recording pool and bought some kind of digital system, the instructions will still work for you. The manufacturers of digital equipment, as a group, have done a wonderful thing. They have made every effort to use analog recording terms that have been around forever. The buttons and functions of these digital machines have familiar names and work in much the same way as their analog counterparts.

In preparing this second edition of the book, I went through the instruction section using my hard disk recorder instead of an analog cassette machine. I'm confident you can use these tips and techniques very effectively to make great recordings with your digital equipment too. You may simply now have the luxury of punch-ins that don't destroy the previous material until you're sure you want to. Or you may have an Undo button that lets you quickly forget and get rid of your most recent mistake.

The General Recording Tips, beginning with Chapter 9, also fair equally well in the digital or analog world. Getting a great recorded sound from a guitar or drum has more to do with understanding the characteristics of that instrument, the quirks of your studio space, and your microphone techniques than whether or not the Record button is on an analog or digital machine. So learn these techniques and make great recordings on any machine.

One basic piece of advice, regardless of what you're doing in the recording process: be patient. One of the main advantages of home recording is that no one is standing over you with a stopwatch in his or her hand, a bell cheerfully ringing for each dollar you spend. Think about what you're committing to tape. Give your ideas a run-through, certainly, but, to my knowledge, planning ahead has never ruined a recording.

Be methodical. Just as you will get used to finding the On/Off switch and hitting the Record button without looking for it, get in the habit of cleaning and degaussing your heads, if you have an analog recorder, and maintaining your transport (analog or digital). I don't mean you should do this every time you lift off the protective cover, but if you do right by the equipment, the equipment will do right by you.

Another aspect of being methodical is keeping a log, not only of the tracks you're working on but of all your tapes and disks. Nothing's more frustrating than knowing you've got great work on tape and not being able to find it. "I know it's around here somewhere. . . ."

With these guidelines established, we're ready to look at some basic recording procedures.

CHAPTER 8

Basic Multitrack Techniques

Before you even begin to think about recording, you have to ask yourself (no, not *that* question) if you've completely unpacked your equipment. Watch out for extra packing materials in the transport or elsewhere on the unit. The cardboard and the pressed styrofoam that once protected the equipment shouldn't get in your way now. And if at all possible, keep the original packaging—if only to transport your gear from time to time.

The owner's manuals should be close at hand when you're first using your equipment (you should have these nearby for the first few weeks, at any rate). Have you got the right type of tape for your machine? *Really?* Find the tape type that is specified for your particular unit and get it. You've laid out good money for this equipment; don't start cutting corners now.

Plug in the AC cord or the power adapter, if your unit uses one (the excitement is almost killing you, isn't it?).

Some of the things we discuss here may seem ridiculously obvious to you, but as you will see, there are lots of right ways to do things in recording—and lots of wrong ones, too. Experience may be a great teacher, but there's no point in reliving the annoyance that so many others have encountered when they decided to add the drum machine *after* they had recorded all the basic tracks. Smarmy Nasty of the Dead Fish Band has been trying to sync his preprogrammed drum part with that absolutely scintillating 8 zillion dB solo for the past six years now with no success. Good luck, Smarms!

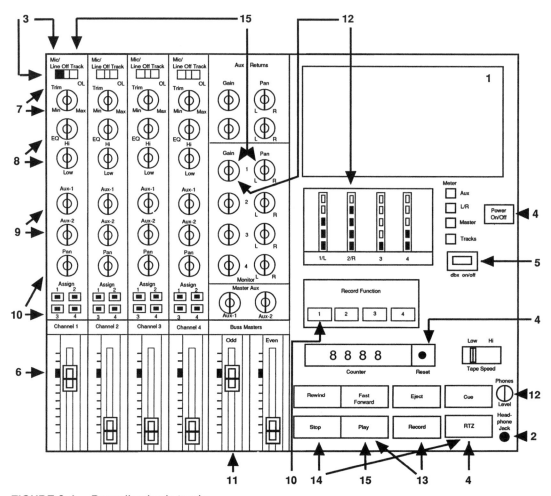

FIGURE 8-1.   Recording basic tracks.

As we go through the process of learning to record basic tracks, refer to Figure 8-1. The numbers below correspond to the numbers on the diagram.

RECORDING BASIC TRACKS

1. Put the tape into the tape compartment (I warned you that we would touch on the obvious, didn't I?). You will probably have to lift a plastic lid to get at the tape transport. Cassette tape transports usually run from left to right, so the tape reel on

the left should be the one full of tape. There will probably be an arrow indicating the direction of tape travel on the lid of the compartment.

2. Find the headphone jack(s). Plug in your headphones. We've already warned you about using two sets of headphones on one headphone jack. Here's another warning: Don't use mono headphones or those little earplug-type units that come with Walkman-type cassette players. These can also damage the headphone circuits in the machine.

3. *With the power still off,* plug your instrument or microphone into Channel 1 of the mixer section. If your unit has separate inputs for mic and line (instrument), switch it to the appropriate setting. Remember what we said earlier on about the different connectors, levels, and impedances on mixer input channels. Make sure that your mic or instrument is switched on and that volume/level controls on the instrument are turned up enough to send a signal to the mixer.

4. Turn the power on. Lights will blink as your portable studio comes to life. Roll some tape by pressing the Play button. Let the tape run for five seconds or so, just enough time to let the leader (the clear tape that won't record anything) roll past the heads and onto the takeup reel. Press the Reset button on your tape counter (Figure 8-2). Does your equipment have any memory or *return-to-zero* (RTZ) functions?* If it does, consult your manual and press the appropriate buttons and/or the tape counter reset so that you can rewind to this spot after recording the first track.

5. You should use noise reduction on your basic tracks. Make sure it is turned on. An LED (little red or green light) will usually light somewhere to show you your noise reduction is operating.

6. Adjust the Channel 1 fader to a position of about number 7 on its scale. This is usually the nominal level for a channel fader.

7. Find the channel's overload indicator (sometimes part of the meter system) and a control called *Trim* or *Input Level.* If your unit doesn't have one of these, perform the adjustment on the channel fader. Your unit may have both level and trim controls. In this case, the level control is probably for tape playback. Your trim control will adjust the mic/line input levels. If your

---

*Return to Zero (RTZ) functions as its name suggests. When you set a memory point in your tape by pressing a Cue or Memory button, and then pressing RTZ, the tape will automatically go into rewind when it reaches the memory spot. The tape will then rewind until it reaches zero, 00:00, on the tape counter.

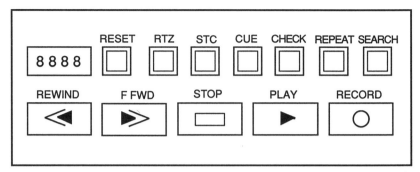

FIGURE 8-2. Transport controls with tape counter and typical return-to-zero and automated functions.

unit has both, you can adjust the level as it comes into the channel with the trim to make sure it is not too hot (distorting the input section of your mixer). The channel fader, on the other hand, makes sure the level going into the program busses is workable after you've used EQ and processing on the signal in the channel.

Play your instrument or speak into your microphone. Turn the trim or level control up until the overload indicator lights. Keep playing or speaking while you adjust trim or level down until the overload light stops flashing. Don't take it too far down now; just until it stops flashing.

8. For the time being, set your EQ controls to their "flat" positions. (This usually means that the pointer should be aimed straight up at 12 o'clock.)

9. We'll ignore any aux or effects controls you may have in your mixer channel for the moment. Adjust them to their off position, usually counterclockwise.

10. Now you need to assign the mixer channel to a recording buss using any assign buttons and the pan control. As we discussed earlier, pan and buss assignment switches work together. A channel must be assigned to a buss for it to reach the recorder. If a channel isn't assigned, the signal goes no further. Pan is used to help balance the channel signal between the left and right (odd and even) busses. If you assign your channel to more than one buss, pan determines how much goes to the left (odd) busses and to the right (even) busses. If you assign to only one buss, use pan to make sure all of the possible signal in the channel goes to the buss assigned by rotating the pan control fully left or right.

If your unit is capable of recording all tracks at once, then you will press the channel assignment button for Buss 1. Sometimes an odd and an even buss are put on the same channel assignment button such as 1 and 2, or 3 and 4. In this case, the pan control is used to route signal only to the left or right buss. So you may press an assignment button marked 1 and 2. Adjust the pan control fully counterclockwise.

If your unit records only two tracks at once, it will have a couple of switches that are record "ready" and record "safe" selectors. Adjust your pan control fully left, and put Track 1 into its record-ready mode. There will usually be an LED light that will blink to let you know that Track 1 is in record-ready mode.

11. Adjust the left master fader on your unit to approximately 7. Your unit may not have separate master faders, or it may have one fader that controls both left and right busses. On large units, such as TASCAM's Studio 8, there may be faders that control the program busses in addition to the stereo master faders. In this case, raise the odd program buss fader to 7 as well as the left master fader to 7.

12. Put on your headphones. Speak into your mic or play your instrument. Adjust the level of sound in your headphones using the headphone level control or the stereo master fader. Make any adjustments necessary to the trim control, as in Step 7. If your unit has a separate monitor section, you will need to adjust any monitor gain controls associated with Channel/Track 1. If you have VU meters on your unit, adjust your instrument/mic level using the channel fader until the meter is reading near 0 when you are speaking or playing (Figure 8-3).

13. You're ready to go! Press the Record and Play buttons on your transport (sometimes only the Record button needs to be pressed). Start playing or speaking into the mic. The record function light will stop blinking and it will stay steadily lighted. If you are simply speaking into the mic, try counting very slowly, leaving plenty of space between each number. When you do your overdub in a few minutes, you'll record something else in these spaces.

14. After recording your first track, press Stop on the transport control. If your unit has a return-to-zero or memory return function, press that button. Your tape will rewind to the spot selected earlier. If your unit doesn't have a return function, press Rewind and roll the tape back to 00:00 on the counter.

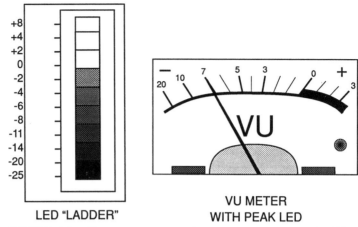

LED "LADDER"   VU METER
                          WITH PEAK LED

FIGURE 8-3. The two most popular meter systems are the VU meter and the LED "ladder," which is a stack of light-emitting diodes.

15. To hear what you've just recorded, turn off the record function switch. (Its LED will go off.) Set your mixer channel input selector to its Tape (also called "Track") position for Track 1. Some units will automatically route the tape return to a monitor section of the mixer. Press Play on the transport and listen through your headphones. Adjust the level in the mixer or the mixer's monitor section. When you've finished listening to your first track, rewind the tape again.

Now you're ready to participate in the magical process created by Les Paul: overdubbing.

OVERDUBBING

This is what you really got this multitrack equipment for—the ability to commit your own arrangements to tape. The idea now is simply to see that both parts will sound as if they were recorded at the same time (Figure 8-4). So you will listen to the part just recorded on Track 1 while recording another on Track 2 or Track 3. The numbered paragraphs that follow correspond to the numbers on Figure 8-5.

1. You may use the same mixer channel to record your next track. If you are using a microphone, leave it plugged into the mic input. The faders, EQ and trim controls should be fine where

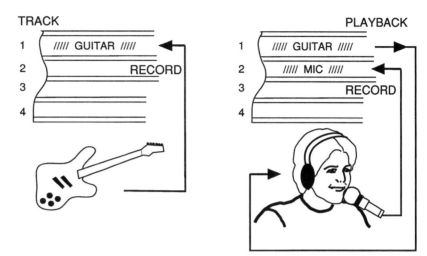

FIGURE 8-4. The process of overdubbing is one of listening to a previously recorded track—the guitar in this example—and recording another part that will go with it.

they are. Rotate the pan control in Channel 1 all the way clockwise (right). This will send Channel 1 to the even-numbered program busses, if your unit has them, and to the right stereo buss. If your mixer channel has assign switches, make sure the channel is assigned to Buss 2 (or 1 and 2).

Note that your unit may have mixer channels permanently assigned to tracks of the recorder. In other words, you may not be able to record to Track 2 using Channel 1 of the mixer. In that case, you will have to plug your mic or instrument into the appropriate mixer channel (probably Channel 2). You will then have to set up the channel as you did the first time through.

2. Set the Track 2 record function switch to its on or ready position (some kind of LED will usually blink, as it did when you recorded Track 1). *Make sure you have turned off the record function switch for Track 1, or else you will erase it.*

3. Raise the right master fader to approximately 7. If your unit has program busses, raise the even buss fader that corresponds to Track 2 to the same level as the master fader, about 7.

4. Press Play on the transport and listen to Track 1. Adjust the level in your headphones. You may want to speak or play your instrument now to set the level for your new Track 2 in your headphones/monitor. When you're done, rewind the tape to zero.

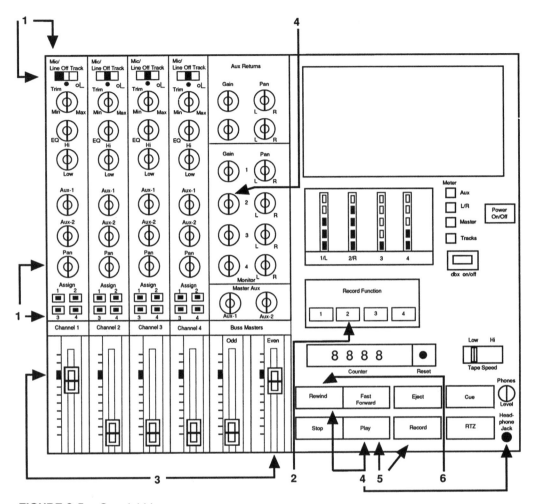

FIGURE 8-5. Overdubbing.

5. You are ready to record Track 2. Press Record (the record function light for Track 2 should stop blinking and stay lighted continuously). Play along with the first take or, if you were counting through a mic, try placing numbers in the pauses left on Track 1.

6. When finished, rewind the tape. Turn off the record function switch for Track 2. Press Play and listen to both Tracks 1 and 2 together.

There you have it: your first home overdub. You can fill another track in just the same way. If you want to experiment, great!

For the purposes of this exercise, though, leave at least one track free for the ping-pong recording technique we'll discuss later.

PUNCH-IN OR INSERT RECORDING

Stretch your imagination a little and suppose that one of your two tracks didn't turn out exactly as planned. Perhaps one of the numbers was spoken out of sequence. Maybe a note crept into your solo that was just a little too far "outside." Whatever the reason, your multitrack allows you to re-record small segments of your previously recorded track. While in play mode, your transport can be put into record mode at the right spot and put back into play mode when the "bad" area has passed (Figure 8-6).

Often, machines come equipped with a footswitch so that your hands can stay on your instrument. One thing to remember about punching in is that any area of your track that you fix will be fixed permanently. Once you have recorded over a section, you can't retrieve the old one. So rehearse your punch-ins. The numbered steps below correspond to the numbers on Figure 8-7.

1. Set up your mixer channel as you did before. If you are about to fix a portion of the overdub, be sure that your setup is as described for Track 2 in the overdub section. You may want to

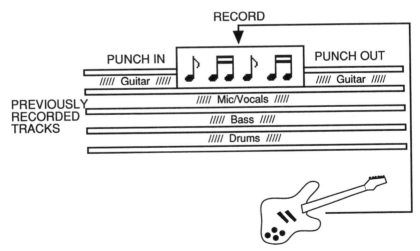

FIGURE 8-6. Punching in a few notes can fix an error in playing on a previously recorded track.

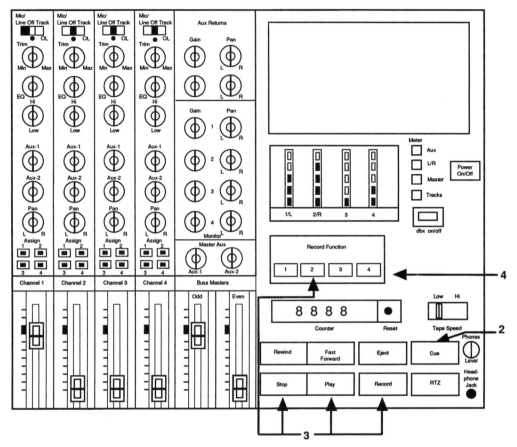

FIGURE 8-7. Punch-in recording.

rehearse the punch-in a few times without pressing the record function switch to its on position. Accidents *do* happen.

2. When you have found the spot you want to fix, set the memory (cue point) there if your equipment has it; if not, reset the counter. On most units, turning on the record function switches the monitor (headphones) from tape to source (from the old track on tape to your instrument/mic input). It's possible, then, to use the record function switch to get a few dry runs before you execute the punch-in itself.

   Your machine may have a switch called Insert or Sync. This feature helps you to hear the parts you need to by switching your headphones from the previously recorded track to the new source material and back again to the old track during the punch-in.

3. After a few dry runs, when you feel confident that you can perform the punch-in, put the Record Ready switch on (its light will blink, if it has one). When the tape nears the point where you want to repair the track, push Record and Play on the transport. If your unit has a footswitch, simply step on it. When you come to the place that you want to revert back to the old track, push Stop on the transport or step on the footswitch again.

4. Once you have corrected the mistake, be sure to turn off any record function switches, returning them to their "safe" position. Rewind the tape and listen. If the punch-in didn't turn out the the way you had hoped it would, try it again. Practice these techniques a lot. Make your mistakes and learn the techniques on this practice material so that you won't mess up on serious attempts later on.

PING-PONGING, COLLAPSING, OR BOUNCING TRACKS

You may only have four tracks on your unit, but with *ping-ponging, collapsing, or bouncing* tracks, you can free used tracks by combining them onto a single vacant track and so make it possible to record more than four different parts in a single arrangement.

Moreover, it's also possible to record new live parts while you're combining previously recorded tracks. So where there were once three discrete tracks, you can have one comprised of four different parts. (Getting confused yet? Good. *That's* why you'll need a log book).

The process involves playing back the previously recorded tracks, say Tracks 1, 2, and 3, while routing them to the vacant Track 4, which is in the record mode. When you're done, and the material is successfully "mixed" to the single track, you can record new material on Tracks 1, 2, and 3 (Figure 8-8).

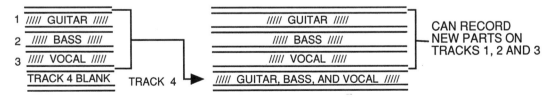

FIGURE 8-8. Through the process of "bouncing," or "ping-ponging," previously recorded tracks may be re-recorded onto any blank track. The old tracks may then be erased and used to record more music.

Bouncing sacrifices a little fidelity, but adds tremendous flexibility to your home studio. Let's see how it's done. Match the steps below with the numbers on Figure 8-9.

1. Set your mixer to receive tape playback for Tracks 1, 2, and 3. This will mean setting the input selectors to Tape. Since we will mix and record Tracks 1, 2, and 3 to Track 4, we will also have to assign the mixer channels of Tracks 1, 2, and 3 to Track 4 using the assignment switches and/or pan control. Rotate the pan controls for all tracks/channels to be bounced fully clockwise, right.

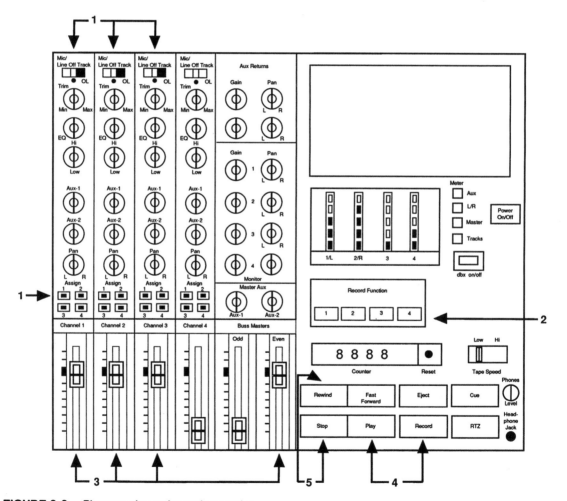

FIGURE 8-9. Ping-ponging or bouncing tracks.

Some units may not allow you to bounce all three tracks to Track 4, or they may have some restriction on bouncing to adjacent tracks (recording on a track that is right next the one playing back). You should still be able to bounce Tracks 1 and 2 to Track 4, though.

2. Turn on the record function switch for Track 4. This may mean setting the right stereo buss record function to its on position.

3. Set the playback levels for Tracks 1, 2, and 3 so that they sound good and balanced to you. If your unit has a rotary level control (knob that turns) for track playback levels, set them to approximately the two o-clock position. If you have faders, set them to approximately 7. Set the program buss and right stereo buss (if your unit has both) to 7. Make sure your meter or LED for Track 4 is reading near zero as you listen to the playback. Make any adjustments necessary to your headphone level.

4. Rewind the tape to zero. Press Record or Record and Play. Your Track 4 record function light should stay on. No other tracks should be in record mode. Your material from Tracks 1, 2, and 3 is now being ping-ponged to Track 4.

Note that if your mixer has sufficient channels, or input flexibility, you can add new live material during the ping-pong process. Connect your instrument or mic to a mixer channel that is free (not being used for tape playback) and assign the channel to Track 4. Play or sing the new part along with Tracks 1, 2, and 3. Your new part will be recorded, along with Tracks 1, 2, and 3, onto Track 4.

Make sure your levels for the new material fit well with the others as they are going to Track 4. Unlike the overdubbing you did before, you cannot repair any mistakes this time around because the new part is imprinted on the same track as the previously recorded material. If you attempt to fix it, you will also be fixing your other work. So, if you make a mistake, you will have to go through the entire piece again.

Be sure to listen to the completed ping-pong to make sure it turned out all right before you record over Tracks 1, 2, and 3 with new material.

5. When the recording is done, press Stop and then press Rewind. Turn off the record function switch for Track 4. Turn the input selector to Tape for the mixer channel that corresponds to Track 4. Turn the input selectors corresponding to Tracks 1, 2, and 3 to Mic/Line. If you want, you can

listen to the results of your ping-pong by pressing Play and adjusting the levels for Track 4 playback.

6. You can repeat the ping-pong procedure by recording new material on Tracks 1 and 2 and then bouncing them to Track 3. Only four tracks, but they can hold as many as seven different parts with only two bounces.

There are a couple of caveats to be aware of with bouncing, though. Every time you do it, what you have on tape will be affected in two ways. First off, even with the best noise reduction system available, you are still going to increase the level of sheer tape noise—quite apart from what you've imprinted on the tape. Secondly, the quality of the original tracks is going to deteriorate with each *generation* (bounce).

Think of the image we used earlier about tracks being like footprints in the sand. Bouncing tracks is a bit like a wave rolling over them—they're still there, but they've lost their edges. If you add a live part as you combine your tracks, you may cover the tape noise, but the old tracks are still going to lose more and more fidelity every time you bounce.

THE MIXDOWN OR REMIX

Remember that second recorder you had to buy? Well, this procedure is the reason why you got it. By mixing down your multitrack tape to stereo, your music can be played on car cassette players, home stereos, and even by those annoying little cassette players with headphones that make people walk in front of moving traffic. Converting your multitrack efforts to the stereo format is called *mixdown* or *remix* (Figure 8-10).

It is impossible to overemphasize the need for a high-quality stereo machine. At this point, you are probably getting a sense of

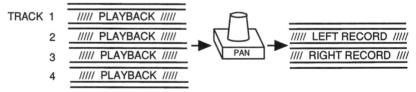

FIGURE 8-10. The process of mixdown, or remix, uses the mixer to blend the music from your multitrack to two tracks of a stereo master recorder.

how much thought and effort will be going into your recording. And, oddly, the more you do, the more finicky you become. Wouldn't it be a real shame to ruin that work by mixing down to an inadequate tape deck?

If your mixdown deck is as good as your multitrack, it can play a role in your actual recording process. We'll let you in on this later.

On to the mixdown. Match the steps below with the numbers in Figure 8-11.

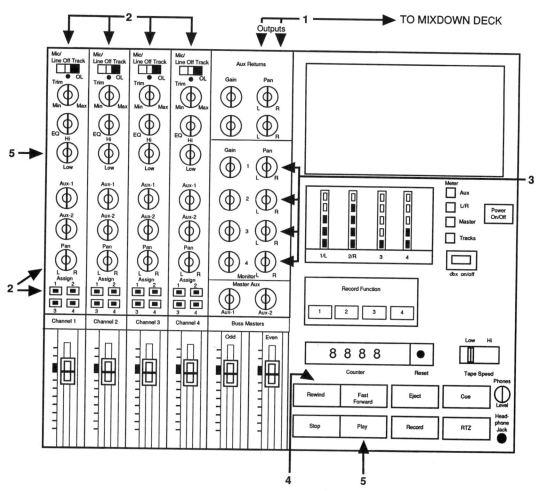

FIGURE 8-11.   Remix or mixdown recording.

1. You'll need to connect your mixdown recorder to the stereo master outputs of the mixer section on your portable studio. These outputs will be labeled *Line Out Left and Right, Stereo Output Left and Right,* or *Master Out Left and Right.* They should be RCA-type connectors, just like those at the inputs of your mixdown deck. Make sure Left Out on the portable studio goes to Left In on the stereo deck and Right Out goes to Right In.

2. Set your mixer channel input selectors to their Tape positions (if your unit has a separate monitor section for tape playback, it may also have a channel input selector position called Remix; that's where you want to set it). We want our tape signals going fully through the mixer channels so that we can adjust the EQ, level, pan, and effects processing. Set your assignment switches to Busses 1 and 2 (or the master left and right busses, if your unit has them). You will use the pan control to determine how much signal goes to which side of the stereo mix.

3. You may want to do the mixdown by listening to your music through the monitor system rather than through headphones. If your portable studio has separate monitor outputs, connect these to your stereo receiver or amplifier. There will probably be a switch that lets you assign the monitor system to listen to different parts of your mix such as the aux or effects mixes and the stereo buss. It will probably be the same one that switches your headphones to the various mixes. Make sure this switch is set to the stereo buss.

   If your unit has only one set of stereo outputs, connect these to the receiver and use its tape dubbing capability to connect to your mixdown deck. That is, there should be inputs and outputs for two tape decks on your receiver. Plug your mixer outputs into one set of inputs and plug your mixdown deck into the other set of outputs—but don't connect them to posts intended for the same machine on your receiver (Tape 1, for example). If your receiver only has one tape post, send the portable studio to the Aux input of the receiver and send from the receiver via the Tape Out on the Tape post.

4. When you're properly connected, rewind the multitrack to zero. Put a fresh, high-quality tape in your mixdown recorder. Put the mixdown recorder in play for 5 seconds or so to roll past the leader. Set the mixdown deck's counter to zero or use its transport memory to mark the spot.

5. Play your multitrack tape, making adjustments to the pan, EQ, and various level controls, until it sounds right to you. You may find that you'll have to move a control at a specific place in the tape as it's playing to make something sound better. Rehearse this a few times. Check and set the record levels of the mixdown deck; your material should be at between −3 and 0 on the meters. When you're ready, rewind both machines to zero. Put the mixdown deck into record mode by pressing Record and Play. Put the multitrack into play mode by pressing Play. Perform any control moves you've rehearsed at the appropriate times.

6. When finished, rewind the mixdown deck and listen to the playback of your stereo master tape. If it's not what you wanted, make your plans as to how you'll fix it and start the mixdown process over again. This is your finished product. Make it the best it can be. Besides, the more you do it the better you'll get at it. Keep practicing.

Whatever copies you send out to Aunt Sarah, Boris your music publisher, or Alphonse the A&R man should be made from your *stereo master;* this is, after all, your music the way you want them to hear it. Store your stereo master with your multitrack master for later use. We'll give you some storage tips later, too.

CHAPTER 9

General Recording Tips

A good, listenable recording is like any other artistic endeavor. It isn't just dynamic performances and great musical arrangements; it's a balancing act in which you bring together all the elements in just the right proportions to create the perfect assemblage of sound.

Some people see this balancing act as a mystical and indescribable process. But while artistic judgment is involved, what recording most often involves is a lot of common sense. We can't give you the experience or the "feel" for balancing the different parts, but with these tips, you can create some very fine recordings.

The various controls on your mixing and recording equipment all affect one another. Turning up one control too high means that you'll have to set the next control in the chain too low. As an illustration, note the following fable of "Golda Lox and the Three Faders."

Once upon a time in a Los Angeles recording school, there studied an aspiring recordist named Golda Lox. One day as Golda went through the various studios at the school, she found herself hungry for a decent-sounding mix.

Golda went into Studio A. There, the mixer channels were set to the 9 or 10 range—*all* of them. But the master faders were set to the 1 or 2 range. Golda listened to the mix and said, "This mix is way too distorted. The channels are pushed too high and the masters are too low" (Figure 9-1).

Golda saw Studio B. She went in and looked at the mixer. This mixer was set with all the channel faders reading about 2 and the master faders reading about 9. Golda listened to the mix. "Oh no,"

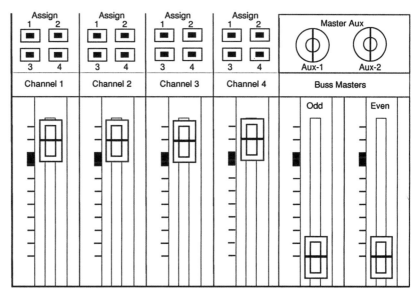

FIGURE 9-1. Channel faders are set too high and master faders are set too low, overdriving the busses.

she cried, "this mix is way too noisy. The channel faders are too low and the masters are too high" (Figure 9-2).

Fearing she had come to the wrong recording school, Golda found herself at last in Studio C. There the mixer was set with its channel faders all hovering around 7. Its master faders were also around the 7 point. Golda listened to the mix and said, "Oh my, that's just right!" And hungry as she was for a great mix, Golda ate it all up (Figure 9-3).

The moral of our story is this: a successful mix will generally show a balance among the faders. If you push something too hard it distorts, so you have to compensate somewhere else—remember the terrible things Golda saw in Studios A and B. The channel faders were so high that the engineer pulled the masters way back.

Similarly, if you don't send enough signal to the next piece in the audio chain, you must boost what it gets. The result is that you will increase the amount of noise in the signal. In Studio B, the engineer, perhaps afraid of sending too much signal from the channels to the busses, kept the channel faders too low. He then had to push the buss fader too high just to get the signal up to an appropriate level for the recorder—hence the even more fearsome *noise*.

Studio C, in our book at least, is the place where the pretty birds will sing and the flowers will turn their happy faces toward the sun.

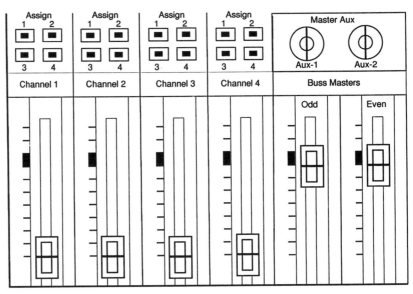

FIGURE 9-2. Channel faders are set too low and master faders are set high, creating noise.

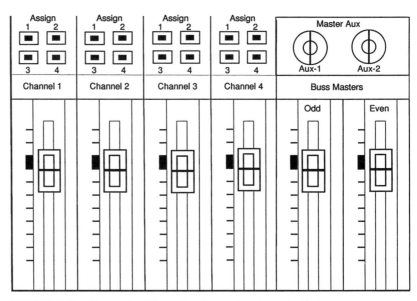

FIGURE 9-3. Correct settings for channel and master faders.

EQUALIZATION

The nice thing about morals in stories is that they can apply to just about anything. So just as a balance between channel and master faders will save you from the hardships of distortion on the one hand and noise on the other, a balanced approach to cutting and boosting various EQ controls will get the best results.

Like the channel and master faders, EQ controls are interactive. You can change the timbre of a signal by cutting or attenuating a frequency as well as by boosting or amplifying one. Say you want a little more brightness from your signal. As it passes through your EQ, your first instinct is to boost some of the higher frequency ranges. While this will make the signal brighter, it may also boost some of the noise in the mid- to high frequencies. By cutting back some of the bass frequencies, you can create a brighter signal because you have left the highs more apparent.

The lesson with equalizing is this: Follow your first instinct (to arrive at a brighter sound, for example) but think of different ways to get that sound *without* touching the high frequency knob. A slight cut in an opposite frequency may achieve better results in the long run.

A tailor starts with a big suit and then nips and tucks it precisely into the perfect fit. This is what you want to do with your EQ system. A little nip here, a slight smidgen of a boost there. The most common mistake among home recordists is how they use their EQ and effects. In both cases, the answer is too much. When they get to their final mixdown, the instruments are so bloated and bleached that they're hard to recognize—let alone listen to.

As we discussed earlier in this book, the term frequency can be thought of in terms of pitch by the musician. Low-frequency ranges are where the bass instruments produce their sound. High frequencies are produced by the high-pitched instruments such as flutes, piccolos, and violins.

Does an equalizer change the pitch of an instrument? No. What it changes is the level (loudness/softness) of a very specific frequency area (range). By boosting a high-frequency control, you are raising the signal level of all the music within the range of that high-frequency control. The effect is a brilliant sound; the high-frequency range is more "present." Boosting a bass frequency range will bring out the bass, kick drum, and low notes of the piano or synthesizer. The frequency chart here illustrates the relative frequency ranges of common instruments (Figure 9-4).

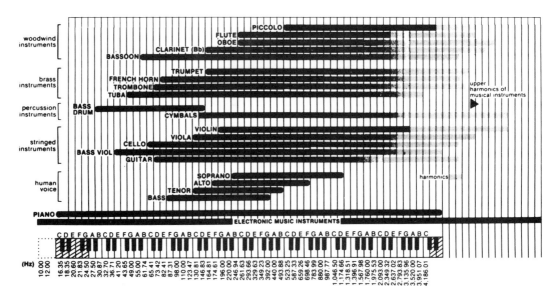

FIGURE 9-4. Instrument pitches and their frequency ranges. Understanding these is the key to effectively utilizing equalizers. (Courtesy of TASCAM, Teac Professional Division)

Here are some general characteristics of various frequency ranges:

20 Hz to 60 Hz: These frequencies are so low that some of us can't hear them at all. While elephants can hear these very distinctly, people tend more to feel these frequencies. Too much boost here will make things sound "partly cloudy"—as if you're hearing music with cotton in your ears.

60 Hz to 500 Hz: This is where pitches and timbres become more evident. Pianos, basses, drums, trumpets, violins, human voices, and many other instruments have fundamental notes/frequencies in this range. This is a very fickle range for equalizing: cut it too much and you will thin out the sound of your music. You'll replace the cotton in your ears with wax. Too much boost, on the other hand, can distort the pure sound of certain instruments, making them sound artificial.

500 Hz to 2.5 kHz: This is the infamous midrange. An awful lot of musical fundamental pitches exist here. Too much boost can really assault the ear, creating what is known as listener fatigue. What sounds fine and bright for a little while becomes grating after a short time. Too much cut and your sound can be either boomy or tinny. Good luck! This is a hard range to master.

2.5 kHz to 6 kHz: This area can be particularly important to home recordists using cassette multitracks because it contributes so much to the perception of brightness or presence. A slight boost at about 5 kHz can add some life to your cassettes, particularly as you are ping-ponging tracks. A little boost can go a long way here, since we tend to perceive these frequencies as being louder than their signal levels would suggest.

6 kHz to 15 kHz: This is the range of harmonics—overtones. The ring of bells and metal-stringed instruments such as guitars and pianos are affected most by changes in this range. Alien noise gremlins also float around here. Too much boost may let noise loose on your music.

READING YOUR METERS

The meters in your recording system are like most electronic measuring devices. They are designed to help us monitor and measure things that our own senses can't quite handle. Your meters tell you signal levels of the audio passing through them. They may also tell you whether or not a signal is peaking as it passes by.

How do meters differ from ears in their performance? Meters are objective. The ear is subjective. We tend to hear some things better than others (Figure 9-5). If a 1 kHz tone, a 100 Hz tone, and a 10 kHz tone were all played for us using the same measurable signal level, we would perceive the 1 kHz tone as being loudest.

The ear is also connected to an extremely sophisticated device that decides *how* we will hear certain things. The brain makes, as Carl Sagan would say, "billions and billions" of decisions about what we will perceive and how we will perceive it every second. The brain averages, it is biased toward certain sounds, it compensates for deficiencies; it is a wonderful but highly opinionated monitor.

What does this mean? Should we disregard what we hear and trust our meters totally? Or, since music is a listening art, should we disregard our meters and trust our ears? The answer is yes to both questions.

As the signal makes its way to tape, meters and overload indicators allow you to monitor your signals carefully. Percussion, synthesizers, and screaming rock vocals must be closely watched

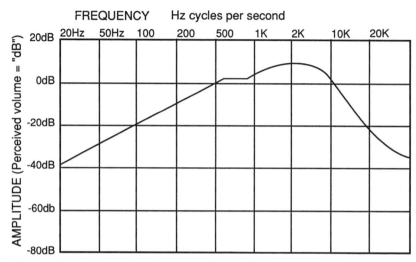

FIGURE 9-5. Human hearing range. Notice that we are particularly sensitive to midrange frequencies (500 Hz to 2.5 kHz). (Courtesy of TASCAM, Teac Professional Division)

for peaks of level that may not alarm your ear but that will alarm your equipment. Let science help you make sure that your signals are manageable.

During mixing down, ping-ponging, and so on, use your ears and artistic judgment. Your music must please you first. If you are just starting out, take heart in the fact that experience counts for a lot here as everywhere else. When in doubt about levels, you might want to trust your meters.

But don't trust your meters blindly. Many meters are accurate, but slow. If a burst of sound passes very quickly through them, they may not be able to fully respond to it. That is why many VU meters are augmented with peak LEDs.

PLANNING YOUR SESSIONS

By proper planning, you can avoid a lot of hassles during your session and save the time you might have otherwise wasted going over mistakes in judgment—like wondering how to add another instrument when there are no tracks left.

Inspiration can be a terrible master. Before you know it, you've combined two instruments on a single track that shouldn't have been, and one beautifully played part is mixed on the same track with an atrocious piece of playing. To make matters worse, you've already wiped the originals.

"Whoopsy daisy!"—or some equivalent thereof—is going to be a common part of your vocabulary early on. What kinds of things do you need to plan? Here are some basic questions you should answer:

- How many tracks will your recording require?
- When and how many times will you ping-pong?
- What instruments can be added while ping-ponging?
- Will this master be stereo or mono?
- How will you pan these instruments? (Don't bounce instruments to the same track if you want to pan them separately.)
- Should you use noise reduction?

Track sheets, available at most recording suppliers, are great tools for planning a session.

Here are some equipment-related points you should take care of ahead of time:

- Do you have an extra set of guitar strings so that you're prepared when one breaks?
- Are you recording with new strings that have been adequately broken in before the session?
- Does any of your equipment need to go to the shop?
- Are there pops and buzzes and squeals that need to be fixed?
- Do all of your audio cords work?
- Do you have enough head cleaner?
- Does your degausser work properly?
- Do you have a sufficient supply of the right kind of tape on hand?

Be prepared. Anything that can go wrong *will* go wrong right in the middle of your most inspired solo in years. Great, spontaneous music requires a lot of careful preparation.

What do you do when the spirit moves you in the middle of the night and you're unprepared? Assuming we're talking musical inspiration here, we suggest always having a "scratch" tape or two around. These can be used as electronic sketch pads for your musical ideas. Don't lose these inspirations, but don't expect them to flow fully realized from your unconscious mind onto the CD racks at your favorite record store. Capture your bursts of musical emotion on a scratch tape. When you have some time, you can plan a session to fully realize the music. Like many great songwriters, you may find that one finished song is the product of many little pieces of inspiration sung or played onto your scratch tapes over a period of weeks or even months.

MAINTAINING YOUR RECORDER

Will your car run great year after year without any tuneups or service? No—of course not! And yet, during all my years at TASCAM, a good half of the machines that came back for repair had problems caused by owner neglect or abuse. It's amazing that the same person who buys a machine with over 2 dB of signal-to-noise ratio performance will never clean the heads or demagnetize the machine.

Cleaning

When tape passes by the heads, it's a bit like rubbing a very fine sandpaper against them because it leaves a little of its oxide material behind. In addition, there are billions of little dust particles floating around in the air (ask anyone with hay fever). These things get deposited on our precious recorder heads. The accumulation of grit will combine with the rubbing action of tape and wear down the surface of your heads unevenly.

How much wear does it take to affect performance? These portable studios are thoroughbreds. Their head gaps and other tolerances are refined to *microns*—and a micron is pretty darn small. It doesn't take very much "sandpapering" to cause problems with performance.

Clean your heads often (and the guides and other hardware, too) every time you use the machine if possible. Use head cleaner available through your recording supplier. Use cotton swabs to wipe off the grit. You should also have rubber cleaner on hand to clean the pinch roller. Don't rely on those cassette tape cleaners that are supposed to clean your machine simply by playing them through one time. They don't work very well.

To clean the heads of your machine, use a cotton swab dipped in head cleaner and simply wipe across the heads until the swab doesn't come back with dirt on it. (You may have to remove the door to the cassette compartment to get at the heads. There should be instructions in your owner's manual on how to do this.) Use several swabs. Don't use so much head cleaner that it is dripping all over the place. Go over the heads a last time with a dry swab to remove any remnants of cleaner.

To clean the pinch roller, get out your swabs and rubber cleaner—*not* head cleaner. You'll need to get the pinch roller to turn for you. To do that, you have to put the transport in play mode and make the machine think a cassette is in the tray. A push rod mechanism senses when a cassette is in the tray, so if you push that sensing arm while you put the machine in play mode, the pinch roller will start spinning. Hold your swab soaked in rubber cleaner against the pinch roller with your free hand while you hold down the sensor with the other. Press the swab on the side of the pinch roller away from the capstan (the thing that pinches against the roller to move the tape). Otherwise, the swab may get pulled into the capstan and tangled up with it. You should also clean the capstan with a swab and head cleaner. Use a clean swab to get all the excess fluids off the capstan and pinch roller (Figure 9-6).

Demagnetizing or Degaussing

When you were in grade school, you were shown how magnetism works. Your teacher took some bar magnets and performed some experiments. One of those experiments may have been to cause the magnet to magnetize another piece of metal. To do this, you simply

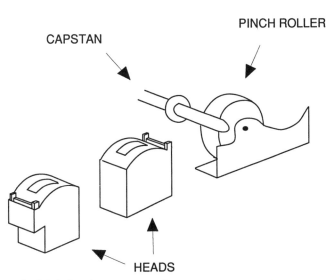

FIGURE 9-6. Components of a cassette transport.

rubbed the magnet along the metal object, a screwdriver or nail perhaps. Soon the screwdriver or nail was a magnet in its own right. There are many metal parts in your recorder that spend their lives rubbing up against magnetic tape. That's their job. That's what you bought them to do.

Here's the problem: if they become magnetized themselves, they will begin to erase your tapes.

Playing a cassette tape 20 to 30 times without demagnetizing (degaussing) the metal parts in the tape path will guarantee that you'll start losing high frequencies through erasure. Playing a cassette ten times without degaussing will deposit enough magnetism (.2 Gauss or so) to hurt the record head's ability. Buy a good degausser and use it (Figure 9-7). Here's how.

Your recorder must always be turned off when you are degaussing. Repeat after me: "My recorder must always be off when I am demagnetizing." When a degausser is turned on, it sends a spike of very high energy out its tip. Stand at least three feet away from your machine when you turn on the demagnetizer. It's not a bad idea to be facing away from your recorder when you turn on the degausser either—I would not joke about something like this. When you shop for your degausser, get one that has a plastic cover on the tip of it. This will help keep the tip from actually touching the parts of your recorder. *Never, ever* touch the heads with the uncovered metal tip of the degausser. It will permanently scar the heads.

Slowly pass the demagnetizer over the heads and other metal parts in the tape path without actually touching any of them, unless your degausser has plastic covering the tip. With a tip, you can

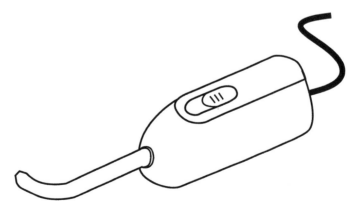

FIGURE 9-7. A demagnetizer. To remove residual magnetism, slowly pass the demagnetizer over the heads and other metal parts in the tape path.

lightly touch the parts. If your degausser doesn't have a plastic covering, use some black electrician's tape to make a covering of your own.

Before you turn off your degausser, walk three feet away, turn around, and then and only then turn it off. If you turn the degausser off or on while it is very close to the heads, you'll blow it big time. The surge of energy from the demagnetizer will put a permanent magnetic charge on the heads that you will never get off. You will have to replace the heads, and that's an expensive proposition.

This is a vital maintenance procedure for your machines, but it is one that entails some risk. Concentrate on the process at hand when you're degaussing. You can joke around with your buddies when you're done.

A recorder that is cleaned and degaussed regularly will last a very long time. And it will perform well within its specifications for a very long time—which is exactly what we want. So commit yourself to properly caring for your recorder.

STORING TAPES

Over a period of time, you will be amazed at the number of tapes you accumulate. You will have scratch tapes filled with ideas. You will have multitrack masters that you might want to remix or add parts to later. And you will have finished stereo masters. You may even have some tapes sent to you by friends in the business. When you think of the hours of work and creativity that went into making these tapes, you begin to realize what a valuable commodity they are. Storing them properly and keeping them straight will be very important to you.

Label and date all your tapes. Keep a file of your track sheets and label them in the same way you labeled the tape. Labels are cheap, so don't be afraid to re-label something if it needs it. Use masking tape if that's all that is around. The first time you go looking for your reggae version of "On Top of Old Smokey" featuring a blistering banjo solo that can't be redone, you'll be happy you labeled your tapes. Otherwise, you'll go through the long and tedious process of hunting and pecking—more a matter of blind luck than anything else and really, *really* aggravating.

Store your tapes in a dry, dust-free place that doesn't get too hot or too cold—what they call in the science trade "room temperature" is about right. Remember, your tapes are a magnetic storage medium. Don't play with your degausser next to them. Other innocent household items might also endanger your tapes. Vacuum cleaners have been known to suck up some dB along with the dust. Their large motors generate incredible amounts of magnetic flux. Keep the motor portion away from your tapes, but don't use this as an excuse not to clean your studio room. Along similar lines, don't store your tapes next to the air conditioner or near the motor on your refrigerator. These two items also have big electric motors that generate a lot of flux.

It's a wild and dangerous world out there—and it's not much safer in the recording studio. A friend once put a pickup from a guitar (it's amazing the junk we all have in our studios) on top of a stack of floppy disks (also a magnetic storage device). That old pickup sat there a couple of days gradually changing the direction and shape of the little magnetic particles on the floppy disks to correspond to the direction and shape of the little magnetic particles in its own powerful magnets. Just when he needed a crucial sequencer file from the very top disk in the stack, he found it full of electro-jibberish. Lost money, lost time, much stress, all developed from this little lapse in common sense and alertness.

Heads up! Magnets are *everywhere*. Even radiators can wipe a tape if you're not careful.

Storing tapes *tails out* is a good idea. Tails out means that the tape is wound so that the end of the tape is the first thing off the reel. The tape is wound at play speed (not fast forward) onto the take up reel and stored that way. To play or record on the tape, it must be rewound to the beginning.

Why waste this time rewinding tape? There are two reasons: As a section of tape lays there on the reel, or cassette reel, it is curled up next to other sections of tape. The closer they are, the more likely they are to interact with one another. This process is called *print-through*. Audio images from one portion of the tape are superimposed on other portions of the tape. By loosely packing the tape (rolling it to the take up reel in play mode) these sections of tape won't be so close together and you will help keep print-through to a minimum. By tails-out storing of the tape, any print-through that does occur tends to be *post-echo*. That is, it follows sound rather than leads it. In this way print-through that does occur tends to be masked by the sounds.

Finally, make copies of your tapes. It is well worth the investment in tape stock—and you never know what can happen. It is so easy not to do. The author knows. A portion of this very book was lost for good because a disk wasn't copied and backed up often enough. True, it happens more often with hard drives than with recording tapes, but *it does happen.*

SPLICING TAPE

Some of you may have an image of the recording engineer madly slicing away at his tape with a razor blade, piles of spent mylar gathering around his ankles. Splice-editing tape is a valuable technique in the audio engineer's arsenal. While it is possible to do splicing on cassette tapes, it is generally a technique associated with open-reel machines.

Splice-editing is done to compile songs from different tapes onto a single tape to send to someone. It is done to rearrange sections within songs, such as moving a verse or chorus part. And it is also done to create a special effect such as reversing the tape. The margin for error is very small when you're using a razor blade. And if you've just ruined your master tape, a razor blade is not the best thing to be holding in your hand; your throat is just a swipe away.

We don't really want to encourage you to perform razor-blade edits, but if you feel you have to live on the edge, here are some tips. Get and use an editing block. It is a metal block with a groove cut in it for the specific size of your tape. Get one for the size of your cassette. You'll notice when you get the block, that there are several cutting slots already there to help you. They look a little like the slots in a miter saw, if you're familiar with them. These slots help you cut matching angles onto your sections of tape for the smoothest splice possible (Figure 9-8).

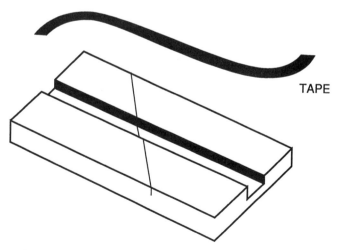

TAPE

FIGURE 9-8. When splicing or razor-blade editing tape, use the appropriately sized editing block.

Get real editing tape from your professional audio store. Don't use household tape—clear, masking, or what-have-you. The stuff will really screw up your tapes and recorder heads, and probably won't stick anyway. It doesn't matter what color editing tape you use unless you want to create a coding system or something.

You will also need some of those grease pencils they sell at the art supply store. Get one or two with light colors, such as white or yellow; they show up well on your tape. Grease pencils are a little messy, but they clean up easily. Your grease pencil is used to mark the spot on your tape that you plan to cut. As you listen to the tape, stop it as precisely as possible at the point where you want to make the edit. The cut will occur on the portion of tape immediately in contact with the playback head. Mark that spot with your grease pencil.

Mark the second cut in the same way at the end of the portion of tape you want to remove. After you've made your marks, put the tape in the editing block and choose an angle to cut. With a single-edged safety razor blade, cut the tape as cleanly as possible. Make both cuts at the same angle.

Match up the two tape ends to be rejoined in the trough of the editing block. They should fit together exactly. Cut a small piece of editing tape from its roll. Make sure the back side of the tape is facing you. You don't want to put editing tape on the side of the tape that faces the heads. Apply your small piece of editing tape to splice the two ends together. Smooth out any bubbles, and make sure the ends of the editing tape are smoothed down. Your edit is finished.

If you've made a mistake, editing tape can usually be peeled off if it hasn't been on the splice too long. So don't panic. Peel off the editing tape and try again.

READING A BLOCK DIAGRAM

You may have noticed the block diagram in your owner's manuals or sales brochures. Most of you assumed it was a schematic used by repair or technical people, but it is really more like a map indicating the pathways your signals take through your unit. As such, it is a vital element of creative mixing and recording. And they are pretty easy to decipher once you get the hang of them.

When you are more familiar with your block, you'll see how blocks are all pretty much the same—even at those giant recording studios. You'll find that a block is the easiest way for you to understand the workings of an unfamiliar piece of gear. When faced with a hookup or routing question about your own gear, you'll find yourself going right to the block diagram. The ability to read a block is a skill well worth the time you'll need to invest. A mixer's block is the one you'll use the most.

You'll notice that some simple symbols represent the various controls on your recorder or mixer; many of them look very much like the thing they represent. The best way to learn to read a block is to trace a few signal paths. Make some copies of your block at the local copy center; get 10 or 15. Using a highlighting pen, trace the path of a signal in your mixer. (A sample mixer's block is shown in Figure 9-9.)

Start with a mic input (it will look a bit like the connector and will be labeled). The first thing you'll hit is a triangle indicating the direction of the signal flow. This triangle represents an amplifier circuit that boosts our low mic levels up to an acceptable level for the mixer. If the triangle has a circle with an arrow passing through attached to it, it may be labeled Trim. This means that it is a variable amplifier with a control on the top panel of your mixer.

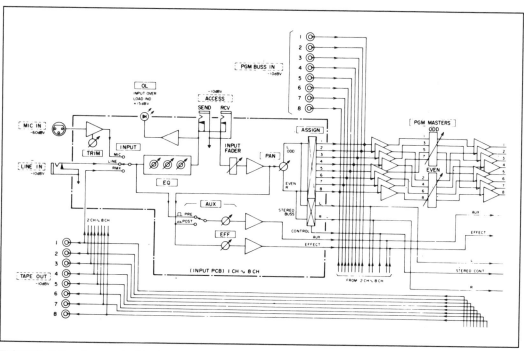

FIGURE 9-9. A sample block diagram from a TASCAM Studio 8. (Courtesy of TASCAM, Teac Professional Division)

The next thing along the path will probably be the input selector switch, which may look like a series of little circles with an arrow that points at one of the circles. The arrow is like a checkpoint: it lets one signal pass while it stops others from moving on. All switches in your system will look similar.

Now it will start to get interesting because you'll see that the signal doesn't pass through the controls of your mixer in the same order as their layout in the channel strip. For some of you, the element following the input selector will be the channel fader. For others, the fader will show up further down the line. The channel fader will be a rectangle with an arrow piercing it—a kind of square version of the trim control. The arrow means that it is a variable control, while the rectangle shows you that it's a sliding, rather than rotary, control. Most of you will then hit an intersection. Your little black line will have a dot with another little black line going somewhere. Unlike the intersection of Highways 30 and 218, your signal can go in all directions at once. Most likely, this is the point where your aux mixes come in, so your signal will go down the aux mix trail as well as continuing along its main path. If you follow it down the aux trail, you'll soon see a circle pierced with an arrow. That's a rotary level control.

About now, you might notice that some of the lines don't have the ever-important dot. Think of these as interstate flyovers with no exits. The lesson, then, is that if the signal is illustrated with the dot, different paths are joined together; without the dot they are not connected.

Next in the channel strip you'll probably see the EQ section. This looks like a series of level controls—circles with arrows. You'll start seeing overload indicators and any access or insert points in this area of the map. Access and Insert will look like line input jacks, but you'll notice they may be connected if there are two of them. These are "switched" jacks which will simply pass the signal along if nothing is plugged into the send jack (or the single insert jack). If something is plugged into the send, the signal detours out of the mixer at this point. It will come back in through the receive jack (or the single insert jack).

If you haven't seen a channel fader yet, you'll run into it at this point. It will usually be accompanied by an amplifier circuit (the triangle). Next comes pan. The pan control looks like a level control—circle and arrow—with a big difference: there are two lines leaving the pan, signifying the division of the signal to the left and right (odd and even) busses.

If your mixer is a simple stereo unit, then the two signal paths from the channel pan will join (see the dots?) two busses (the left and right master busses). You'll notice that other mixer channels as well as aux mixes join the stereo busses. These busses will go to faders, amplifiers, and output connectors.

If your mixer has multiple busses (four or eight), you will see a series of assignment switches after the pan control. These switches may look like a box with an "X" in it, or they may look like the switches we've seen earlier (little circles with a pointing arrow). From these assignment switches, you'll see four or eight summed busses, instead of just the two stereo busses. Then you'll see the program buss faders and amplifiers. You may also see stereo master faders. Notice that the left stereo master fader controls all the odd-numbered busses while the right controls the even-numbered busses. At the end of the line are the outputs.

You've just taken a very brief tour of the mixer using the block as a road map. You may have been surprised that certain controls weren't where you pictured they'd be in the signal flow sequence. The beauty of a block is that it shows you the machine's inner workings.

Now take some colored markers and photo-copies of the block and trace some other signal hookups. Try tracing the way you'd hook up some effects using the aux or effects submixers and their inputs and outputs. Are there extra buss inputs that might be used to hook up a line-level source?

This is the kind of thing you can learn from reading your blocks.

ACOUSTICS

Huge amounts of research have been devoted to the subject of *acoustics,* the way sound acts in a particular environment. Whenever you use microphones to pick up the sound of an instrument or voice, you will also be picking up the reflected sound waves in the room. These reflections, when recorded with the original sound, create what is called room ambience.

The ambient sound depends on the size of the room, its construction, and the way it's furnished. In professional recording studios, much attention and much money is spent designing the acoustical performance of the rooms. As home recordists, we're lucky if we have an extra bedroom or a section of the garage to set aside for our studio.

What we can do is be deeply aware of the ambience of the room or rooms we use, then we can learn a few basic techniques to control the worst acoustical problems. Use a scratch tape to make a few recordings in your intended studio room. When you listen to the tapes, do you hear things rattling around? Do some frequencies seem to boom out while others fade away?

You may be lucky and have a room that is either controllable with very little effort or acceptable as is (no use fixing what ain't broke). As you make some of the following changes to your room, make new tapes to check out the results.

The first thing to do is remove anything that will rattle, buzz, or hum. Loose picture frames, shelves with little bric-a-brac, lampshades that aren't tightened down, metal waste baskets, loose pieces of paper; all of these things will make noise at the wrong time—while you're recording. Anything loose will rattle if the room is filled with bass sounds or anything playing at high volume. So tighten up the room.

If your studio room isn't carpeted, you should invest in some carpet or carpet scraps to cover the floor. Hard parallel surfaces bounce sound waves around the room at incredible rates. Some of these reflected waves will meet and cancel each other out, causing drop-outs at certain frequencies. Other waves will gain energy through the reflection process, which will cause them to sound much louder. The scientific reasons for this are very complex. No matter; the point you have to remember is that a live room with hard parallel surfaces is very difficult to control. In the home situation, you'll want to start getting control by carpeting the floor.

Stay away from walls or other smooth reflective surfaces when using your mics. Place your mic position somewhere near the center of the room away from the source of the reflected sound. If you still find that you are getting booming reflections and other aural maladies, you may need "the tent."

The tent is a technique I learned from Dick Rosmini, an expert on home recording and author of scores of documents, owner's manuals, and booklets over the years for recording enthusiasts. His *Multitrack Primer,* written for TASCAM, was for many years the only available text for home recording enthusiasts.

You make the tent by mounting some eye bolts high up on opposing walls (two bolts per wall about six feet apart). After stringing up some clothesline between the eye bolts, you can create the tent by throwing some material over the lines (Figure 9-10).

Dick suggests using shag carpet with the shag material facing in, but the combination of my allergies and the heat generated by the carpet has always led me to use furniture-movers' blankets. You have to get big ones, and sometimes stitch two or three together, but they work pretty well. You can also use clothes pins to hold up the

FIGURE 9-10.   By hanging carpeting or heavy blankets over a clothesline or thick cord, you can create a small, inexpensive soundproofed area for recording acoustic instruments and vocals.

moving blankets instead of stitching them together. The tent is the least expensive isolation booth known to man. It works great for those important vocals or "dry" acoustic guitar tracks.

In preparing your room, make sure you have fairly heavy drapes over any windows. Glass is terrific at reflecting sound, so a good wad of material over the windows will do a great deal for your room (good drapes will also keep bad guys from seeing the goodies you have in your studio).

If there is a closet in your recording room, open the door when you record. Hanging clothes are great at dampening sound, while the open closet door will mute troublesome bass frequencies.

If you have ever been in a recording studio, you may have noticed all the little portable walls, like short room dividers, that studios use. These are acoustic baffles, and they help control the movement and reflections of sound waves. Some of the best baffles you can use in your home studio are very large pillows or cushions from the living room couch. If this is going to cause problems with a spouse or roommate, you may want to buy some large pillows at the neighborhood thrift shop—you know, the kind that passed as living room furniture in the '60s (Figure 9-11).

With four or five of these pillows you can tackle some really tough problems—like miking a big guitar speaker cabinet. Some guitarists just can't get their sound unless some giant cabinet is roaring away at top volume. Don't fight it. Aim the thing into your clothes closet, or a corner of the room, put the mic in front of the cabinet, and then smother the thing with your big pillows.

The next problem is noise leaking into your recording room from the outside world. Cars passing, the neighborhood kids—that kind of thing. If such leakage is terrible, you may be in for some major home building projects. If your drapes are not enough to keep outside noise from coming in, you might first try leaving your storm windows in. If that is still not enough, you may have to build some

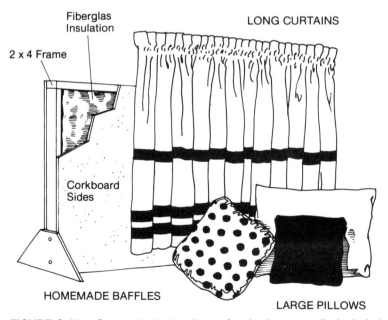

FIGURE 9-11. Sound-deadening items for the home studio include large pillows, heavy drapes, and home-made baffles and window coverings.

baffle-type window coverings for the inside. Plywood or particle board with poly foam works best. Cut the board to fit snuggly in your window opening and use Velcro or those screen-holder wing-nuts to mount it in the window.

For noise coming from inside the house, you might want to put some weather stripping around the door to stop people running up and down the hallway outside from being immortalized on your tapes. If you have a hollow-core door, you may want to line the inside surface of it with cork or foam. If you have kids playing in the basement, their screams and yelps may come straight at you through your furnace ducts. You might have to block off these heating/cooling vents. If you start sweating or freezing, depending upon the season, remember this: it's your art and somebody's got to suffer.

Although there is much more you can do to make your studio room soundproof, at this point the alterations start to become permanent. For example, you can cover the walls with egg carton bottoms and then cover them with drapes or other fabric. You can put in a false ceiling that is not parallel to the floor and is made of sound-deadening material. You can build a false floor with insulation and air space.

Before you start making these kinds of alterations, you had better make sure they are worth the effort and expense. Perhaps you should simply rent a previously soundproofed or more naturally acceptable facility. Maybe an area of the garage or basement should be permanently designated as the studio so that you are not tearing up the guest room. Once you get started down the road to acoustic perfection, you'll find that it's easy to go crazy during the journey. Acoustic perfection doesn't exist, so you must decide where to draw the line in your search. What level of performance can you ultimately live with? Recording screaming kids along with screaming guitars may seem aesthetically appropriate, but it might not impress your music publisher. We suggest that you do the simple things outlined above, but that any permanent alterations to your studio room be considered very carefully.

PHASE CANCELLATION

Whenever you combine two or more signals from the same source—for example, the use of close and distant mics—you run the risk of phase cancellation. When these signals are combined on a track, they will sometimes cancel or accentuate certain frequencies. The reasons for this are too complex to go into here, but if you notice that the signal sounds funny when combined on a buss or track, go back to the mixer. Bring the close mic up with the fader and take the distant mic channel down to zero. As the track plays, bring up the distant mic channel fader. As the distant mic comes in, you may notice the unpleasant effect. Some notes may seem like they're fighting their way through a pillow to get to you, or the whole track may start to fade out. You have two choices: either move the distant mic and record the track again or do without the distant mic sound entirely.

ALTERNATE USES OF THE MIXDOWN RECORDER

One of the handiest tools in your home studio is the mixdown deck. There is no reason *not* to use it while you're recording your basic tracks. What are some of the tasks your second recorder can perform for you during basic tracking?

External track bouncing is one of them. Just as you can mix three tracks to the vacant fourth track on your multitrack in an internal track bounce or ping-pong, you can use the second recorder to bounce tracks and still keep a stereo image. You can fill up all four tracks and add a live part while you're bouncing so that you increase the number of tracks per generation.

If you're using a sequencer (or computer with sequencing software) synchronized to the tape, you can bounce to your mixdown deck three tracks from your multitrack and all of your sequenced tracks, plus any live instrument tracks you might add.

You can then transfer your two stereo tracks back to the multitrack and begin adding more tracks—you can, that is, if you are using a stereo machine with a compatible format. If your mixdown machine is a cassette deck and your multitrack is a four-track cassette, you can transfer the tape itself from the mixdown deck to the multitrack. This won't work, of course, if your multitrack is a double-speed deck (unless it is switchable to standard speed and you're willing to continue building tracks at lower fidelity and speed).

As a rule, an external track bounce will give you better fidelity than an internal one. Your mixdown recorder may have separate record and playback heads. When you do an internal bounce, you are using the "sync" head, which is doubling as both record and playback head. Performance in sync mode is not up to the performance of separate heads. If you have to bounce the stereo tracks back to the multitrack, you may loose some of the advantage. If your mixdown deck is an open-reel machine or a DAT machine, you will experience real benefits from external bounces.

You can also use your second deck to create many effects. Nice, high-fidelity delays and flanges are possible using the second machine. If you wanted to add delay to a track (or three), run the playback out from your mixer and on to your mixdown deck. Your mixdown deck should be operating at a slower speed than your multitrack. Switch the monitor/output of the mixdown deck to the playback head. This will be the Tape position if your machine has a tape/source switch. Now, send this playback head signal *back* to your mixer.

You will have assigned the channels from your multitrack to two outputs of the mixer. One will be the send to the mixdown deck and the other will be a send back to another track of the multitrack. You will now assign the returning signal from the mixdown deck to the output feeding the multitrack. Since the record and playback heads are offset, you'll get a nice tape echo when combining the signal from the mixdown deck with the bounced signal from the other track(s) of the multitrack.

Playing with the speed of the mixdown deck will get you some interesting flanging effects. Assuming you're set up as in the delay above, you'll leave one set of signals alone by assigning them from the mixer back to the bounce track of the multitrack. The signal is also going to your mixdown deck. You can monitor the record head and use the variable tape speed of the deck to slow it down and speed it back up slightly. What's produced, when the variable speed track is combined with the unaffected tracks in the mixer, is a very nice, smooth flanging effect. In the days gone by, engineers varied the speed by applying their thumb to the reel flange (hence the name). Not all cassette decks have variable tape speed, however.

You can also perform the function by varying the speed of the multitrack, but you must first record the tracks to your mixdown deck; and then you must get the multitrack and mixdown deck to play in sync. That can be tricky when you're using the old "line 'em up by ear and push Play" method of synchronizing.

Finally, your second machine can serve as a kind of *musique concrète* sampler. By recording interesting noises, animal sounds, musical excerpts, rhythms and so on, you can drop them in at appropriate places in your compositions. You need only be quick on the transport buttons and willing to experiment.

CHAPTER **10**

Recording Drums and Drum Machines

We're beginning with drums and drum machines because rhythm section instruments—drums or percussion, bass, and such harmonic accompaniment instruments as rhythm guitar and keyboards—are the first to go to tape. There are a couple of reasons for this. Drum tracks will help the other instruments play the tune with the proper rhythm and feel. And since rhythm tracks tend to end up somewhat back in the final mix, they are likely candidates for any bouncing that will go on.

Another reason, one pertaining particularly to the use of the drum machine, is that this will provide a kind of click track to maintain the time and the beat. You can't begin to record without the click or the drum machine to set the meter.

That having been said, it's always a good idea to record any drums—machine or human—with some other instruments. If you are using a drum machine, accompanying bass and rhythm parts will help remove some of the "machine-ness" of the sound. If you're working by yourself, record the drum machine parts along with a track of your primary instrument (guitar, bass, keyboards, or whatever).

If you are a drummer and you are using a drum machine, play the hi-hats and ride cymbal "live" along with the drum machine. This will add a human dimension to the groove and will also help compensate for one of the few inadequacies of drum machine sounds: the ride cymbal. And if you are using a sequencer to perform some bass and keyboard parts in sync with your drum machine for the first track, your cymbals will be the only non-mechanized instruments in the initial tracks.

Drums should get two tracks. This way, you can place the various drum instruments in a real stereo image. Bass drum and snare drum sounds are usually placed in the center of the stereo landscape so they will be panned to dead center with the signals ending up equally on the left and right sides. Pan cymbals and tom-toms to varying degrees from left to right to get a spread-out feeling. Their sounds will end up in unequal, varying amounts on the two tracks designated for drum recording. Be careful about panning to the extreme left or right, as this tends to sound artificial.

DRUM MACHINES

Drum machines are a blessing and a curse for the home recordist. The blessing comes in that you don't have to have a forest of microphones, all of which have to be equalized and mixed in order to capture the gutsy beat of your song (Figure 10-1). A few cables and connectors will bring you all the bass drum, hi-hat, snare, toms, and cymbals you need. Some stereo drum machines even have panning built in so you don't even have to worry about that on your mixer.

So what do you have to look out for when mixing and recording drum machines? First of all, the audio levels of some drum machines can get really hot. Watch the input trim and channel overload lights in your mixer, particularly at the very first smack of the drum. Bass drums, snare drums, and low toms are the main culprits, but any accentuated drum beat (or one that is struck hard if your drum machine has velocity-sensitive pads) can really send fire into the audio channel.

The best setup for your mixer and drum machine is to use at least four channels of the mixer. Run the bass drum and snare drum through their own channels and the rest in the other two (Figure 10-2). If you have six mixer channels, run the cymbals through two channels; run the toms and other drums through two other channels. You can then process the bass and snare separately and image the cymbals and toms, while still grouping them together for EQ and processing.

If four channels are all you can spare, use one each for the bass and snare. You then must decide whether stereo imaging or processing is more important to you for the rest of the kit. If you

FIGURE 10-1. Roland R–70 drum machine (Courtesy of Roland Corp. US)

play a lot of rolls on the toms, you may want to use the stereo panning capability by running the cymbals and toms out the drum machine's stereo outs and into two mixer channels. This way you can image them properly, but then you may run into roadblocks when it comes to EQ and processing. Using four mixer channels, you could also run bass and snare separately, and then run the cymbals through a channel and pan them slightly left. The toms could then go through another channel and be panned slightly right. You won't get those big right-to-left rolling fills on the toms, but you'll have a pretty realistic sounding drum kit.

Your noise reduction system may have some difficulty dealing with the highly percussive and transient audio signals coming from your drum machine. If there is a problem, it will show up as a breathy noise after the drum sound has begun to die away. The cumulative effect of this pumping and breathing may really muddy up your drum tracks. Experiment a little with your drum tracks using the noise reduction system. You may find that you'll have to do without it as far as the drums go.

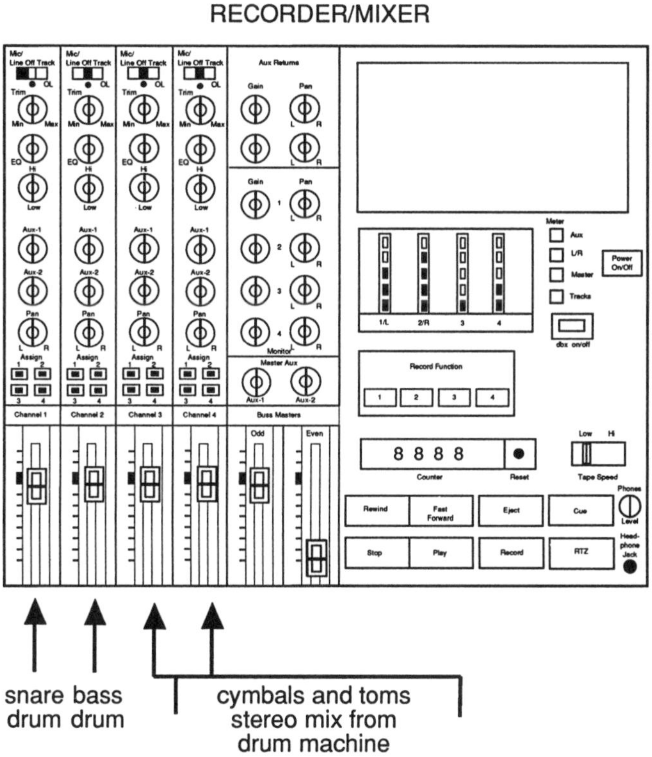

RECORDER/MIXER

snare bass
drum drum

cymbals and toms
stereo mix from
drum machine

FIGURE 10-2. A basic mixer setup for sounds from a drum machine.

Snare Drum

The right drum sound from a machine is often the result of proper EQ and processing, but it can also be a matter of using the drum machine's features creatively. For example, some drum machines offer a dry, thin-sounding acoustic-type snare and a big, booming, gated-reverb snare. And there are times that neither of these are appropriate. Try using the thinner snare and program one of the higher-pitched toms to strike at the same time. Tune the tom to the snare and run it through the same drum machine output and mixer input as the snare. The two sounds will blend to make a big, deep, but acoustic-sounding snare.

In a similar vein, but trickier to pull off, you can combine the sound of an acoustic snare drum and your drum machine snare drum without ever playing the acoustic snare with a stick. This is done in overdubs. Run the drum machine snare track in playback and out to a small monitor speaker. Place the monitor speaker facing down on the top head of the snare drum. Put your mic about ten inches below the snares. As the drum machine snare part is played back, the sound from the speaker will cause the drum heads and snares to vibrate. Run your mic and its mixer channel to another track of the recorder and record it. If you like what you hear in the playback, you can bounce the two snare tracks together onto a single track. You can also bounce the live snare and previously recorded snare together on the first pass.

How do you equalize and process your drum machine snare? The author prefers the tight, deep snare sound of the great drummer Bill Bruford. Bruford's snare always pops on the back beat. It also has substance in the lower frequency ranges so that you feel it as well as hear it. But the lower frequencies don't cause it to boom or ring into the next rhythmic event. Remember that in most cases, drums are the pop and drive of the rhythm, so you want them to have clarity and punch, particularly in the snare and bass drum.

Getting a drum machine snare to pop, but still have fullness, can be a little tricky. Although some of today's drum machines have great snare sounds right out of the box, let's assume yours needs a little help. The snare has a couple of distinct elements that affect the sound: the drum itself and the rattling wire snares underneath. The drum sound can be brought forward by boosting the EQ in the sub-200 Hz range. As I said before, this is one of the areas where we really *feel* sound.

The snares themselves ring and rattle in the upper frequency ranges. You'll start finding them somewhere around 5 kHz. We have to be careful up here, however. A lot of noise gremlins live above the 5 kHz range. If your drum machine is not a "sampled" drum machine—that is, digitally encoded from a real drum set—you must be extra careful. Manufacturers use noise generators to synthesize the sounds of snare drums and cymbals. If you boost this area too much, you'll be adding a lot of noise to your mix.

What do you do if your drum machine doesn't have the famous gated-reverb sound made famous by producer Peter McIan on the Men at Work recordings and by Phil Collins? Don't despair. A simple noise gate, even one packaged as a guitar foot pedal effect, can be used along with reverb to get the job done. Run the separate drum machine snare output, or mixer channel aux output, to the reverb. Run the output of the reverb to the input of the noise gate. Set the gate to close down quickly on the release side of the sound, then send the gate's output back to the mixer's aux input or to the channel input. Experiment with release times until you get the desired effect.

Bass Drum

When it comes to the bass drum, the author prefers a bass drum that isn't boomy and is free of processing (such as reverb). The bass drum must really be distinct on every beat if your music is to have a groove. Much more important than EQ or processing is tuning the bass drum. A bass drum should be high-pitched enough so that it pops, but not so high that it loses its rich tone. A bass drum, like all drums, should be tuned in the key of the song being recorded. You'll find that this makes a big difference in the way your drum machine or acoustic drums sound in your recordings.

Boosting the EQ in the 100 Hz to 200 Hz range will add chest-thumping punch to your bass sounds, but don't get carried away. If you ping-pong these drum parts a few times, the bass frequencies may get accentuated to a point at which the sound will start booming and becoming indistinct. Certain kinds of music use a boomier bass drum, most notably heavy metal. If this is your style, then you may not mind so much.

In some drum machines, you really lose the sense that the bass drum is played with a mallet. Instead, the sound just seems to emanate from the machine. The pop of the drum pedal hitting the head can be found in the upper midrange to high frequencies: somewhere between 1.5 kHz and 5 kHz. Boost it a little if you want the beater back in your beat, but bear in mind that this is listener's fatigue territory, so be subtle.

Tom-Toms

When it comes to the tom-toms, you may find yourself wanting to add some more effects to them. While I don't much care for processed bass or snare drums, toms benefit greatly from reverb and delay effects. They help highlight the ornamental nature of toms while separating the sound from the vital, beat-keeping functions of the snare and bass. Experiment with reverb and delay effects on your toms. But beware of creating multiple delays that conflict with the beat of the song. A short delay that fattens the sound without creating a distinct drum strike works best.

As with the bass drum, the tom needs to be tuned with the other instruments. Start tuning them with specific pitches in the song's key and lower them by thirds or fourths as you go down from high to low toms. You will be running your toms together through one or two mixer channels, so you'll be equalizing more than one drum at a time. If you can get the toms to sound good as they come off the drum machine by tuning them well, you may be better off leaving them alone as you record them. Toms are pitched in the range of other instruments, so you must be careful with EQ, particularly in the midrange frequencies. If you have a sampled drum machine where you can really hear the attack of the stick, you may want to accentuate it. You'll find the stick sound quite high up in the frequency range—roughly 7 kHz to 10 kHz. Watch out for noise and brittleness in this territory, though.

Cymbals

Cymbals tend to be the weakest sounds on drum machines. The crash cymbals, for example, tend to have too short a decay time. Or if the decay time is long enough, the decay sounds very artificial or noisy as it rings on. Ride cymbals lose the distinctive "ping" sound of the stick hitting metal. And they tend to have a mushy over-ring sound. The hi-hats tend to sound either like pie tins or aluminum washers clanking. It's tough to get a nice clean hi-hat sound that can define sixteenth notes well. And it's much tougher to get an opening/closing hi-hat sound that actually sounds like a drummer working the pedal on the hat stand.

But is the situation completely hopeless? The machines are getting better. You may want to make the cymbal sounds your first priority when shopping for a drum machine. If you find a machine that does two out of three cymbals well, you might consider buying a real cymbal and stick to replace the deficient one. Playing a cymbal part live can be a lot of fun for a non-drummer; it can add the right amount of human error to the drum track, too. If you're serious about having your own studio, it's not a bad idea to have a small drum set with a good set of the three basic cymbals: ride, crash, and hi-hats.

With regard to EQ, the relevant frequency ranges for your drum machine's cymbals are in the upper stratosphere—around 10 kHz. Unfortunately this is also where a lot of noise lives. In some drum machines, particularly those that synthesize the sounds, noise is added to the sound of cymbals to help them sizzle. Boosting frequencies up high may make your cymbals sound worse instead of better. But this high range is where you have to search for clarity if your cymbals are mushy. Cymbals really have to accent the beat. To do so, they must be clear and precise at the point of attack. This is what you're listening for. Ride cymbals also shouldn't ring over into succeeding beats too much. This is why it's difficult not only to find a drum machine with a good ride cymbal, but also to find a *drummer* that plays a good ride cymbal. A good drummer can make a mediocre ride sound good by the way he strikes and controls the cymbal. Nothing much can help a bad drummer and a bad cymbal.

If you are interested in making your cymbals sound different, you can try processing them with effects. Flangers and phase shifters can sound very nice here. Be careful with any regeneration or resonance controls on your flanger or phaser, though. These functions can turn a nice washing, sweeping sound into a roaring monster.

A Brief Word About Sync

Your drum machine may have a set of connectors labeled Sync or Tape Sync. These can be very useful when recording overdubs using your drum machine. The output of the sync connector sends a recordable code, like an electronic metronome, to your tape machine. Your drum machine can then read this code back, using it to "know" where the basic beat is. Most of these codes are strictly metronomic, however. They don't tell the machine what measure is being played; they simply give the machine a reference that tells it, "Here's the next beat." This type of code is sometimes called FSK, which stands for *frequency shift key.*

There are two important ways you can use this code. First, it's possible to hear and use your drum parts without actually recording them until mixdown. What's the advantage? You can save tracks, perhaps even a bounce. Instead of using two or more tracks for drums, you simply listen to them while you record your other parts. Then when you're ready to mix down, you can record the tracks as well as your "live" drums straight to the mixdown deck or on available tracks of the multitrack. By avoiding unnecessary ping-ponging, you may preserve the punchiness of your drum tracks.

So how do you proceed? Write your drum part on the drum machine. Play it, but record only the sync signal to a track of your recorder. Rewind the tape and plug the output of your sync track into the sync input of the drum machine. Reset the drum machine to the first beat of the first measure. The drum machine may have an external Sync Start button or switch, which you'll need to activate. When you play back your tape, the drum machine should follow along with the sync code by playing its drum part.

For the second use of the code, you may have a really elaborate percussion part for your tune. Your drum machine may be limited by the number of instruments it can play at a given time. You can record your first drum tracks to the multitrack and simultaneously record your sync track to an available track. Reload your drum machine with the additional sounds. Here, you have two choices: you can run the sync track back into the drum machine and record the new percussion sounds to an available track, or you can ping-pong the old and new together onto the available track.

We will discuss this type of sync, or *virtual-track,* recording in later chapters as we add MIDI to the home studio. We will also discuss in greater detail the differences between all these brands of technological alphabet soup: MIDI, FSK, and SMPTE.

RECORDING ACOUSTIC DRUMS

Recording acoustic drums begins with microphones or some kind of specialized pickup system.

Since mics don't discriminate, they pick up everything in their area that makes sound. So the first thing you need to do with an acoustic drum set is troubleshoot it for strange noises and squeaks. Hi-hat and bass drum pedals are notorious for emitting odd squeaks and rattles; a little oil can't hurt. Another common source of noise is the drum throne, the drummer's stool: these tend to groan every time the drummer moves (and drummers move a lot).

Indeed, all of the drum kit's hardware must get a once-over for tightening and lubrication. Strong adults take sticks and beat the heck out of these things, so it is common for stands and other hardware to wind up bent and loose. When this happens, pieces have a natural tendency to rattle. Tighten everything and fix what's broken or you'll end up with a lot of "rattle and hum" without the benefit of U-2 to perform it.

The drum heads and mufflers will also need attention. If the drummer has been out gigging with his set for a while, the heads are probably dented from innumerable stick strikes. These dents change the way the head vibrates, and the change is not for the better. Dents will sometimes even "grab" a stick a little, creating a double strike. So replace any drum heads that need it—probably all of them. Use basic white-coated heads such as Remo Ambassador or Emperor. Fiber or layered heads (pin stripes with oil layered between) sound very dull when you record them. Control Sound heads (with the black dot in the center) can sound fine if they're not too worn; they seem to have a little extra "pop" with the initial strike. When the black-dot heads get worn and dented, however, they seem to sound worse than any others. Worn black-dot heads will buzz noticeably as they vibrate.

When you change the heads, make sure the mufflers are tight and in good condition. They can rattle when improperly adjusted. This is also your chance to take a look at the clamps and tuning tension rods. Are they rattling around or are they in good shape? And make sure drums aren't placed too close together. When they're struck, they tend to clank together for some added (and unwanted) percussion. Toms mounted on bass drums and snare drums too close to bass drums are particularly good at clanking.

One element of acoustic drums almost always overlooked is their tuning. When drummers play live, they tend to tune the drum until it rings best. They usually don't worry about tuning to particular keys or pitches because they may play in many keys before the night is over. But *recording* drums is a very different story. Tuning them can be vital to the sound of the drum track. Well-tuned drums that vibrate with, and not against, the pitches of the other instruments will sound clean and precise. They will add punch and liveliness to the track. Poorly tuned drums will sound dull and lifeless.

At this point, you can probably see why drum machines are such a blessing to people who record. But controlling the pitch and sound is only the beginning of the drum-set saga. Now we have to put our mics to use. If you have our recommended minimum complement of one dynamic cardioid and one PZM, you'll want to use them both. You'll use the dynamic mic to pick up the bass drum and the PZM as an overhead mic for the rest of the drums (Figure 10-3).

The dynamic will actually go inside the bass drum. Remove the front head of the bass drum, if it's still there, and use a boom mic stand to place the mic close to the beater head of the bass drum—but not touching. If you don't have a boom stand, or you're using it elsewhere, you can put one or two of your furniture-moving blankets or a large pillow into the bottom of the bass drum. The dynamic mic can then be put on top of the pillow or blankets, with its element facing the beater head. (Even if you're using a boom, it's a good idea to lay a blanket or pillow in the bottom of the bass drum to dampen it, as shown in Figure 10-3.) When you've got the mic placed inside, use another blanket to cover the outside opening completely. Just drape the blanket completely over the front of the drum.

Place the PZM overhead to pick up everything except the bass drum. A PZM tends to hear everything equally, so it's no problem having the cymbals closer to it than, say, the snare. For best results, use a boom stand and place the PZM directly over the drum set at a height of six to seven feet. The PZM's plate should be parallel to the floor. Tell the drummer not to groan and grunt while playing because the PZM will pick that up, too.

FIGURE 10-3. Miking drums with a PZM mic as an overhead and a dynamic mic for the bass drum.

You can vary the height of the PZM above the set. A greater height will allow you to pick up more room ambience if you want it. But be careful about putting the PZM too close to the ceiling. The effect will be to create a much larger plate with massive bass response. If your ceiling is acoustically treated, you may not have this problem.

For one reason or another, the overhead placement may not work for you. If so, try mounting the PZM three or four feet in front of the drum set about four feet off the floor, just above the top level of the toms.

Should some friend offer you his footlocker full of mics for your session with the drummer, you will have more choice of mic placement. The most basic expansion of our two-mic setup would be to add another overhead. Move the first one off-center to one side of the set. Add the second to the other side. These two overheads will help you create some stereo imaging (Figure 10-4).

If your mic locker overfloweth, you can consider close miking each drum. For this configuration, you'll need a lot of mic stands. The bass drum placement stays the same as in our two-mic array. Use a dynamic mic for the bass drum and snare drum. Use condenser mics for the cymbals, particularly the hi-hats. The toms can be picked up with either dynamics or condensers, but don't mix mic

FIGURE 10-4. Miking drums with two mics positioned overhead and a single mic in the bass drum.

types on a drum grouping—in other words, don't use two dynamics and two condensers to mic four toms.

Place the drum mics about eight inches over the rims (Figure 10-5). Point the mic at the head but place it out of the drummer's way. The snare and hi-hat mics are particularly bothersome to place and still keep out of the way of the drummer. Keep the snare mic to the drummer's left (if he is a right-handed drummer) away from his toms. That way he won't smack the mic on the way to a tom roll. When placing the hi-hat mic, you should try to keep it from picking up the snare as much as possible. Aim the mic's element across the top of the hi-hat and toward the front of the drum set. You shouldn't have any trouble with tom placements if the drummer consistently hits the center of his toms. Crash cymbal and ride cymbal mics are really just our overheads brought in a little closer. If you have even more mics, you could add some "room" mics to the array. Room mics placed at a distance from the drum set and, when mixed at lower levels with the other mics, will give the impression of

FIGURE 10-5. Close-miking the snare drum. The mic should be about eight inches over the rim, pointed at the head.

the drums being played in a large room or stage. They pick up the reflected sound waves, but they also pick up a lot of other room noises. As a result, they can be more of a problem than they are worth if you have a one-room studio.

MIXING AND EQUALIZING YOUR DRUMS

It's easy to get carried away with drum sounds. Here's why: they tend to be recorded first, either by themselves or with one or two other instruments. At first, the drums may sound "small" because they are so exposed. The temptation is to start trying to fatten the drum sound, but you have to resist, particularly if you are going to ping-pong the drum tracks. Once you have bounced enormous-sounding toms, huge gated-reverb snares, and chest-exploding bass drums together with the bass guitar and keyboard parts, they are joined forever (unless, of course, you've done your bounce using your mixdown deck and removed the tape with the basic drum tracks for later). Too bad if you don't like what the drums sound like then: you're stuck with it. So as a rule, you should record your drums dry, without effects or too much room ambience.

Similarly, if you start off with very powerful drum sounds, you may find yourself involved in a power struggle that is the audio equivalent of World War III. The bass can't be wimpy against such a sound, and the keyboard part has to come on strong to complement the bass and drums. And then, of course, the guitarist will have to follow the same crunchy, high-volume footsteps. And the vocals? Get screaming kids, if you want to compete with this crew. The end result of this audio is a mega-decibel distorted wall of sound.

If you're using a two-mic setup, you have two distinctly different drum channels in your mixer: the bass drum and everything else. The bass drum channels can be equalized and mixed as we suggested in the drum machine section. For more chest thumping, boost a little around 200 Hz. If your portable studio has only high and low controls, you will find it difficult to bring out 200 Hz by raising the low control. You will also accentuate many other frequencies, which will dilute the desired effect. In this case, you're better off leaving the bass drum as it is recorded, letting it go to the track without any EQ.

When it comes to using your equalizer for the overhead mic channel, you are working with a lot of drums and frequencies. Everything, from low floor toms to cymbals, is in the same channel, and they all should be there in a relatively good balance. Listen first to the overall sound. Does any drum or cymbal sound too prominent? If so, you may want to cut its EQ. Since you can't deal with all these instruments individually because they are already mixed together, you will have to strictly prioritize the instrument sounds based on the song.

As a general rule, you must hear the snare and the hi-hats clearly. The snare usually keeps the backbeat while the hats cut the time into smaller rhythmic values. Along with the bass drum, these instruments are the foundation of your drum track. In some patterns, the ride cymbal takes the over the role of the hi-hats, so the ride may take priority.

You should find the snare in the 5 kHz range. This is roughly where the wire snares under the drum make their sound. Since this is the unique aspect of the snare drum, accentuating the snares makes the snare drum cut through better. The hi-hat and ride are found at even higher frequencies, around 10 kHz. Boosting a little here will help the cymbals come through better. If your machine has only high and low EQ controls, you may want to try rolling off the low very slightly. This may rob your toms of some body, but it will bring out the snare and cymbals.

If the snare is just not coming through, you may have to have a heart-to-heart with the drummer. Encourage him to hit the snare harder. This will not only raise its level, it will also make it pop more. If the drummer is good, he will be able to help you get the balance and definition you need from the various instruments. In this way, you can leave the track alone until the mixdown or ping-pong stage.

When you are tempted to process acoustic drums that you've picked up using the two-mic method, don't do it. At least, don't do it at this stage of the game. Adding reverb, flange, or anything else now will only muddy the waters later. Keep the acoustic drum track dry for the moment. If you've close-miked the set, you could add some processing as we did with the drum machine. But if you had a lot of mics, you may have set up some room mics. The room mics will give you better ambience than digital reverbs will at this stage of our recording.

The long and short of it is this: It's very easy to sabotage the sound of a drum track. Think about it. You've recorded a good drummer. When you play back the tape, you want the drums to sound the way they did when the drummer was playing them live. Screwing around with the EQ and the processors may give some short relief, but in the long haul, don't you really want to wonder: Is it live, or is it Memorex?

CHAPTER **11**

Recording Keyboards

Back in the dawn of recorded time, about 30 years ago, when Fats Domino found his freedom up on Blueberry Hill, there were really only three kinds of keyboards—pianos (grands and uprights both), Farfisa-style electric organs, and your basic ecclesiastical variety with thousands of pipes and bellows and Lord only knows what else.

Technology has altered this landscape irrevocably, first with the development of the synthesizer, then with the mysterious development of the sampler, which covered the same ground as the Farfisa and early synths, but which then began to infringe on the territory of the acoustic piano, the strings, woodwinds, the church organ, and a host of other sounds that haven't even been heard yet.

One character remarked about a recent session with a synth whiz: "I said, 'With all these sounds we got on tape, the only thing we're missing is the kitchen sink.' Bert [the synth player] rubbed his chin and said, 'Yeah. I know what you mean.' Then he rummaged in his bag of diskettes and said, 'Would a babbling brook do?' So now we've got running water on the track."

We talk about keyboards, but the only similarity between the piano and the synth is the keyboard. From recording to equalizing, the two are very different beasts indeed.

RECORDING THE SYNTHESIZER

For our purposes here, "synthesizers" will refer to digital pianos, samplers, organs, and those consumer one-finger-chord instruments.

Pianos will be covered later. Regardless of the way keyboards generate their sounds, we are concerned here with keyboard instruments that send a line-level signal out their audio jacks. As such, these instruments, like drum machines, are recorded "direct."

Synths are deceptively simple to record. All you really need is a cable with a quarter-inch connector on each end. One end goes in the synthesizer and the other into the high-impedance input of the mixer. In the case of a stereo instrument, you'll need two cords.

The trouble starts when it comes to matching output levels of the instruments to input levels of the mixer. There isn't much standardization among electronic keyboard makers in terms of audio output levels. Most of them have a nominal level that is around 0 dBV. These nominal levels aren't a problem for a mixer. But some synthesizers have a dynamic, velocity-sensing keyboard capable of producing incredibly hot outputs. A dynamic keyboard gets louder when you press the keys harder. When you combine these dynamics with certain *patches,* or sounds—particularly very percussive sounds with a lot of high-frequency information—you may end up with a signal that will cause problems for your mixer.

The first tip for recording synthesizers is to watch your levels. If the synth has a dynamic keyboard, check out the levels when the keyboard is played hard. Remember, people play softer when they're rehearsing than they do when they are performing. Use the input pad or trim control to set an acceptable level. Don't let the level creep up during the recording process.

As a second tip, we suggest you be careful of the noise levels generated by some synths. Lower-cost units will have pretty poor audio circuits. Though they may sound fine in the living room or with the band, when you record them their noisiness becomes obvious. If your unit runs on batteries, always use the AC adapter when you record; a low or interrupted power supply will make the unit even noisier.

But even high-priced synths will generate some noise in their higher-frequency ranges. Patches such as string sounds, flutes, whistles, pan flutes, cymbals, and so on will really put the "hiss" on your tape.

Two ways to help the noise problem are to keep levels under control and use a noise gate. Many synthesists in the studio use a good limiter. If you are having little luck trying to get the noise out of your high-frequency patch, you might try running the signal through a direct box, using the low-impedance input on your mixer. However, many of you won't have this kind of input on your portable studio. A noise reduction system is pretty helpful in dealing with your synthesizer's noise, but be careful when applying it to a very percussive patch. You might end up with the kind of "pumping and breathing" found with drum machines.

Once we have defeated the distortion and noise problems, we are then faced with the human problem. When most of us first start recording synthesizers, we tend to get infatuated with their sound and capabilities. Before we know it, there are synth tracks everywhere. They begin to dominate the music.

Synthesizers are powerful instruments that are much more often over- than under-utilized. It takes great skill to record numerous synths at different frequency ranges and still come out with a clean and coherent recording. Quincy Jones, Michael Boddicker, Dave Grusin, Peter McIan, Suzanne Ciani, and Michael Stearn are producers and performers whose synthesizer work is often multilayered, but always beautiful, clean, and coherent. Listen to their recordings to get an idea of how multiple synth voices can be tastefully and imaginatively arranged.

You probably have a single synthesizer that you will use over and over again to add tracks. Since every synth has its own sound characteristics, using the same unit on multiple tracks will highlight the peculiarities of that sound to the point of caricature. This is why professional synthesists will use several different instruments to create layered effects.

Granted, you may not have the money to keep an array of different synths on hand. What you *can* do, though, is exercise restraint when arranging synth parts. Don't layer multiple pads (a kind of ambient chordal background) using the same synth. By layering these nondescript pads, you make the background very mushy. It will also make it difficult for the voices and lead instruments to cut through all this mush. So try to accomplish your ambient pads using as few tracks as possible.

Equalizing Synthesizers

When it comes to EQ, remember that your synth has tone generating and modifying circuits far more sophisticated than EQ found on portable studios. Whenever possible, edit the sound for tone on the synth and record it flat.

What are you looking for in synth sounds? In live performance, you are often looking for "fill"—you may want sounds that help create a full and powerful performance. In recording, however, you must search for definition and clarity.

Definition can be added to a synth part by accentuating the higher frequencies, 8 kHz to 10 kHz. But you must be careful playing around in this range, since synths have some noise there. Some sounds already have noise built in. Flutes, for example, just don't sound like flutes without the breath of the player. The breath sound is provided by adding noise to the patch. Violins and cellos don't sound much like themselves without the sound of the bow sliding across the strings. The bow is added by using noise generators in the synthesizer. This level of noise is essential to good sound, but by layering or EQing, we can easily emphasize the noise to the point of distraction.

Some digital synthesizers can use a shot of warmth. This can be added by boosting frequencies from 100 Hz to about 500 Hz. If you're working with a raucous bass part, however, you'll start red lights flashing all over your mixer.

Effects are so popular with keyboardists that many synths on the market have built-in reverb, chorus, delay, and so on. Many of these sound great, of course. Chorus can really make a synthesized string part sound nice and lush. A little short delay can add some pop and excitement to lead and bass lines. And reverb sounds good on just about anything.

Using effects during the basic tracking procedure is called "printing [recording] wet." It was a definite no-no in the old days—about five years ago—since it is extremely hard to control the interaction of different effects, particularly reverbs of different depths, when the tracks are mixed together. For this reason, engineers and performers used to record "dry" during basic tracks. Later, they would apply some reverb to the monitor mix, but they left the tracks dry until the mixdown stage.

There's an implicit tip here, isn't there? It's not that it is wrong to record basic tracks with effects. But when it comes to putting some nice reverb in during mixdown, you may have a bit of a problem with the already existing reverb and other effects.

RECORDING THE PIANO

By "piano" we mean the big, heavy thing that can double for a piece of furniture, that comes with only one sound, and that has been thrilling musical enthusiasts for generations.

Because each piano is one-of-a-kind, it is easy to get used to a particular instrument—the one in your parents' living room, for example, that now sits in your recording room. You need to sit down for a session or two of strong and critical listening to make sure this is the piano sound you really want. It's probably full of rattles and buzzes and hasn't been tuned in two years. When was it last voiced by a quality piano technician? Probably not since it left the factory in 1930.

Giving the piano a complete physical may be the place to begin—from technician to tuner. It's no excuse to say, "But it was in tune when I bought it." So was your guitar.

Seek and destroy those rattles, buzzes, and squeaks. Use felt wedges to stop any body panels from rattling. As for the front panels and kick boards, you can just take them out while you're recording. Check the pedals and hammers for squeaks. Check the bench, too; it can sometimes rattle.

Now comes the time to pass judgment on the old friend. Get someone else to play the piano, while you stand back and listen. Move around the room and find spots where the piano really sounds good.

Assuming that you've judged your piano worthy of recording, make some notes on where you were standing when the piano sounded its best. Also make some subjective observations about the piano's tone. Is it bright, or mellow? Loud or soft?

The easiest and often most effective way to mic a piano with our recommended selection of mics is to use the PZM on a stand at chest height, placed in one of the spots you noted as sounding great. That's right—just one good, full-range mic placed in a sweet spot in the room.

If you must isolate the piano because there will be other instruments performing in the room at the same time, there are a couple of things to do. If you're just using your PZM, you can attach it to the lid (or the support rod of a grand), and cover the piano with your blankets (Figure 11-1). With an upright, you can place the mic where the front panel was, dead center. Cover the mic and the piano with the moving blankets. You will still probably get some bleed from the other instruments or vocals onto your piano tracks, so in the end, it's a good idea to record them separately using overdubbing.

Using two mics on a piano is pretty easy. A matching pair of condenser mics would be ideal, but your dynamic and PZM will do the trick as well. Use the dynamic for the bass strings and the PZM for the treble. If you have an upright, take off the front panel and put the mics beside one another in the middle of the piano facing the strings. Rotate the mics so that their elements face toward the bass (dynamic mic) and treble (PZM) ends of the instrument. You will notice you've created a kind of X pattern with the mics (Figure 11-2). You can mic the sound board side at the back of the piano using two mics in a similar X pattern. Miking the sound board will give you a more mellow, romantic sounding piano.

FIGURE 11-1.   Miking a grand piano with a PZM mic. After positioning the mic, cover the piano with packing blankets to isolate the sound.

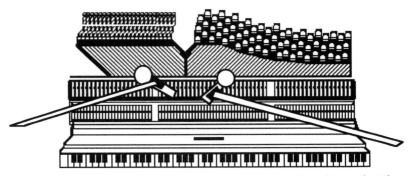

FIGURE 11-2.   Double-miking an upright piano. Place the mics so that they face the bass and treble ends of the instrument.

When it comes to miking a grand piano, the standard approach is to pop open the lid as far as the lid support will let you, and then use two mics, one for treble and the other for bass. Point both straight down at the strings. To isolate, cover the piano with your moving blankets. *For a brighter sound,* move the mics toward the hammers. *For a mellower sound,* move them away from the hammers toward the center of the harp. This is a standard rule for any piano.

Processing and Equalizing a Piano

A piano gives you a really broad audio landscape. You've got low lows and high highs, with all the other notes/frequencies in between. As we've said about other instruments, if you've placed your mics properly and the instrument sounds good in the first place, it should sound good on your tape.

Because of their extreme range, pianos have a tendency to crowd other instruments, particularly when they are played with a lot of sustain. Those pedal points can ring and cascade in a beautiful way in your living room, but they take up lots of space on your tracks. Get your pianist to play the part with as little pedal action as possible.

Watch out for ringing bass notes that are in unison with your bass player's part. Any notes the piano and bass hit together will really jump in level. And if the notes are slightly out of tune with one another, you'll get some serious beating. So while the pianist is laying off on the pedals, he might go light on some of the bass notes, too.

Before you begin to use EQ on your piano part, determine the style of the song. Rock and country pianos tend to be very bright while jazz and classical pianos are mellower. You should also be clear as to whether your piano is to compete with other instruments for center stage or if it will be part of the backup.

A piano really needs to cut if it is competing with guitars and synthesizers. To help a piano cut through, roll off the frequencies near 200 Hz and boost the frequencies at around 5 kHz and 10 kHz.

If the piano is the total support for a vocal, then you'll want to roll off the vocal frequencies of the piano a little, around 500 Hz. Add some warmth to the background by boosting slightly at 100 Hz. This will allow some space for the vocal to come forth and add some bottom to make it all feel nice and warm. If you lose clarity by boosting at 100 Hz, take it back.

If you feel overwhelmed by the need to process the sound of your piano, count to ten and resist the urge. It just doesn't make a lot of sense to process. While flangers, harmonizers, delays, and chorus sound great on synthesizers and samplers, they just tend to muck up the sound of a piano. A certain amount of compression may be useful, but go lightly. In the context of rock, you may need to tighten the dynamics of the piano track to keep it from dominating everything. If you compress the piano too heavily, though, you'll cause the notes to sustain over their fellows. This can make the piano track a muddy mess, particularly if the piano player used a lot of the sustain pedal.

In short, try to get the piano to sound good in the room, eliminate the noises and rattles, try to get that good sound on tape exactly as you hear it, go lightly with the EQ, and don't process it unless you really have to.

CHAPTER **12**

Recording Guitars and Basses

Just as there are different approaches to playing guitar and bass, there are many different ways to record these instruments. The method depends on what kind of feel you want, what kind of sound you're going for, and the physical requirements of the particular instrument. For example, the electric guitar fanatic who raves endlessly about the sound of his pre-CBS Fender Twin Reverb amplifier may require that you mike the amp itself. You can also run the electric guitar through a Rockman-style preamp before sending it into the board. A session bass player, however, may simply line his instrument direct into the mixer. Acoustic steel and nylon-stringed guitars have their own set of requirements and compatible devices designed to capture their sound. Upright acoustic basses have some very fine pickups as well as the tried-and-true method of using microphones.

INSTRUMENT MAINTENANCE

But before you worry about mics and pickups and how to get the instrument on tape, you should check out the condition of the instrument, starting with the strings. Whatever else people say, I maintain that guitars require new strings for each session. As it is, a new set of strings lasts only a few days when the instrument is played a lot. Old strings sound dead, play dead, and can't hold their tuning. Old strings have a nasty habit of breaking. In short, old strings are a pain. You can wipe down the strings with a soft cotton cloth but that only delays the inevitable—so why sweat it when you're making the tape of a lifetime? Go wild! Buy three or even four sets of strings. You'll need them. Dull strings *might* work for some rhythm parts, but solos are a no-no without new strings. This is true for both acoustics and electrics.

Basses, particularly acoustic basses, don't require string changes as often. Electric basses, however, are a little more like guitars in terms of string life. Round-wound electric bass strings are particularly fast to deteriorate, but they have the brightest sound to begin with. You may want to consider outfitting your bass with "half-round" strings for recording. They work great for many styles (only the hardest of rock styles may suffer). They last longer than straight round-wounds and carry a more consistent tone in the long run. And you'll find the half-rounds eliminate some of the finger squeaks caused by movement of the hand on the fingerboard.

Finger squeaks can be very annoying and very prominent on guitar and electric bass tracks. While EQ and a noise gate will help, the real solution is to avoid creating the squeaks in the first place. Part of the solution can be found in better playing techniques. Part of the answer is mechanical. Half-round bass strings offer less of the surface texture that causes the noise. Electric and acoustic guitarists, however, need to find a way to make the fingers glide better over the strings. Some musicians use a spray-on lubricant that you can apply to the strings and the fretboard. Indeed, some producers have suggested putting cooking oil or household lubricating oil lightly on the strings with a cloth. A classical guitar teacher once suggested that a little drop of baby oil on the fingertips of the fretboard hand is helpful. He suggested letting the drop soak in for a few seconds before wiping off the excess. This works better, in the author's opinion, than putting oil all over the strings.

Another cause of the squeaking problem is perspiration. Keeping your hands dry helps keep down the ruckus. Perspiration is the body's way of cleaning dirt and foreign matter out of your pores. So accumulations of grit, smog, and other material all come out along with those beads of sweat. The stuff builds up on the strings and back of the neck and it begins to actually grab at your hand. Drops of baby oil for the calluses on the fingertips, and baby powder for the rest of the hand, are helpful solutions.

An electronic tuner is a must for your studio. Chromatic tuners are best, because you can use them on other instruments, but a tuner of any kind is vital if you record guitars and basses often. It's all too easy to finalize an overdub that's not in tune with the previous tracks.

But there's another reason for using the tuner. The performance of a guitar or bass can be ruined by imperfect intonation. The bridge piece of the instrument must be adjusted so that the twelfth fret plays a true octave above the open string. The harmonics must ring true as well. If you find the guitar or bass is difficult to tune or it doesn't hold its tuning even with new strings, you might be having problems with the neck or you need to have the instrument "set up" properly. This is intricate stuff, so avoid doing it yourself unless you really know what you're doing.

Another reason for making sure your instrument—bass or guitar—is set up properly is the problem of dead spots, where notes die away before they should while others ring unusually loudly. Electric basses are notorious for dead spots. Having the instrument set up well will eliminate this problem.

TO MIC OR NOT TO MIC

Not so long ago, the standard rule was: Put mics in front of the guitar amps and record the bass direct (straight into the mixer), but technology—bless its battery-operated heart—has given us more options. Guitarists just couldn't get the sound of the moving speaker by any means other than putting a mic square in front of the cabinet. This mic was usually accompanied by a more distant mic to pick up a little of the room ambience (which is how George Martin caught Lennon's feedback at the beginning of "I Feel Fine").

This still isn't a bad way to go. For many reasons, though, guitar and bass are both being recorded direct more often. For example, if you are like me, you may not be able to blast away in your studio at all hours of the day and night. Recording guitar direct through a Rockman is a good compromise. The Rockman, a device invented by design engineer and Boston-band-leader Tom Scholz, combines the powerful sound of distorted amps with several other guitar effects in a single black box. The audio output of the box is the perfect level for your mixer. It's possible to lay down some devastating guitar tracks with nary a peep coming from your studio. Rockman also makes a small amplifier that offers numerous sound processing options at low volumes (Figure 12-1).

In addition to the Rockman, there are several other even more sophisticated devices for recording guitarists. Rack-mounted

FIGURE 12-1. Zoom 9150 MIDI controllable guitar preamp and processor (Courtesy of Samson Technologies)

multi-effects modules are the current rage. These units have reverb, delay, distortion, flanging, chorus, EQ, and so on, all in the same box. Some of them have highly developed "speaker emulation" circuits where the signal coming out of them resembles the sound of moving air you get from putting a mic in front of a speaker cabinet. Some of them are very, very good.

For years, bass has been recorded direct. Often, for the benefit of the musicians, the bass is plugged into a direct box with one feed going to the amp in the studio and the other going to the mixer. This way, the bassist gets to feel his instrument as he plays it. In some studios, the practice is to place the drummer and bass in the same room divided by baffles. If the bass sounds too dull, you can put a mic in front of the cabinet and mix that sound with the direct signal.

For the same reasons—recreating the sound of playing live— you or your electric guitarist may insist on miking the guitar amp.

Properly placed mics still provide the absolutely best way to record an acoustic guitar or bass.

MIKING THE ELECTRIC BASS

To mic an electric bass, use your dynamic cardioid. Get the bass speaker cabinet up off the floor a little by using one of your big pillows or a chair. Point the dynamic mic at the cone of the bass speaker (Figure 12-2). Set the bass amp to give a full sound, but keep the level of the amp down. Bass frequencies are tough on the small-diameter diaphragms in microphones. High levels just makes the problem worse.

Now start listening for the noises. Bass amp cabinets tend to rattle and buzz, especially if they have any casters or metal handles. Get some sheets of protective foam wrap from a moving supply house (U-haul has them) and use some gaffer's tape to wrap the foam around the handles and casters. Check the grate or fabric and frame on the speaker cover; these often rattle. Tighten them down, or remove them. Those plastic name plates that manufacturers use to boast their name often rattle as well. Take those off or stuff them with foam. If you used the chair instead of the pillow to raise the speaker cabinet, make sure the chair doesn't rattle.

The pillow is a better choice than a chair for another reason: it helps cut down reflections from the floor.

After tracking down the noises, you should deaden the area around the speaker. Bass frequencies tend to bounce around a small space and get real "boomy" in the process. Use your moving blankets to build a tent over the cabinet and mic stand. You could also use your clothes closet by putting the speaker in there and covering it. Remember to get any unused metal hangers out of there. Another way is to point the speaker into a corner of the room and stack all your big pillows up in the corner. Position the mic facing the cone, then cover the whole lot with your moving blanket.

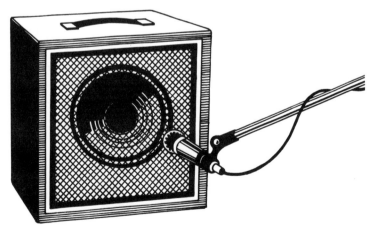

FIGURE 12-2. Miking a bass amplifier cabinet. Point the mic at the cone of the bass speaker.

RECORDING THE ACOUSTIC BASS

Recording an acoustic upright bass is fairly tricky. If you don't get the bright sounds of the strings being struck, the bass will sound dead. If you don't get the resonance of the body of the bass, it will sound thin. And you never want to pick up a lot of room echoes. What's the best way to proceed?

Bring out your tent—the one made out of moving blankets and clothes line—and place your bassist square in the middle. Make sure he or she has got some carpet under foot. The best bet is

FIGURE 12-3. Miking an acoustic bass. Place a dynamic mic about a foot away from the bass; place a PZM mic about two or three feet away at chest height.

to use both the dynamic mic and the PZM to record the acoustic bass. Put the dynamic on a stand about a foot away from the bass and aim it at the spot where the bassist's hand plucks the strings (Figure 12-3). Now, place the PZM on a stand roughly two or three feet away at chest height. The dynamic will pick up the attack of the strings, while the PZM will pick up the body resonances. If the bass has a good pickup, you don't need the dynamic. If you want the bass to be fuller-sounding (more "bassy"), you can cut a piece of cardboard (two feet square or so), and attach it to the PZM's flat plate surface. Most PZMs have a hole or hook arrangement for these kinds of attachments. This will effectively increase the plate area of the PZM and so increase the bass response somewhat.

If you can't or don't want to use the tent, then use an open clothes closet. Place your mics as above, only inside the closet. The bassist will face the clothes closet, standing about three feet from it. Put the dynamic in front of the bass at the distance of a foot. The clothes closet will act as a bass sound trap. If you don't want the bassist to think you're a total bum, you might hang some of your better clothes in there.

MIKING THE ELECTRIC GUITAR

With the exception of the keyboard, the guitar is capable of the most varied and exciting timbres of any instrument you will record. Just when you thought you'd heard it all, along comes a Joe Satriani or an Alan Holdsworth with some new, mind-blowing sound. Check out some good guitar recordings—Satriani, Holdsworth, Andy Summers, Mark Knopfler, Stanley Jordan, Earl Klugh, Joe Pass, John Renbourn, Roy Buchanan, and Richard Thompson will give you a few different places to start. The guitar is an incredibly versatile instrument. Listening to the jazz, folk, and rock players will, I hope, inspire you to go for some different sounds—at least every once in a while.

I talked a few moments ago about recording guitars directly using either a Rockman device or going directly into the mixer (with or without a direct box). Before doing that, let's first try putting a microphone in front of a speaker cabinet. A lot of the same issues apply here as with recording electric bass with a mic. Troubleshoot the amp casing and cabinet for rattles and buzzes. Check the condition of the speaker. Constant, relentless volume doesn't just wear out hearing, you know. It can loosen speakers to the point where they don't have the clarity and precision of yore. This isn't really noticeable in a nightclub, but becomes apparent when you try to get a crisp edge to the guitar sound while recording.

Speakers that have spent too much time in nightclubs will also be coated with the residue of millions of cigarettes. The constant pushing and pulling motion of the speaker cone actually sucks the air from the club in towards the cone itself. The residue is a tarry substance that permeates the paper element of the speaker cone. Smoking isn't any better for speakers than it is for people.

Once you know that your speaker cabinet is free of noises and that it will reproduce all the crisp, clean sounds you might want to push through it, you need to consider the room and your other surroundings. For the sake of argument, let's say that your guitarist plays regularly through a large amp using four or eight 12-inch speakers such as a Marshall "stack." To get the perquisite "crunch," he needs to turn the amp up to a level that will threaten the fertility of any life form within two blocks—around 11 on the control. Very few home studios can handle these levels successfully. Things that have never rattled in your house before, like the roof, will rattle now. In my youth, my band routinely practiced at these levels. During one rehearsal, we even brought the house down—literally. The ceiling came crashing down on the band. Fortunately, no one was seriously hurt.

One friend built a very large plywood three-quarter-inch box and lined it with about eight inches of foam. He added Sonex sound panels to the sides and dropped his four-by-twelve speaker cabinet inside. Then he placed a microphone in front of the speakers and ran the mic and amp cords out a little hole and sealed the box up tight. The result was that he could roar away without disturbing the neighbors. Of course, the box takes up the space of a small car, but people will go to extremes for the love of pure crunch.

So how do you record a cranked Marshall stack? Short of extreme measures, you might try using smaller amps at lower levels or recording direct using a Rockman or one of the current crop of guitar multi-effects processors. The processors are particularly effective if they have some kind of speaker emulation circuit, especially if your sound doesn't require three stages of distortion (preamp, power amp, and speaker). If it just doesn't have the feel of real without the power amp tubes and the speakers breaking up, there is yet one more avenue to explore.

There is a product that can take the speaker output of your amp and convert it to a line-level signal for your mixer. At the same time, it gives the amp the kind of loading it needs to get from a speaker. An example of one of these units is made by GT Electronics and is called, appropriately enough, the Speaker Emulator.

Meanwhile, back at the mic, after you've found a place to put the amp where you can play it really loud, and you've found and corrected all the noises and rattles, you put your dynamic cardioid in front of the box. If your cabinet has a number of speakers, you may want to find out which one gives you the best sound. If they are all about the same, pick one that is furthest away from the floor and aim your dynamic cardioid at its cone. But don't aim it dead-center; rather, aim it about three inches in front (Figure 12-4). This will help keep your microphone from distorting. Get out your moving blankets and cover the cabinet and mic copiously.

Now you have to worry about overloading the mic. High sound-pressure levels are where dynamic mics excel—don't even think about miking your speaker cabinet with a condenser. If you've gone this far and you're still missing something, you're probably lacking ambience. You can use a distant mic in conjunction with your dynamic or you may want to try adding just a taste of reverb or very short delay. If the effects don't provide what you need, you'll have to add a PZM about three or four feet away from the speaker at chest height. Put your big pillows on the floor between the speaker cabinet and the distant mic.

Controlling the Frenzied Guitar Player

Before we move on the gentler climes of the acoustic guitar, we should caution you about a major affliction that strikes electric guitarists. The primary symptom is a kind of all-out frenzy that occurs when the guitarist is soloing or trying to thrash out powerful background chords.

FIGURE 12-4.   Miking a guitar amplifier cabinet. Aim the microphone at the cone of the speaker.

During soloing, the affliction takes the form of non-rhythmic finger-tapping that causes notes to lose their individual identity. Although you may be tempted to scream when this happens, you may only spur the player on to heightened musical tantrums. So stop your recorder and in a calm, soothing voice, tell him you're after something different and special, and you're sure he can do it.

In pursuit of power chord backgrounds, electric guitarists have been known to hit the strings so hard that pieces of finger-flesh fly around the room. Pete Townshend's signature stage routine—"windmill" power chording—seems to have inspired a whole generation of players. Occasionally they need to be reminded that Townshend doesn't play like that in the studio. When they hit the strings with the delicacy of a chain saw, all kinds of extraneous noises end up on the tape. The strings go out of tune, or at least sound out of tune, and the lower notes muddle together and sound really awful.

Again, stop the recorder, count to three, and with your most soothing tones remind the guitarist of the need to play with finesse. The sound is coming through just fine on tape.

And if that doesn't work, boost his headphone cue-mix level to a point where his ears will explode if he hits the guitar that hard again. Of course, he may be three-quarters deaf already, so it may be just your tough luck.

MIKING THE ACOUSTIC GUITAR

Ah, the sound of nature . . .

There are three different techniques for getting acoustic guitars on tape in your home studio: a pickup system made for acoustic guitars (found in most music stores); using one or two mics; combining the pickup system with one or two mics. But despite many of the terrific advances in pickup technology, nothing sounds better than properly miking the instrument when it comes to recording.

Using your dynamic and PZM mics, you can get some very nice results. Place the dynamic, or a second condenser if you have one, close by. Put it level with the sound hole of the guitar, but positioned either toward the headstock or the butt of the guitar (Figure 12-5). Aim the mic back at the sound hole, if it is placed toward the headstock. Aim the mic toward the corner of the bridge if it is positioned toward the butt of the guitar. The first position is more traditional (toward the headstock aimed at the soundhole), but aiming the mic at the corner of the bridge can work well, too.

FIGURE 12-5. Miking an acoustic guitar. Place the mic at the level of the sound hole. Put another mic—a PZM—on a stand about four to six feet away at the guitarist's eye level.

Put the second mic, your PZM, on a mic stand at eye level to the guitarist, roughly four to six feet away. You may or may not want to use the tent to record your acoustic guitar. It depends on the sound of your recording room.

The two-mic system gives you the biggest, most life-like recording of an acoustic guitar. The second mic also captures sounds you may not want—grunts and groans from the guitarist, the sound of one foot tapping, and so on. On the other hand, some of these noises can enhance a recording by making it very human and exciting. Just watch and listen to Richie Havens singing "Freedom" on the *Woodstock* video. You can really hear the grunts, the elbow and hand pounding the guitar body, the foot stomping, and the sound of the pick across the strings. You can hear it all, and it sounds wonderful. Whether these noises work depends on the kind of music, the setting, and the effect you are trying to achieve.

In a single-mic situation, use the close mic position. If the guitar is equipped with a pickup system, you can use it effectively with a close mic. Running the pickup through a different mixer channel and processing it differently sometimes lends the air of two

FIGURE 12-6. Miking an acoustic guitar with a single PZM mic. It should be on a stand at about chest height three feet in front of the guitar.

guitars playing the same part. A chorus effect also sounds nice on the pickup signal, particularly when it is mixed to support the close-mic signal.

If you find that you have to record a vocal along with the guitar, and you want to use your dynamic for the vocal, just put your PZM on a stand at about chest height three feet in front of the guitar (Figure 12-6). You'll be amazed how well it picks up the guitar. If the guitarist and the vocalist are the same person, you're better off recording the tracks separately.

Besides, you can always use the practice overdubbing.

USING EQ AND PROCESSORS FOR BASS AND GUITAR

If you have worked hard to get the sound you want on the basic track, you shouldn't need much EQ for either guitar or bass. But if you want to twiddle with the EQ knobs some, here are some basic guidelines.

Bass Processing

When you record the bass, try to get the fullness of the low frequencies from the amp or bass itself. If you start boosting the 100 Hz range with the portable studio EQ, you will end up with a very boomy, muddy sound that will only get worse as you bounce the track. Unless you have expensive parametric equalizers with very narrow bandwidths, you just won't be able to do much with the low end of the bass.

Boosting the midrange a little can help the bass in terms of note definition, particularly with busy bass parts. When complex figures are played, the bass tends to rumble rather than express a discrete series of notes. Some midrange boost will clarify the line. But don't make the bass too "honky." Round-wound bass strings will really honk at you if you boost them much in the upper midrange.

Wait until you're ready to ping-pong the bass part to boost frequencies around 5 kHz. A slight boost when ping-ponging, or the use of a commercially available exciter, helps maintain brightness. When you're recording your basic tracks, it's not a bad idea to roll off the frequencies above 10 kHz. Attenuate them 6 dB to 12 dB. As always, there's nothing much there but noise.

The two most often used processors for bass are the compressor and the flanger, which we discussed in Chapter Four. The compressor limits the level (loudness) of the signal, dropping the highs and raising the lows. In short, it evens out the peaks and valleys of level in the sound. This is particularly helpful in the slapping and popping bass style, because the pops are so much louder than many of the slaps. But use compression with care. Compressing a bass tends to make lower pitched notes sustain and can therefore muddy up the track.

A limited amount of flanging can make the bass sound like two basses are playing the same track, a little like a chorus. A radical flanger can make it sound otherworldly. Experiment to find effects you like. Envelope filters also sound good on funky bass tracks.

Guitar Processing

As with the bass, getting the right sound from the guitar amp or the mics will save you time when you start equalizing. You can enhance the sound somewhat on the way through the mixer to the basic track, and on the way to a bounce or mixdown. The low E note of a guitar is approximately 82 Hz, so if you want to emphasize those rock and roll fifths played on the E and A strings, you should start looking around 100 Hz. Keep any boost here to a minimum—perhaps 3 dB. Any more than that and things start to get ugly.

Unless the guitar sounds really dull, avoid boosting any of the mid- or high-range frequencies. With an acoustic guitar, you can add some sparkle with a little push at the 10 kHz range.

If you're interested in effects and signal processing for guitar, just go into any music store and look at the endless rows of brightly colored pedals, all waiting impatiently like presents under a tree. These boxes are so seductive that they can make an effects pedal junkie out of the stoutest soul. Beware! These boxes are noisy, their levels are inconsistent, and most of their owners don't know how to control them.

If you're a guitarist and you can't do without your effects fix, you might get one of those rack-mount multi-effects processors designed for guitar. They are usually quiet, their level is consistent, and they have some nice out-of-the-box factory programs. Owning one will help you learn its applications. Be mindful, however; none of us is immune to the addiction. Before you know it, you'll be flanging the church choir.

The hit parade of electric guitar effects begins with the distortion pedal. There must be a hundred different versions of this unit on the market today. Regardless of the model, just remember that one distorted guitar will take up a lot of room in your musical arrangement. Two won't leave much room for anything else.

The chorus, which produces a very lush effect not unlike the flanger, has become very popular. It has the curious effect of softening the overall sound. Some of the stereo units have really marvelous panning that can add further lushness to the sound. The only warning, other than for overuse, is that some of the less expensive units on the market can be quite noisy.

Digital delays are another effects hit. They can be subtle, as in the case of simple short delays for pre-delay reverb or doubling. With slightly longer delays, they can create slapback echoes, while still longer delays will repeat whole passages of notes in a kind of audio waterfall. Delays are commonly used with hefty amounts of distortion in heavy metal music.

Other effects which have fallen out of fashion or are too new to be exploited or are just waiting to be rediscovered include: phase shifters (Jimi Hendrix and Robin Trower), pitch shifters (Trevor Rabin), wah-wah pedals (Jimi Hendrix), talk boxes (Peter Frampton), and echoplexes (Jimmy Page). Many of these are worth a listen when you're searching to find that special sound to set your tracks apart.

CHAPTER 13

Recording Acoustic Instruments and Voice

While the current rage is to use electronic keyboards to play the parts of string, brass, or woodwind players, you could do worse than to try and find musicians who play the *real* thing if you can't do it yourself.

MIKING ACOUSTIC INSTRUMENTS

Before you start sticking mics down the bell of a sax or wrapping a mic in a sponge and wedging it under the bridge of a cello, listen to the instrument in the room in which it will be recorded. Much as you did when assessing your piano, you should make notes or mark spots where the instrument sounds best to you. Put your PZM on one of these spots, placing it at about chin height. See if you can capture that nice sound on tape.

If you have too much room ambience with the instrument on the track, you'll want to bring out your tent. You still need a little air with the sound, so don't jam a mic in the bell of a horn. Place the PZM one foot to three feet away from the instrument. If you have several instruments playing at once, place them so that they are all equidistant from the mic. You may want to use several mics for an ensemble.

Here are some things to watch out for. We've often seen flutes miked right up near the sound hole. Having tried it myself, all you'll get is a lot of wind and mouth noises from the flute player. Back off

FIGURE 13-1. Miking a flute. Aim the mic toward the center of the instrument.

the mic a foot and aim it toward the center of the instrument (Figure 13-1).

A mic in the bell of a sax may look great with Clarence Clemmons on stage, but it doesn't work well in the studio. Much of the instrument's sound comes from the holes in the body of the horn. Again, back off and focus on the body. If you get too close to brass players, they can tear your head off with one note (these horns are always louder than you imagine). These characters sometimes turn their heads slightly, which causes the bottom to drop out. Get a brass player who is used to holding still in front of a mic. Then back off a bit (Figure 13-2).

Inexperienced violin players tend to move and rock back and forth. They've seen too many gypsy movies. Get them to hold still and back off the mic. Cello players bang their knees against their instruments and the buttons on their clothes may scrape against the back. Get the player to wear soft clothes or a cotton jogging suit to the session.

Regardless of the string instrument, get a player who can play *in tune*. You may be able to fix them using a chorus effect or harmonizer, but the best fix is a player who can play.

Mandolins and dobros should be recorded in the same way as the acoustic guitar. Banjos, too, but be careful with these instruments. Players tend to drag a finger or two across the head of the

FIGURE 13-2.   Miking a saxophone. Aim the mic toward the body of the instrument.

banjo when they play. Since the head of a banjo is the resonator, like a drum head, it can make a really ugly noise on your track. Try to get the player to stop dragging his finger.

Cheap banjos tend to rattle and buzz, so make sure everything is tight. And keep in mind that banjos are very loud; they can distort some mics.

RECORDING VOICES

If you are recording a voice, it is probably going to be the most important single element in your work. Take a great deal of care to get the most out of this instrument during the recording and to place it properly during the mixdown.

Start by trying to get a good idea of the special qualities of the voice. Does it have extra warmth or resonance in the lower registers? Do the high notes get shrill or harsh? Rock singers have a tendency to scream on the high notes. Screaming tightens the throat and usually restricts resonance. It's very difficult to be objective about your own voice, so you may want to get another opinion.

These observations should help you determine the necessary EQ settings and types of processing you will want to use. If you use the same singer a great deal, keep a record of what you've done. That way, you can set up in advance, cutting down on prep time.

You can use the dynamic mic to record a solo voice or any backups that are done one at a time. It's a really good idea to isolate the vocal track as much as possible, so the tent will come in handy here. Put the dynamic about nose height, 12 inches away from the singer, and aim it at the singer's upper lip.

One reason for this is to get the singer to sing facing up. It helps maintain breath support. The higher mic position also seems to capture "head tones" better. These are higher notes that seem to emanate from the throat on up. Even with head tones, though, good posture and breath support will bring fullness and resonance to the sound (Figure 13-3).

Never let a vocalist hold the mic. Forget the protests and claims of "years of experience." He's only going to bang it around and move it in a way that may look good on stage but that sounds terrible on tape. In the studio, *nobody* holds the mic.

This is probably the point where we should say that no amount of brilliant mic placement, EQ, or other recording wizardry will help a bad performance. If you've got someone in your studio, friend or not, who just can't cut the vocal, then get another singer. Even the charismatic front man who sounds good belting it out on stage with a heavy metal band might not be able to cut it in the studio. On the other hand, a person with a soft voice that has a lot of character may sound great—Michael Jackson, Suzanne Vega, Michael McDonald, Mark Knopfler, and Donald Fagen all come to mind.

A bar stool can come in handy here. If you do a number of takes, the singer may want to take a load off; others like to sit right

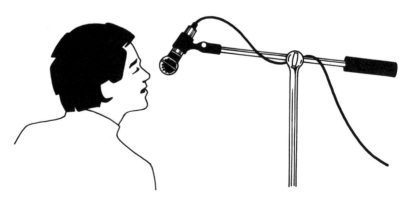

FIGURE 13-3. Miking a solo vocal. The vocalist should sing facing up into the mic.

from the start. Be sure to adjust the microphone's height (the beauty of the bar stool, however, is that the singer is just about the same height sitting as standing). Another benefit of the stool is that it helps keep the singer from creeping up on the mic. Singers love to get close to those mics.

A good music stand will save the singer from clenching the lyric sheet, and while rustling may be appropriate for "Autumn Leaves," paper noises as a rule don't help recordings.

Be sure to set up a good cue mix for the singer so that he or she can hear the vocal and the backing track clearly. It's also a good idea to add some reverb to the cue mix. Making it sound fairly close to the final track helps the singer reach for that something extra to make the track happen.

Once you're set up, start listening to the singer warm up. Have him sing some phrase or practice the lyrics a bit while you set up your mixer. Does he or she pop the P's or hiss the S's? If so, the time has come to trot out your homemade pop filter: a wire clothes hanger bent into a circle with a woman's stocking stretched over it. When placed between the singer and the mic, this will do a good job of stopping the exploding P's and the lighted-fuse S's. There are commercially produced versions of this if a stocking is not readily available.

You should do background vocals one at a time; however, if you've got a group of people who are used to singing together and you want to capture that spontaneity, you can mic them as a group. Place them in a semicircle around the mic, and make sure none of the singers gets too close to the mic. If the singers are used to working together, then no single voice should overpower any others. You may want to use your PZM as an additional distant mic for the group. Place it higher than the dynamic and about three to four feet away. (You can also use this technique with a particularly strong voice, one with a lot of character and overtones. When you EQ the distant mic, you can focus on the overtones and room sound.)

PROCESSING AND SETTING EQ FOR VOICES

Most voices have a two-octave range and will change tonal characteristics at least three times while progressing through that range. With each change in the voice comes a new challenge. Working EQ effectively within two octaves can be tough enough with the average EQ circuits in most portable studios. In all likelihood, only one of your controls will affect the voice's fundamental range—the midrange. The extreme bass and treble controls will only affect the warmth or brilliance of the voice.

In other words, unless you have a parametric equalizer, it's very difficult to work with the voice. Even with a parametric you have to use a narrow bandwidth and very moderate cuts and boosts.

On the bass end, there just isn't much audio to work with. Most voices don't have any push below 200 Hz. You'll find if you try to boost this area though, that you'll be boosting the *proximity effect*. The proximity effect adds a kind of boomy, muddy quality to the voice. Take your dynamic and just speak into it as you move it closer to your mouth. When you get close to your mouth, you'll notice that the bass comes up dramatically and unpleasantly. That's what we mean by proximity effect. If you keep the vocalist away from the mic in the first place, you're going to have little of this effect on your track. However, if you boost the EQ around 200 Hz, you'll bring it right back in. If you're searching to add a little warmth, you should try between 300 Hz and 500 Hz. As you get to 500 Hz, you start to hit the frequencies of the voice itself.

Rock singers can often use a little roll-off in the frequencies between 1 kHz to 3 kHz. Things get pretty unpleasant in that range if the vocalist is used to screaming out rock songs all night—the sound is very shrill. Even trained singers can be deficient in this area. Female singers have a problem closer to the 3 kHz side of this range. These notes just seem to blaze across the room like they're on a beam of light. They seem to be more directional and piercing than other notes sung by the same vocalist.

Above the 3 kHz area is the realm of pops and hisses. It's a good idea to just leave the frequencies from 4 kHz to 10 kHz alone—unless, of course, you have further problems with pops and so on. Then you can lightly attenuate frequencies here to help alleviate those noises.

Nice things can be done in the 10-kHz-and-over range. Your portable studio probably has a high EQ control of the shelving type that is positioned at 10 kHz. This shelving control will boost or cut all the frequencies above 10 kHz. Some boost up here can really bring out the sparkle in a vocal. If you intend to ping-pong the voice at any point, boost this area by 3 dB to 6 dB. You'll also pick up some presence, room ambience, and any reverb that you've applied to the vocal by boosting here.

Because the human voice is our primary communication tool, it's important to retain its intelligibility and human-ness. Try to tread very lightly when processing your vocal tracks—beyond reverb, of course. As you saw from the EQ settings, the idea here is moderation.

Not every singer is a trained singer, and not every trained singer has learned to use a microphone properly. You may run into faults in the singer's ability to keep dynamic levels under control and tone consistent. The tone problem can generally be attacked with judicious use of EQ as suggested above. The dynamic problem may require a compressor. Using a compressor on vocals demands a high-quality unit and a soft ratio with a very moderate gain reduction. In this way the compressor won't steal the show by making the vocal sound like some creepy, overly compressed FM radio program.

In terms of faulty mic technique, you've eliminated a lot of those problems by not letting the singer hold the mic. Watch him so that he doesn't sneak up on the mic and start causing proximity effect. As a rule, singers tend to shout the higher notes in their range. The higher in pitch, the louder they shout. If you have a step-wise melody, you can often just ride the channel fader a bit to keep the level under control; if not, you may have to resort to the compressor. An experienced performer will probably have developed the habit of moving away from the mic as the notes get higher. Nothing replaces great vocal technique, but a few tricks of the performing trade can make the most out a situation.

In addition to reverb, proper EQ, and soft compression, is there anything else necessary to process the voice? Anything can be used, of course, but the best vocal effects are usually the most subtle. A chorus effect can sound good on backing vocals; it will make them sound a little thicker and will help backing vocals blend together. Digital or tape delay can also sound good. Echo triggered rhythmically so that the repeats come on the beats of the measure can be particularly fine. Experiment with some of these effects by dubbing some vocals to one of your scratch tapes. Then, when you're into a project, you'll have already done your experimenting. The journey generally goes better when you know where you are going.

CHAPTER 14

MIDI (Musical Instrument Digital Interface) and Your Studio

Often, the more you learn to operate your home studio, the more you will want to record. The biggest problem you'll encounter is that unless you're capable of playing a number of instruments and have them all on hand (do you work in a music store, by any chance?), you may not be able to use all the colors of the musical palette. Oh, you may learn to create some unusual musical effects—recording a guitar at half-speed, for example, and running it through various effects will give you some interesting sounds—but you soon will tire of guitar-derived music. Guitar with peanut butter, guitar with jelly, guitar soup, guitar stew.

And if you get to the point where you bring in other players, you're also going to come to the day when you need a drummer and every drummer you know is either out of town or not returning your calls.

It may be difficult or impossible to record without the help of some other musicians. But do you really want to depend on other musicians for your own musical fulfillment? Why wait for them? You don't have to. Electronic musical instruments now offer the exciting option of making fully orchestrated and arranged music by yourself at home.

Probably because they are so difficult to record well, drums became the first instruments to get automated. Some of you probably remember the early drum machines—black boxes sporting a variety of little candy-colored buttons with labels such as "Tango,

Enka, Waltz," and the famous "Rock I." Although the initial sounds weren't good enough to end up on professional recordings, they were good enough to help the songwriter work out an arrangement. They could also sit in a track until a live drummer replaced the sound of spit in a frying pan (cymbals) and a hat hitting the floor (drums) with the real thing.

In other words, the first drum machines were glorified metronomes for practicing musicians that eventually opened the door to an entire industry of automated drums. It wasn't long before other instruments would come under the threat of the push button.

Early sequencers (enabling the user to arrange, sequence, and edit sound) produced single strings of sixteenth notes that seemed more robotic than musical. When sequencers achieved the capacity to render numerous parts simultaneously (polyphony, circa 1981) the music realized on them began to sound as if it were played by a human being. Musicians everywhere began to long for the opportunity to automate bass and harmony parts. This practice became prevalent just as the portable studio, which appeared on the market in 1979, was beginning to revolutionize the recording industry. It was a match made in Heaven.

Before the relationship could be consummated, however, manufacturers of electronic musical instruments had to bury their silicon hatchets and agree upon a standard of information-sharing among their products—not unlike the ASCII code that allows IBM and Apple computers to communicate over telephone lines.

The result was MIDI (Musical Instrument Digital Interface). With the standardization of musical digital signal (circa 1983), a single musician/composer alone could drive a bank of drum machines and synths from a single controller (generally a keyboard) at once. No longer would composers need to hire a room full of musicians simply to hear with their own ears the music that had been echoing through their minds. With the addition of a portable studio to keep a permanent record of the music, the world could benefit from a flood of new sounds and new composers sharing with us the message of their muses. Well, though we haven't entered a new cultural Renaissance, the opportunities for musical expression have never been more affordable or more powerful.

Nowadays you can't go into a music store without being confronted with an intimidating barrage of buzz words and gobbledygook. Something that should make a musician's life easier has wound up making it more complex and confusing. If we can

cut through the jargon for a minute, we think you'll see that
MIDI isn't that tough.

HOW MIDI WORKS

MIDI is a language of numbers. Since it's a digital language, the
numbers it uses are just zeros and ones, which are strung together in groups of varying sizes that are called bits, bytes, and
words. And because this is stuff that even your computer can
understand, you can now bring your home computer (won't your
significant other just love you to death?) into your studio to talk
to your drum machine and synth(s) by sending streams of information via the MIDI controller card and the MIDI cable.

If you could hear MIDI, it would sound like Morse Code on
pep pills: very fast, very high-pitched, and very nonmusical. So
what's going down the MIDI cable if it's not music? Basically,
what's going down the cable are instructions that tell your instruments what to play. If you press the middle-C on a MIDI keyboard, the MIDI code for that pitch is sent down the line. If you
have a velocity-sensing keyboard, then MIDI will transmit a
number representing how hard you are hitting the key. Pitch
bend or modulation wheels, patch change buttons, and so on all
work the same way—as a series of instructions.

The instrument that is receiving the MIDI signals will, in
turn, interpret the instructions. It will play its middle-C at the
velocity suggested by the sending keyboard. It will bend pitches
and change patches and do lots more besides if and when you ask
it to. But if an instrument wasn't designed to understand certain
words in the MIDI language (velocity, for example), it will not
execute those functions.

Some instruments—most notably sequencers and computers running sequencing software—are designed only to process
data itself. They don't make sounds themselves, but they keep
track of all the data sent to them until they're commanded to
send it back down the MIDI cable.

In some cases, MIDI commands are more like suggestions.
When you push a program/patch change button on your sending
unit, this message gets sent down the line. If the receiving unit is
capable of responding to patch change MIDI commands, it will
change. But will the second unit make the same sound as the
sending unit? Not likely. These are, after all, two different
machines, each equipped with its own collection of sounds. Patch

18 on the second is not going to be Patch 18 on the first.

In recent years, makers of MIDI instruments have attempted to let the instruments talk to each other in depth. "General MIDI" was created to allow instruments by various makers to exchange sounds or patches. This has been only partly successful; some instruments, such as those by Roland and Yamaha, still have difficulty communicating through General MIDI.

Lighting systems, guitar processors, mixing consoles, and even recorder transports now speak MIDI. The MIDI commands called MIDI Continuous Controller (MCC), MIDI Machine Control (MMC), and MIDI Time Code have made it possible to control almost every aspect of a performance or recording via MIDI.

MIDI Messages

There are two basic types of MIDI messages: channel messages and system messages. The data that are sent on MIDI's 16 channels relate to the musical notes and their performance. (Note that there are now many multiples of the basic 16 channels available on most MIDI systems.) A MIDI channel is like the channel on your television. A sound module or other MIDI instrument may be instructed to respond to only those messages that come on a certain channel, just like your tube. Although the television receives all the channels on the dial at all times, its screen only shows the one you select. Similarly, a sound module set to MIDI channel 2 would only play those music messages that come to it with the channel 2 assignment. Channel commands are directions aimed at the individual instruments—they have unusual names like note on/off, control change, pitch wheel change, and aftertouch; they also include mode messages such as local on/off, all notes off, and select for the MIDI modes.

System messages address the system shell from which the channel commands are sent. System messages include such bizarre expressions as system exclusive (data dumps that will send out all the numbers in the units memory and so on). One realm of system message is *system common,* by which you issue such commands as song position pointer, song select, and tune request. *System real time* deals with the actions of sequencers and computer: the timing clock, start, stop, continue, and active sensing.

That's a lot of information and certainly a long way from the fairly straightforward wish to have a set up that will play the bass, drum, and keyboard parts for you while you play the guitar.

These functions are zealous attempts by manufacturers to push the limits of MIDI development. Sometimes it boils down to their desire to create a feature that their competitors don't have. Not every machine can do all of these things, nor would you necessarily want it to. These commands get sent only if the sending instrument is capable of generating them. And only those functions the receiving unit understands will be translated and performed. That's why every MIDI-equipped instrument is supposed to come with what's called a *MIDI implementation chart*. The chart will tell you what your instrument will send and what it will receive (Figure 14-1).

TYPES OF MIDI INSTRUMENTS

Though there seems to be an endless array of MIDI instruments and applications, all these instruments fall into a few categories:

- *Sound modules* are anything that makes sound, such as a synthesizer or sampler.

- *Controllers* are the instruments you play: keyboards, drum pads, guitars, anything that will send performance data from the human to the machine.

- *Sequencers* provide the storage place for all the numbers you generate with your controllers; the sequencer may be "dedicated" or it may be computer-running sequencer software.

- *Peripherals* are MIDI patch bays, MIDI mergers, synchronizers, lighting controllers, and the like.

- *Signal Processors* are the delays, reverbs, and so on that will accept MIDI data.

Often, you'll find a single box that offers a combination of these functions. A drum machine, for example, is a controller, a sound module, and a sequencer. That is, you can play it (so it's a controller); it generates sounds (making it a sound module); and you can program patterns (so it's a sequencer). A synthesizer can be a keyboard controller and a sound module. Some "work station" instruments may also include signal processors, sequencers, and peripherals.

Model X7000   MIDI Implementation Chart   Version :1.0

Function ...		Transmitted	Recognized	Remarks
Basic Channel	Default Changed	1 1 - 16	1 1 - 16	
Mode	Default Messages Altered	MODE 3 **************	MODE 3	
Note Number : True voice		36 - 96 * **************	0 - 127 0 - 99	Key Transpose ±7
Velocity	Note ON Note OFF	○ 9nH v=1-127 ○ 8nH v=0-127	○ 9nH v=1-127 × 8nH v=0-127, 9n v=0	8nH: Velocity Release
After Touch	Key's Ch's	× ×	× ○	
Pitch Bender		○	○	
Control Change	1 7 64	○ ○	○ ○ ○	Modulation Wheel Volume Control Sustain Pedal
Prog Change : True #		○ (0 - 31) **************	○ 0 - 31	
System Exclusive		○	○	Sampling Data
System : Song Pos : Song Sel Common : Tune		× × ×	× × ×	
System :Clock Real Time :Commands		× ×	× ×	
Aux :Local ON/OFF :All Notes OFF Mes- :Active Sense sages:Reset		× × × ×	○ ○ × ×	123
Notes				

Mode 1 : OMNI ON, POLY   Mode 2 : OMNI ON, MONO   ○: Yes
Mode 3 : OMNI OFF, PLLY   Mode 4 : OMNI OFF, MONO   ×: no

FIGURE 14-1. A MIDI implementation chart. (Courtesy of Akai Electric Co., Ltd.)

Sound Modules

Samples, synthesizers, organs, digital pianos, and drum machines are all sound modules. They are MIDI sound modules only if they have a MIDI "in" jack. This jack means that the sound module can be controlled (played) from any device that sends MIDI—a keyboard, drum pad, guitar synthesizer, or sequencer. Some sound modules, such as keyboards and drum machines, have their own controllers. And even though a synth may have its own keyboard, it may be controlled from another keyboard via MIDI. MIDI controllers are also made using guitars and wind instruments.

Sound modules are categorized by the way they create their sounds. A *sampler* is a sound module that uses a digital recording system to create its sounds. The sound played is a sample of a sound that could be heard in nature or on another recording medium, such as CD, record, or tape. You could sample your dog Sammie's barks and use them as a sound for bass lines or percussion accents. Or you could sample the sound of a French horn and then play the sound from the sampler's controller. Both Sammie and the French horn would sound very realistic.

Some samplers are playback units only; they are not able to record their own new sound samples. Most of the current model drum machines are now sample players that concentrate on playing back percussion samples.

A *synthesizer* is a sound module that uses an electronic means to construct a sound from its various parts. Starting with a blank audio slate, the synthesist creates a waveform and modifies it until the desired sound emerges. Various forms of synthesizers have developed over the years and you will hear many names thrown around loosely by partially informed music store salespeople. Your main concern is that the sound module is capable of creating sounds that you like no matter what type of synthesis is used to create them.

Analog synthesis refers to machines made with analog electronics, which means they are controlled by linear voltage rather than by numbers (digits). Analog synthesizers are characterized by big fat bass, pseudo-strings, pseudo-brass, and screaming lead lines à la Chick Corea and Jan Hammer. The pseudo-strings and pseudo-brass sounds are often called "pads." So, next time you saunter by that nice old Memory Moog or Jupiter-8 in the music store, say wistfully, "Love those string pads on the old analog stuff." This will show the salesman you're not to be trifled with.

Before synthesizers became "totally digital," they went

through a stage of being partially digital and partially analog. These units had digital counting oscillators (DCOs) with analog filters (VCFs) and amplifiers (VCAs). The Roland Juno-60 and JX-3P are examples of this. These units make sounds that are similar to the fat strings, brass, and bass of the fully analog synthesizers. They tend to be a little "thinner" sounding, but they stay in tune better.

In today's market, with the exception of some of the audio circuitry, synthesizers are totally digital. FM synthesis, created at Stanford University and successfully marketed by Yamaha, has passed its prime as a method of choice for generating great sounds through synthesis. FM (Frequency Modulation) is a way of combining waveforms to create other waveforms. In Yamaha's DX series of synthesizers, for example, sine waves of various frequencies are modulated by one another in various combinations to create the final waveform sound. These combinations are called algorithms. (I know, I know! I'll stop in a minute.)

FM's more popular sounds seem to be characterized by a bright, shimmering, metallic quality. Some very nice bells and tine piano (Rhodes-type) sounds are found on most FM menus. All in all, FM is a synthesis system of great potential, but also of great complexity. There are, however, thousands of prepackaged sounds available for FM synthesizers. So, if you run into a bargain, you won't necessarily have to learn to program the thing in order to make great music with FM.

The current crop of popular synthesizers base their operation on sampled waveforms, or partial waveforms. These sound increments are combined and then filtered, amplified, and modulated by the rest of the circuits to create the finished product. The systems of filtering and so on have become very sophisticated. Many instruments offer "models" of various instrumental characteristics in their filter and modulation sections. A variety of synthesizers from Roland, Ensoniq, and Korg all use variations on this theme.

Most current sound modules are *multitimbral*. This means that they can play several sounds simultaneously—not just pads, but bass, chords, drums, and melody all at the same time. For your purposes, you'll want your sound module to have multiple audio outputs, so you can route a snare drum or bass drum, for example, to be processed by any effects devices. You could also equalize a string or a bass part separately. If the sound module you are considering is multitimbral but doesn't have multiple audio outputs, you may be better off considering a separate drum machine—but even that will require separate audio outputs if you want to do anything special with the bass and snare drum sounds.

Drum Machines

As mentioned earlier, a drum machine is more than a sound module that specializes in percussion sounds, it is also a controller and a sequencer. Its pads take the place of keys as on a synthesizer or sampler. And in the kind of drum machine you need for your home studio, the pads are velocity-sensitive—the harder you hit, the louder they go. This is a very important feature if you want to make your drum machine parts sound more human.

In terms of the sounds themselves, choose quality over quantity. It may be fun to have timbales and shakers, but a great sounding basic "kit" is what you need 90 percent of the time (unless, of course, your muse speaks to you only in salsa, tango, and samba rhythms). Go for the dry-sounding set rather than the drum machine filled with heavily processed sounds. The latter will sound more spectacular in the music store, but it may dominate all your tracks at home. It's better to have something you can process yourself than to have something you're trying vainly to de-process.

Multiple outputs are a must. But you don't necessarily need outputs for every instrument sound. Four outputs—a pair for stereo and two monos—will do the job. This way you can process your bass and snare separately in the ways discussed earlier. Or you could pull a troublesome cymbal sound out one of the sepa-

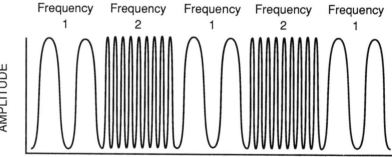

rate outputs. The remaining instruments can keep the stereo panorama that they are assigned in the drum machine. In this setup, you're only using four mixer channels as well.

Because a drum machine is also a sequencer, it will store and play back patterns and compositions using its own sounds. Its memory functions are usually organized as both individual patterns of one to several bars, and as songs, which are structured as arrangements of individual patterns. You can, therefore, program your entire composition into the drum machine. When done, get your recorder and mixer ready and record the part.

The sequencer sections of many drum machines have a function called sync or tape sync (Figure 14-2). Tape sync is used to overdub drum parts with your drum machine. This is a terrific function for home studio applications, and it's so easy to use. Here's how:

1. As you record the first pass of your drum part, use another track to record the signal that comes from the sync output. Simply connect the tape sync output to the input of the track on the recorder you will want to use for the sync signal (it's not a great idea to run sync signals through your mixer). These sync signals aren't musical; in fact, they're pretty annoying. Record sync on track 4 (at a lower level than you would music; say, -3 on the VU meter. On some drum machines, you may want to record it even softer, at about -7 on the VU).

2. After the first track is recorded, connect the output of track 4 to the tape sync input of the drum machine.

3. Rewind the tape, program your overdub part on the drum machine, and when ready, roll the tape and press start on the drum machine. There may be a special button to be used when the drum machine is to start and stay synchronized to its own code. Look for Sync Start, or Ext. Start, or some similar function button.

Don't be confused. There are a number of different things that are called sync. With very few exceptions, the sync code on most drum machines is not MIDI Time Code or SMPTE or one of the more elaborate sync codes you learn about shortly. Its technical name is FSK (Frequency Shift Key), and it is simply a recordable electronic metronome. Each pulse of the frequency shift tells the drum machine to advance one beat. This is why you must reset the drum machine and rewind the tape machine before you can overdub.

You may find the drum machine sync useful when you want to separately process more instruments than your drum machine has outputs. Let's say your machine has four outputs. You've got the bass drum and snare assigned separately. The toms are going out the stereo (summed) outputs. But you really want to process the cymbals for EQ and reverb. The sync feature allows you to record the drums on the first pass and the cymbals as an over-dub. Simply shut down the cymbal part for the first pass, then delete or turn down the drum instruments for the second pass. The only problem with this arrangement is that it eats up a lot of tracks and you'll be forced into ping-ponging early in the record-ing process.

Controllers

Various controllers have been designed to accommodate the musical abilities of different kinds of musicians. There are con-trollers that play like guitars, or keyboards, or drums, or saxes, or trumpets (Figure 14-3). These controllers work to varying

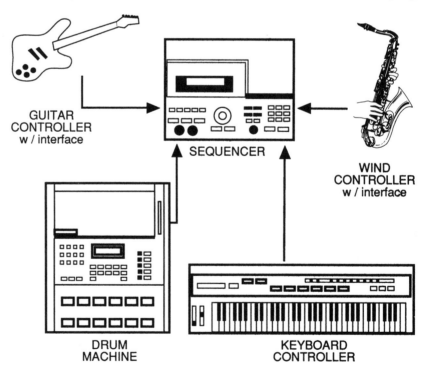

FIGURE 14-3. MIDI controllers.

degrees of efficiency, but their mutual goal is to translate musical expression into MIDI code. Frankly, though, there's a lot more nuance and expression than most MIDI controllers are capable of translating. You've heard the phrase "Something was lost in the translation." It's a common occurrence in MIDI-land, and a common source of disappointment for MIDI users. But try to see the glass as half full rather than half empty, and your MIDI experiments will end up being much more rewarding.

As mentioned earlier, MIDI has a wide variety of messages; there is a lot more to it than just note on/note off commands. For example, controls that communicate how hard a key or string or wind instrument is played, or how hard a pad controller is struck, are very important. Many controllers also send messages for how quickly the key (or string) is released. And if a key is held down and then secondary pressure is applied, there is a control called aftertouch that can send this information. What's important for you to keep in mind is that not all controllers are capable of sending all these messages. So any shopping for controllers should include a look at the unit's MIDI implementation chart.

Other controls may add to your possibilities for expression, but they should be used appropriately. Pitch bend and modulation controls may not have any relevance to a piano sound, but in MIDI-land, your pianolike keyboard may be playing violin or synthesized sounds that could use these controls. Those of you with a composer's view of the MIDI process should look at the attributes of a controller from the perspective of the sound. Just as an arranger must realize that a flute cannot play notes in the bass range, the MIDI composer/arranger should play the sound.

This is also true for the players who are not as interested in MIDI as in having a controller that plays like their main instrument. The tendency here is to continue playing the controller as if it were a piano, guitar, or saxophone and ignore the particular sound it is producing. Lightning-fast finger-tapping guitar leads don't work with sounds that resemble lush string sections. McCoy Tyner–style blocks of chords won't work with a flute ensemble sound or with human whistling. Though some of the accidents that happen when technique and instrument sound collide are exciting and creative, most are just bloody messes that end up in the audio emergency room.

So what do you need from a MIDI controller for your home studio?

1. The unit should be polyphonic and able to send individual signals to your sound modules and sequencer. (Beware:

some older units do not do this.)

2. It should be capable of rendering velocity (loudness and soft-ness), pitch bend, and modulation data.

3. It must send on any MIDI channel, and it should support all the MIDI modes.

4. If possible, it should have the feature that allows you to send program-change data to switch the sound of your sound module from the controller. (This is not essential, but is helpful nonetheless.)

5. Similarly, the unit should be capable of handling mapping, zones, or key ranges. This effectively divides the controller into different registers that send via different MIDI chan-nels. This allows you, for example, to play a bass part with the left hand of a keyboard (or the low strings of a guitar) and other parts with the right hand.

Beyond these functions, the controller should match up well with the multitimbral sound module. It should be able to send mes-sages that will make the sound module operate to its optimum efficiency. See how the MIDI implementation sheets for the sound module and the controller match up. Take particular notice of how the "transmit" signals of the controller match with the "receive" signals of the sound module.

If you are on an unlimited budget, you should also get a con-troller that matches your own level of expressive capability. As a rule, controllers that allow accomplished players to execute their techniques are very expensive. Keyboard controllers with real piano action, 88 keys, and all the pitch wheels, MIDI controls, and so on, cost over a thousand dollars. Guitar controllers that work well are in the same range. Wind controllers run about the same, and have the limitation inherent in horns: they're mono-phonic. Organ-touch keyboards found on most synthesizers usu-ally have about five octaves worth of keys, but are much less expensive than their "tactile" cousins.

Because it is so easy to spend thousands on a MIDI system without knowing what you're getting, you might do best to start with a simple keyboard controller, one that comes with a sound module in a synthesizer or sampler, and then gradually come up to speed in terms of sequencing and different controller types.

Sequencers

A sequencer may be a stand-alone unit or a package of software and MIDI interface for a computer. Though it is often called a digital recorder, a sequencer makes no sound on its own. A sequencer records the actions—not the sound—of the performance.

In that sense, sequencers resemble our multitrack (Figure 14-4). Manufacturers use the term *track* to refer to segmented portions of the sequencer's song memory. But as used here, the term has only a very loose relation to the term as it applies to recorders. In the first MIDI sequencers, each new pass or part or MIDI channel assignment required a new track. A player could merge tracks in a process similar to ping-ponging. And as in ping-ponging, the early sequencers couldn't unmerge.

Today's MIDI sequencers can merge many parts together,

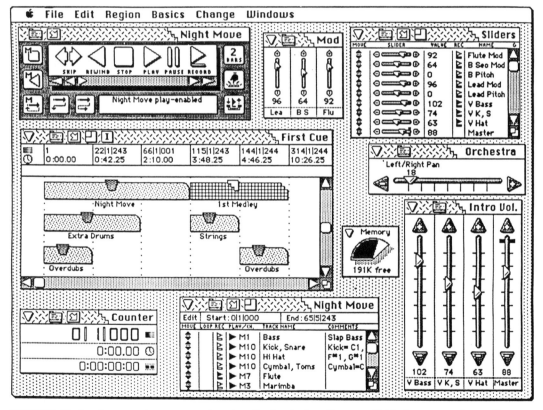

FIGURE 14-4. A computer screen showing the basic functions available in sequencing software. Note the recorder-like graphics in the upper left corner and other functions borrowed from multi-tracking. This display is from "Performer" by Mark of the Unicorn. (Performer is a registered trademark of Mark of the Unicorn, Inc. Courtesy of Mark of the Unicorn)

even those with different MIDI channel assignments, and later separate them again for editing or other purposes. Obviously, those of you who are using those ancient sequencers will have to plan your mergers just as carefully as you plan your track bounces on the multitrack. In a sequencer that allows you to merge, unmerge, and edit with real flexibility, the number of tracks it has doesn't matter at all. There are now software programs for computers boasting 64 or 96 tracks. Who cares? The marketing department, that's who. But you shouldn't care if you can get what you need from a sequencer that has two tracks.

And though its operating commands sometimes resemble those of the portable studio, the kinds of things you can do with those commands are vastly different. When you edit on the sequencer, you can take advantage of some kind of time correction or autocorrection capability. Often called quantization, the program will "correct" small errors in the rhythmic value of the music you enter into the sequencer. If you are a little shaky on the playing end, you can set your sequencer to a note value (sixteenths or thirty-seconds). The sequencer will then move the note values entered to the closest sixteenth or thirty-second note. This feature is great if you're a guitarist using a keyboard controller, or a nonexperienced drum machine user.

A sequencer's ability to correct time depends upon its degree of resolution—as indeed does its ability to enter any note's rhythmic value. You will see a number that may be followed by "bpq," which means "beats per quarter-note." Regardless of the tempo, the sequencer will divide each quarter-note into this many smaller increments. Sequencers should have a minimum of 24 bpq, with a more useful resolution of about 96 bpq. The larger the number of bpq, the greater expression and variance available to any given note. Sequencers should have a minimum of 24 bpq; some even boast 384 or greater bpq, but this may be more than you need. Such very fine resolution allows sequenced tracks, particularly drum tracks, to sound more alive. It is the deviations (some might say the imperfections) that make parts swing with a human feel. A sequencer that operates at 96 bpq will be more than adequate for your needs.

Remember the two kinds of MIDI messages, channel messages and system messages? Your sequencer should let you change your mind, or experiment with channel messages. In your sequencer's event-editing section, you should be able to change such things as note value (pitch), note on/off (rhythm), pitch bend, modulation, aftertouch response, the MIDI Mode, and so on. If you decide that the "C" in the second measure should be a

"C#," you should be able to change it without playing it again. The more channel message or event editing capability your sequencer has, the better.

Your sequencer should also have some form of "copy" editing. A sequencer's ability to copy a bar or series of bars to another place in the score will save you from having to enter the same part over and over again. If it can copy whole verse and chorus segments, all the better, because it will also save some memory, providing the sequencer is designed to put the copy command itself into memory and not the entire string of notes.

Your sequencer should also be able to punch in—just as you punch in on your multitrack. On most sequencers with this feature, you have an ability to audition the change before eliminating the old section. The sequencer saves both sections until you make a final decision as to which one you prefer.

Step-time recording on a MIDI sequencer is a very useful feature for those sections you simply can't seem to perform at any speed, even with the option of time correction and event editing. In step-time recording, the note's pitch and rhythm are entered separately. In other words, you pick a sixteenth note from a selection of notes, and then press the "C#" key. The resulting sixteenth note "C#" is then entered into the sequence. You construct your music in this way until you have completed an entire musical phrase. Step-time recording can be a terrific help if you are not the world's greatest sight reader and you are entering music into your sequencer from sheet music.

Two useful but nonessential features are Multiple MIDI Outputs and disk-storage capability. Having more than one MIDI output helps relieve the pressure of having lots of parts coming through the same serial interface. As a serial interface code, MIDI sends its material in a one-at-a-time manner. Although it is not usually a problem, elaborate parts with multiple sound modules and drum machines can cause a little traffic jam at MIDI junction.

Disk-storage capability is obviously handy. When working on a piece, it is very convenient to be able to store it to disk, stop working, and come back later. If you have a friend with the same sequencer or sequencer software, you can take disks back and forth. Whether you get a sequencer with a disk drive or not, make sure your sequencer has a "nonvolatile" memory. A volatile memory loses all its data every time it is turned off, or power is interrupted for whatever reason. If you don't get a disk drive on which to store your sequences, at least get a sequencer that won't drive you crazy by dumping your hard work just before you record it because the guitar player tripped over the power cord.

Synchronization

Another good function—though not essential—is some kind of tape synchronization. Variously called sync or tape sync (as on the drum machine), this feature produces a recordable signal that can be used to create sequencer overdubs using your MIDI equipment. MIDI itself is not recordable, because at 32 Kilobaud, MIDI produces a pitch well beyond the range of human hearing and multitrack recorders, so the data signal must be incorporated in a form that can be captured on tape and yet give off the necessary cues for your MIDI instruments.

The two most common recordable signals are FSK (discussed under drum machines) and SMPTE (pronounced sim-tee; it stands for Society of Motion Picture and Television Engineers). SMPTE was devised to help synchronize audio with visual images.

SMPTE provides time references of hours, minutes, seconds, frames, fields, and bits (Figure 14-5) with points being defined with very fine resolution. Sequencers can use SMPTE to stop and start, go to a specific frame to perform a function, and repeat a section between two SMPTE locations. There is a type of SMTPE called VITC (pronounced vit-see; this stands for vertically integrated time code), which is embedded into the video signal recorded to video tape. Though you won't be using this, you might encounter LTC (longitudinal time code), which is recorded on the audio tracks of video tape and is easily recorded by our tape machines.

A late addition to the MIDI code specification called MTC (MIDI Time Code) has been used very effectively with SMPTE for synchronization purposes. Since it is embedded in the MIDI data stream, MTC is not recordable either, except by digital machines.

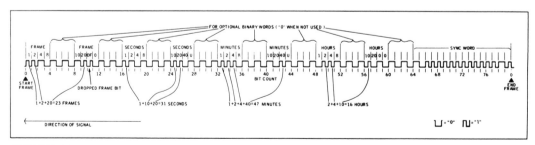

FIGURE 14-5. An example of SMPTE Edit Code for one video frame. The smallest increment of SMPTE data is a "bit"; there are 80 of them per frame. Different bits and groups of bits communicate information about the frame. (Courtesy of TASCAM, Teac Professional Division)

MTC does give code pointers or directions to measures, beats, and other musical references. These musical references can be correlated by a machine made to read both SMPTE and MTC, so that a sequencer can give very precise directions to find locations on tape using the musical references with which we are familiar.

A growing number of recorders, particularly digital hard-disk-based recorders, implement MTC control of their transports and supply MIDI connection points. Using a sequencer with one of these systems is a breeze because MIDI can be used as "house" control system. If you don't have machines capable of using MTC in this way, SMPTE provides a recordable sync signal with amazing resolution.

FSK, mentioned earlier, is a kind of recordable metronome that drum machines and sequencers can read from, and write to, tape. However, it can be frustrating to find specific locations on tape; you have to go back to the beginning of the song every time. Smart FSK, developed by J. L. Cooper and others, helps correlate the FSK signal to MTC to give it more flexibility and some location finding skills. If you have one of Jim's peripheral boxes, you may be able to perform some reasonable overdubs with your sequencer without the benefit of SMPTE.

STORING MIDI DATA

The amount of information that either the disk or the sequencer memory must hold depends upon the sophistication of the controller that sends the code to the sequencer in the first place. If your controller is capable of generating polyphonic aftertouch and multiple key ranges across multiple MIDI channels, then your MIDI messages to the sequencer will be much more complex than those of a controller that sends only note on and note off.

Each and every instruction—note on, note off, pitch, velocity, value, and so on—generates its own MIDI information that must be stored and transmitted. Though some manufacturers express the memory capacity of their sequencers in notes, the average note they describe probably only has four or five MIDI events. Any use of continuous controllers such as pitch bend or aftertouch will eat up memory quickly because the final note may involve hundreds of MIDI events.

When MIDI was new, so was most personal computer technology. Consequently, memory was expensive. A sequencer of 10,000-note memory was considered pretty large (and it was also pretty expensive). Ten thousand notes might get you through a simple arrangement of a pop song, but not much more. Now that computer memory and disk drives have become so inexpensive, the storage capacity of your sequencer or computer can be huge by comparison to these early sequencers.

Types of Sequencers

By now, you're probably asking, "But how can I actually use a sequencer with my hands-on recording?" Sequencers are the "brains" of MIDI and come in two basic forms: dedicated sequencers, which are units specifically geared for sequencing, and sequencing software for use with a personal computer.

In the current market, dedicated sequencers are slotted at the extremely high end of the market (the AKAI MPC-60) or at the very low end (as exemplified by simple sequencers used with home digital pianos). The computer running sequencer software has become the de facto standard. The reasons for this are many and include:

- Computers have some form of massive data storage capability, usually a disk drive or hard drive.

- Computer software programs for MIDI sequencing generally offer more flexibility and editing power than dedicated sequencers.

- Software is easier to update or replace in a computer-based sequencing system.

- Many sequencing programs will work with other programs that will print music in the form of lead sheets.

- With a modem, you can transmit your MIDI sequence to anywhere the phone lines reach.

You can also use the computer for such MIDI tasks as sound editing programs for your synthesizers and samplers, studio management programs, and video/audio cue sheet and synchronization programs. And there are a number of music education programs available for computers, many of them with MIDI implementation. You can use a computer to improve your ear training, composition, or basic performance skills.

Both the Macintosh and IBM (DOS and Windows) computers are heavily supported by MIDI manufacturers. A choice between them should probably be based upon your non-MIDI uses for the computer and your budget.

MIDI PERIPHERALS

The enthusiastic push of MIDI users into more complex uses of the code and compatible instruments also brought demands for peripherals that would help expand capabilities. Jim Cooper (of J. L. Cooper Electronics) and other creative people make a living out of plugging the gaps in the MIDI development race. There always seems to be some gizmo needed to fill a missing link in the production chain (sometimes they plug holes that you didn't even know were there). In addition to the synchronizing peripherals mentioned earlier, there are a number of units that support, route, or alter the MIDI signal in some way (Figure 14-6).

When first developed, the MIDI code was not expected to support the large and complex systems that many people now have assembled. Early MIDI synthesizers had two simple MIDI connectors, In and Out. Users found that when several of these

FIGURE 14-6. MIDI peripherals. *Top*: the J.L. Cooper MSB Plus REV 2 is a MIDI patch bay/switching system. *Bottom*: the J.L. Cooper Fadermaster provides slider control over numerous kinds of MIDI equipment. (Courtesy of J.L. Cooper Electronics)

instruments were connected there were noticeable delays. Each instrument in a chain of instruments connected Out-to-In-Out-to-In, would process the MIDI signal completely through its own circuits. This processing and passing on held up the show so much that the last instruments in the chain played audibly behind and out of sync with the others. MIDI Thru was created to alleviate this problem.

Many first-generation MIDI instruments didn't implement the code very thoroughly. They may have transmitted on only one MIDI channel, or only used one MIDI mode, or misinterpreted an aspect of the MIDI code. The third-party developers and manufacturers were the first ones to address these needs. Boxes that reassigned MIDI channels were created for synths such as the first DX-7s that only transmitted on one MIDI channel. Channel filters stripped away unwanted information from MIDI signals sent in Omni Mode.

In short, a whole industry has grown up to address the anomalies of MIDI. MIDI now controls lighting systems and digital recorders, among many other things, and the industry in peripherals continues to grow and evolve along with MIDI itself.

SIGNAL PROCESSING AND OTHER MIDI-CONTROLLABLE DEVICES

Quite a number of devices can now be controlled to varying degrees by MIDI. Mixers, lighting systems, digital reverbs, and other signal processors have all been made to respond to some form of command. The degree to which these units respond may be small. A digital reverb may, for example, respond to a MIDI patch change command that will switch it from a "hall" reverb setting to a "small room" reverb setting. A lighting controller might respond to MIDI by switching off the green spots and switching on the blue spots because of a program change command in the MIDI sequence. A mixer might mute some channels while releasing the muting of others in response to MIDI.

These program change responses are sometimes called snapshots. They rely on some kind of "memory" to be present in the device to take a kind of picture (snapshot) of the positions of all the knobs and other controls. The mixer, lighting controller, or signal processor must be able to store these snapshots of its own settings. In such a device, you would use the parameter controls of the device to create what you felt was a setup. You would then "write" (store the picture of) that setup into the unit's memory bank. Most units assign some kind of number to these patches/snapshots. If the unit's memory was then capable of responding to MIDI patch change commands, you could have your sequencer or controller switch through the various numbered patches without having to do so from the unit's control panel.

Let's say that you have a great flute patch on your synthesizer and you'd really like to hear a concert-hall-type reverb on it. You're only using the flute patch for a brief solo, and you prefer another reverb setting for the string patch you're using as a chord pad during the rest of the piece. You could program the reverb so that it would switch to the appropriate concert-hall reverb, and back to something else in response to the patch change commands of the synthesizer.

Some of these MIDI controllable devices will respond to "real-time" controller commands (called MIDI Continuous Controller, or MCC). Rather than merely stepping through static snapshots, these devices can follow graduated commands. Instead of simply switching from green to blue spots, for example, the greens will gradually fade down as the blues gradually brighten up. Similarly, you can program one mixer's channel to fade off while another one is brought up to nominal.

Extensive use of continuous controllers is becoming commonplace, and the prospects for future use are very exciting. Complete theatrical productions can be performed using extensive computer, or sequencer, control of lights, video machines, synthesizers, samplers, mixers, signal processors, and so on. A complete Broadway musical could be run with only the singers and dancers performing "live."

In one sense, the prospect is a little scary. Will orchestra pits of the future become barren of human life? Will we be overrun with canned productions? Or will the availability of this technology stimulate more productions of greater creative intensity? Will artists, musicians, and writers be able to produce their own creations? Will the major record labels lose their totalitarian control of music creation and distribution? Will we finally hear something new on the radio and in the "record" stores?

It's up to us, isn't it? Us, that is, and our little machines. . .

CHAPTER 15

Buying the Right MIDI Gear

Now that you have some sense of various MIDI-compatible devices and a little taste of what they can bring to your own recording work, you can start to develop a plan for outfitting your home studio with MIDI.

The first thing you need is a multitimbral sound module. Whether it's a synthesizer, sampler, or digital piano is an artistic choice that's up to you. In the realm of percussion, though, there really is no choice: you will want sampled drum sounds. At the time of this writing, most of the drum machines and percussion sections of multitimbral module are based on sampled sounds. Some of the older synthesizer sound-based drum machines are still around; the Roland "TR" series machines are very popular in the rap, hip-hop, and house music scenes. Unless you're into these musical styles, your best bet is a sample-based percussion section.

The decision concerning whether to acquire a separate drum machine or an integrated unit may hinge on one of two considerations: whether separate audio outputs are available, or whether you will need a drum machine with its own sequencer section and preprogrammed rhythm parts. As we've said often (but not often enough, or we wouldn't be saying it again), separate outputs are essential to the recording process. This is especially true if your sound module will also be producing the drum sounds (see Chapter 10).

Many synthesizer and sampler sound modules with separate audio outputs are quite expensive, so you might be better off from a financial standpoint looking into a drum machine with separate outputs and a sound module with stereo outputs. You can then be sure of the integrity of your drum tracks and still have stereo synth capability.

Many of you will want a drum machine because they have preprogrammed patterns for basic rhythms. Why? If you're not a drummer, you may not know how to get the "groove" you want. Having some basic patterns already loaded into the unit is really helpful. This kind of memory doesn't come with all multitimbral modules.

CHOOSING A SEQUENCER

Many of the best sequencers on the market come in the form of hardware and software packages for computers. There are good choices available whether you have a Windows- or a Macintosh-based computer. If you are intent on a stand-alone sequencer, then shop at the high end of the market (such as the Akai MPC-60). Make sure the unit has lots of memory and lots of disk-drive storage.

Some kind of sync-to-tape function is essential to your successful use of MIDI sequencing in your home studio, because a single good sound module can be used again and again through the multitrack processes of overdubbing and bouncing to create finished tapes of amazing sonic sophistication and professionalism. But to do this, your sequencer must be able to play a second, third, and fourth part in sync with the first part. When you are considering the value of tape sync in terms of dollars and cents, consider the value of another sound module or two. In the next chapter, we'll show you how sync works to keep your arrangements afloat.

We've already spent some time looking into synchronization (see Chapter 14). The two most viable options for your basic sync system are SMPTE and MIDI Time Code. As we've mentioned, ad nauseum, MTC is not a recordable signal. In order to use it effectively with analog recorders, the analog recorders must have transports that can be controlled by MIDI. In other words, the recorders must have MIDI inputs and be able to respond to MIDI signals. In an MTC system, your sequencer will be the master and your recorder will follow its commands.

SMPTE, on the other hand, is a recordable signal. In a SMPTE-based system, the time code is recorded on the multi-

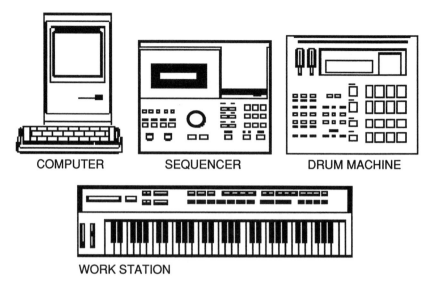

COMPUTER   SEQUENCER   DRUM MACHINE

WORK STATION

FIGURE 15-1. Sequencers and units with sequencing capability.

track and it becomes the master. Your sequencer must have the ability to read SMPTE coming from the recorder and translate it into MIDI for its own use. Many MIDI interfaces offer SMPTE as an option, and many software packages utilize SMPTE as well.

Either MTC or SMPTE will work well for you, but you must make sure all your modules and transports (recorders) understand whichever sync language you choose. A selection of sequencers is shown in Figure 15-1.

CHOOSING A CONTROLLER

The controller you use should suit your playing style, but should not hinder your arranging and composing style. As we said before, you need to learn how to play the sounds as opposed to the instrument. If you're a guitarist, you might make a beeline for a guitar synthesizer/contoller. But chances are that you will play the same melodic lines you would on a guitar, complete with the same hammer-ons, finger-tapping, string bends, and chord voicings. It is sometimes easier to break out of styles appropriate only to your own instruments if you use a different controller. Hence the horn player or guitarist may be better off using a keyboard controller for MIDI.

Apart from the type of controller, there are some things that your MIDI controller absolutely must do. It must send velocity MIDI data. Without the ability to convey how hard a key or a string is hit down the line, your MIDI controller speaks in a boring monotone, like some pedantic old teacher. There will be no dynamics, no accents, no excitement. It must have a sufficient number of keys, or notes, so that you can play your arrangements without too much transposing in the sequencer or computer. If it is a keyboard controller, a minimum of 61 keys should get you by.

Your controller should also send pitch bend and modulation data. If it doesn't, it will seriously hamper your ability to articulate instruments with vibrato and pitch nuances. Sustain and damper pedal operations should also be available if it is a keyboard controller.

Finally, your controller must be able to send on any MIDI channel or you'll be reassigning channels in your sequencer instead of making music.

You may think all the above features are not necessary in a controller. And it's true that not all these features are necessary to making some kind of music with MIDI. But you *will* need them all. There are controllers that do more. Decide for yourself the value of additional features to your own situation.

SUMMARY OF FEATURES

The basic MIDI system for your home studio, then, should consist of a multitimbral sound module, possibly a drum machine, a sequencer or computer with interface and software, and a controller (Figure 15-2). Here is a summary of the required characteristics for each item:

Sound Module and Drum Machine

- Multitimbral

- Sampled drum sounds

- Multiple audio outputs or separate drum and harmony modules

- Preprogrammed rhythm patterns or separate drum machine

Sequencer

- MIDI Time Code or SMPTE sync

- Lots of storage, including a disk drive or hard drive
- Multiple MIDI outputs
- Ability to control MIDI peripherals and transports
- Ability to edit (including copy and delete) any parameter of MIDI

Controller

- Compatibility with your playing skills and style
- Musical flexibility
- Dynamic velocity
- Sufficient number of keys (for keyboardist)
- Ability to send pitch-bend and modulation data
- Ability to send on every MIDI channel

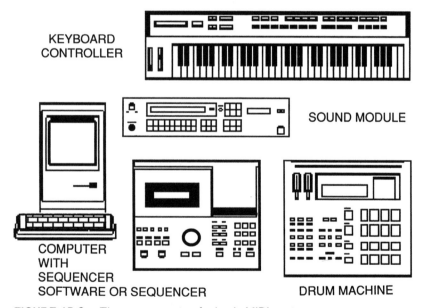

FIGURE 15-2. The components of a basic MIDI system.

WORK STATIONS

It is important to consider a few words on the the product concept known as the work station. Several companies have marketed MIDI instruments that combine, in one box, a controller, a sequencer, and a sound module with drum sounds (Figure 15-3). Some also have digital effects processors for reverb and so on. These units, whether based on a sampler or synthesizer, can be very effective and very cost effective. You must evaluate these units in the same way you would evaluate separate boxes. An inadequate sequencer doesn't become adequate because it is boxed with controller and a sound module.

The term *work station* is also applied to some digital recording products. These units are usually hard-disk-based (utilizing computer hard drives instead of tape). Along with their recording capability, they often include digital sound processing, mixing, and waveform editing (a sampler function). If all the sections are up to snuff, then the work station can be a good investment.

Many of these work stations are "software updateable." This means that as new developments occur, their internal software can be brought up to date by loading a new system disk from the manufacturer. If the work station is not able to be updated, this is a strike against it. It is much easier to update a single component in your system than it is to replace your whole MIDI system.

FIGURE 15-3. Roland XP-50 Music Workstation (Courtesy of Roland Corp. US)

CHAPTER 16

Recording with MIDI

When you start using MIDI in your recording, you may find that you're actually recording in two stages. The latter stage we've already spoken about—the tracks that actually get printed to tape; we'll talk about that some more in a moment. But with sequencing technology, there is a primary stage of recording in which you prepare what are known as *virtual tracks*—the preprogrammed parts which your sequencing drum machine, synth, or computer will store in memory before you commit to tape. It is this feature of *virtual recording* that leads sequencing program designers and engineers to recreate the recording environment in their software—what with all their Stops, Starts, Punch-ins, and so on.

For example, you've probably been using a drum machine by now to create your drum tracks on tape. You programmed the parts using the drum machine's internal memory, building layers of bass drum, snare, hi-hat, and tom-tom, and arranging it in a song sequence. In so doing, you created *virtual tracks* made up for the different instruments in your digital drum kit. Similarly, you use a sequencer, drum machine, and sound module to create a complete arrangement for a song before going to real tracks on tape (Figure 16-1). To commit them to tape, all you have to do is press Start on your instrument and Record on your portable studio.

Ah! If only it were *that* easy . . .

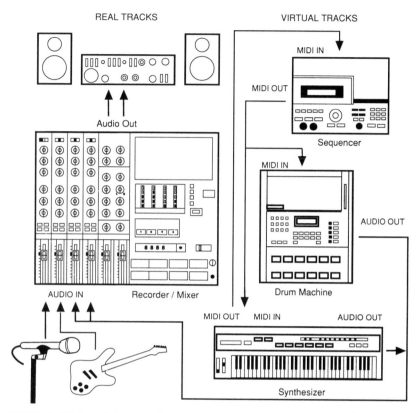

FIGURE 16-1. *Virtual tracks* are preprogrammed parts stored in a sequencer's memory. They may later be transferred to *real tracks* on tape.

PROGRAMMING DRUM MACHINE PARTS

Putting your sequenced composition down on tape should be simple. But first you have to create the sequenced parts, starting with the drum machine. You can program the drum machine by playing its pads either in *real time* (the way the world works—play it as it will sound) or in *step time*.

Real-Time Programming

In real-time programming, you do the following:

1. Make sure you know which pads correspond to the bass drum and snare sounds you want to play. Put the drum machine into

one of its *write* modes—either a *pattern* or *song/track* mode. A *pattern* is usually one or two measures long. It can be repeated over and over, or it can be connected to other patterns to form a song or complete composition. Let's first do a pattern.

2. If you want a fairly basic pattern, there will probably be a preprogrammed one that closely resembles what you have in mind. If there is, you may only need to change a few beats to make it *exactly* what you want.

    Let's assume the preprogrammed cymbal parts are fine, but you'd like to vary the bass and snare a bit. You can erase the bass and snare parts on most drum machines and leave the cymbal parts intact. Instruments are erasable with an Erase or Clear button. It usually means holding down the Clear button and the button that corresponds to the instrument you want to erase.

3. You are now ready to write your bass drum and snare parts into the pattern memory of your drum machine. If you have some cymbals (or other parts) to use as guidelines, make sure you know where the first beat of the measure falls. If you are starting with a clean pattern, activate the metronome function of your drum machine. The metronome will click along showing you the timing, but it will not be included in the pattern.

4. Play the bass drum with one hand and the snare with the other hand by tapping the pads that correspond to their sounds. In *pattern write* mode, the drum machine will store where you played the bass and snare in the course of the pattern. You only need play through the one or two measures that constitute the pattern's length. Repeat these steps for additional drum instruments you might want to include.

5. After you have compiled the patterns you want to use in your song, you then have to assemble them, using the *song* or *track* memory function of the drum machine.

    The trick here is knowing how long (in terms of numbers of measures) your song is and how long you want each pattern to play before changing to the next. As you assemble your chain of patterns, you might stop and play along with the machine to make sure you haven't added an extra two measures or dropped a few by mistake. Commands in this portion of programming include the infamous "Repeat how many times?" Often, by simply calling up the pattern, you've already told the machine to play it once. If you want it to occur twice, then you tell the machine to repeat it *one time*. Other machines, however, will ask you how many times you want the pattern to play. Then you tell it the number of times you want it played, with none of the higher math found in the other type of machines. In this way, you assemble all the patterns for the entire song.

6. Now you can record the drums to your multitrack by hooking up the drum machine's audio outputs to your portable studio, putting the multitrack in record mode, and pressing Play on the drum machine. Or, as we described in Chapter Ten, you might want to record a track of the drum machine's tape sync code so you can overdub the drum sounds in order to process some or all of its individual parts.

Step-Time Programming

Drum machines and most sequencers can also be programmed in step time. In real time, the drum machine repeats the material exactly as you played it. In step time, you tell the drum machine what you want played on a beat-by-beat basis (Figure 16-2).

In essence, what you're doing is narrating the action. On Beat 1, you hit the hi-hat; on Beat 2, you close it. Every event in the drum part is described separately. The result is that it takes a lot

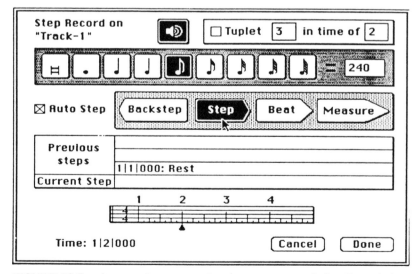

FIGURE 16-2. A computer screen showing a sequencer's functions during step-time editing and recording. Each aspect of the event is entered. This display is from "Performer" by Mark of the Unicorn. (Performer is a registered trademark of Mark of the Unicorn, Inc. Courtesy of Mark of the Unicorn)

more time to compose the part into the machine than it does to actually play it.

Once you've described the measure in terms of its smallest parts (eighth notes or quarter notes are most common), you then tell the drum machine to "Play the bass drum here," or "Rest for a quarter note here," and so proceed step-by-step through the entire musical measure. After you've composed all of your patterns in this way, you assemble them together just as you do for the real-time drum part.

PROGRAMMING THE BASS PART ON THE SEQUENCER

You can also program most sequencers in either real time or step time. Few sequencers have built-in pads or keys, however, so you need to hook up some kind of controller to send the data to the sequencer.

1. The MIDI OUT of your controller should be connected to the MIDI IN of your sequencer. This allows the sequencer to receive what you play on the controller (Figure 16-3). If your controller is a synthesizer or sampler with a built-in sound module, you will be able to hear the parts you are playing as they go into the sequencer.

    If you have a separate controller that doesn't generate any sound, you may want to add a sound module to this setup (it's a little weird playing a part without hearing any corresponding sound; and then, of course, you can never be sure if you hit

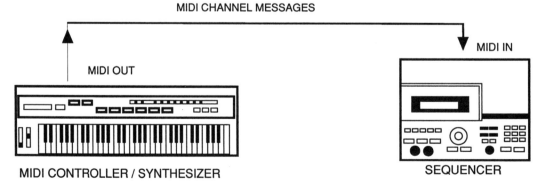

FIGURE 16-3. Basic sequencer recording using a synthesizer/controller and a single sequencer.

a bad note or two). Connect the MIDI OUT of the controller to the MIDI IN of the sound module. Connect MIDI THRU or OUT of the sound module to MIDI IN of the sequencer.

2. For your first part—the bass—set your keyboard to transmit (send) MIDI Channel 1 to the sequencer. Set the bass sound you want to Channel 1 on the sound module, or select a bass program on your synthesizer/sampler keyboard.

3. Select a track on your sequencer, or computer with sequencing software. Let's make it Track 1, but it could just as easily be Track 12. Set that track to receive MIDI Channel 1.

4. Press Record on the sequencer. You should hear one or two bars of metronome clicks before you play the music. (Does your unit gives you a count of one or two bars? Find out.) When finished, press Stop on the sequencer.

To hear the virtual bass track, connect the MIDI OUT of your sequencer to the MIDI IN of your sound module. You may want to fix any mistakes or embellish the bass part before moving on to your harmony parts.

SEQUENCER OVERDUBBING AND PUNCHING-IN

The procedures for MIDI overdubbing and punch-in tend to vary from sequencer to sequencer. Consult your manual, but the usual procedure for overdubs involves assigning a new sequencer track, say Track 2. Instruct Track 2 on the sequencer to receive MIDI Channel 1. Play the additional material and merge the tracks together.

As on the portable studio, punch-ins are done on the same track as the original material. Step-time recording is very handy when it comes to punch-ins. You can simply go to the punch-in point using the sequencer's counter and "scrolling" function. When you have isolated the problem area, you can fix it by changing pitch, duration, even articulation—just as if you were fixing a measure of music on paper. You may also opt to play the note correctly.

Most sequencers will also allow you the option of playing the sequence from the beginning, and when the punch-in point comes, pushing the Record button, just like punching-in on the multitrack. After the problem section has passed, disable the record function. Many sequencers will let you automate the punch-in and punch-out points using the sequencer's counter, which often reads out in measures and beats. This feature will be called *Auto Record, Auto Punch-in,* or something similar.

Programming the Harmony Part

Here is the procedure for adding parts to your MIDI arrangement:

1. Select MIDI Channel 2 on your controller and Track 2 (or Track 3 if you've used Track 2 for a bass overdub) on your sequencer.

2. Choose a *patch* (instrument sound) on your sound module or keyboard and assign it to MIDI Channel 2.

3. Connect the MIDI OUT of your sequencer to the MIDI IN of your sound module, so you can hear your bass part. To play back the bass while you are recording a new harmony part, your sound module must be multi-timbral (or, at the very least, capable of splitting its keyboard and play two different sounds at once). It must be able to send on the different MIDI channels so that your harmony part can be recorded by the sequencer, and later played back using a different sound. (Your keyboard may play multiple sounds, but may not have the ability to assign each sound its own MIDI channel number for later separate playback from the sequencer. This is why we made a big deal about getting multi-timbral sound modules and controllers that can send on all MIDI channels).

4. Now you're ready to play your harmony part. Set Track 2 on the sequencer to its record mode. Pressing the Record button on most sequencers will also start the playback of Track 1. You'll get your count-in, too. If Track 1 is still assigned to MIDI Channel 1, you should be able to hear your bass part via your sound module. Play your harmony part on the controller.

   It should sound all right if you have both the controller and the harmony patch in the sound module assigned to MIDI Channel 2. Your harmony part is now being recorded on Track 2 of the sequencer.

5. When you are done recording your harmony part, your sound module should already be assigned to listen to the playback. Make sure the sound module is in MIDI Mode 4—OMNI OFF MONO—so that both your bass and harmony will play back simultaneously. Press Play on the sequencer; your bass line and harmony line should play back just as you played them. If you want to add more parts, simply repeat the above steps by

assigning consecutive MIDI channels and sequencer track numbers. Most sequencers will let you merge tracks together, so that you can free some up for more overdubs. The merging process usually retains the MIDI channel information so that the merging shouldn't mess up your sound module's ability to play back.

TIME CORRECTING ON THE SEQUENCER

Many sequencers have an editing feature called *auto correct, time correct,* or *quantization.* This feature, also found on drum machines, corrects errors in rhythm made during the recording of your sequencer tracks by aligning all your missed rhythms to the smallest note value you select. In addition to the obvious value of correcting playing mistakes, time correction is very useful for making sure that multiple sequencer tracks are lined up properly. The rate of quantization, as we also discussed earlier, varies from as little as two parts per quarter note to as high as 360 parts per quarter note.

The time correction, or quantization, process is easy:

1. Determine, if you can, the shortest rhythmic value in the music you recorded, whether it be a sixteenth note, an eighth-note, or some other subdivision. Set the sequencer's time correction level for that value (sixteenth note, for example).

    Play back the tracks and listen. Do they sound better? Are they choppy and only slightly better than before? You may need to set the time correction's resolution to a smaller (faster) note value, say thirty-second notes. Now listen again.

2. As you get to smaller resolutions, you may notice that the occasional note seems to have shifted its position slightly in the arrangement. This means that you missed its timing so badly that the auto correct function read it as part of a different subdivision of the beat. You'll have to punch-in to correct this mistake in rhythm.

USING A DRUM MACHINE WITH A SEQUENCER

There are two ways to get your drum machine to play with your sequencer. The first is to use the drum machine's own memory to play the drum parts. The drum machine must know when to start and stop, and what the tempo is of the other parts that it must play with. The sequencer must be able to say, "Okay, drum machine, get ready to start playing the part you have in your memory. Here we go: 1 and 2 and 3 and 4 and go!" It must also be able to keep counting to the drum machine, and when the end of the song is near, it must be able to say, "Get ready to stop, drum machine . . . Stop!"

The second method of using a drum machine with your sequencer involves using the drum machine as a passive sound module. In other words, the drum machine will play back the individual drum sounds upon the command of the sequencer. The sequencer will play the drum machine just as it would any other sound module. The sequencer will see the different drum instruments merely as different musical notes—a bass drum could be assigned to the C note in the first octave of your controller, the snare drum assigned D, and so on. Whenever that C note is played, the bass drum will sound, and the D will sound the snare. By assigning the drum machine its own MIDI channel and sequencer track, it can be played by the sequencer just as the bass and harmony parts were.

Let's assume that you would like to use the drum machine's internal memory. After all, you have those neat patterns already programmed in.

The method for syncing a drum machine to a sequencer is to make either the drum machine the "master" and the sequencer the "slave," or the reverse.

1. To make the drum machine the master tempo controller, you must tell the sequencer to respond to an "external clock." You are telling the sequencer, "Wait until you hear the start command from this drum machine that I have plugged into your MIDI IN." You are also saying, "When you hear the start command, start playing the tracks in your memory along with the drum machine. Be sure to let the drum machine count the tempo now." There will be a switch marked *Internal/External Clock.* Move it to the external position.

2. The MIDI OUT of the drum machine should be connected to the MIDI IN of the sequencer. MIDI OUT of the sequencer is then connected to MIDI IN of the sound module or synthesizer (Figure 16-4).

3. When you press Start on the drum machine, your sequencer will also start, playing the bass and harmony parts on the

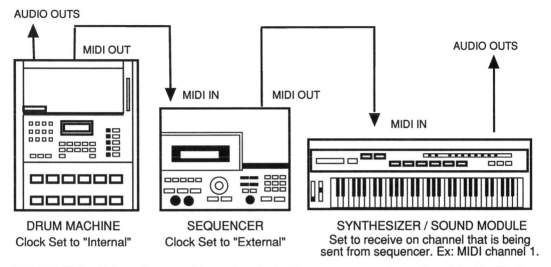

AUDIO OUTS

MIDI OUT

MIDI IN   MIDI OUT

AUDIO OUTS

MIDI IN

DRUM MACHINE	SEQUENCER	SYNTHESIZER / SOUND MODULE
Clock Set to "Internal"	Clock Set to "External"	Set to receive on channel that is being sent from sequencer. Ex: MIDI channel 1.

FIGURE 16-4. Using a drum machine as "master" with a sequencer and sound module. Starting the drum machine will also start the sequencer, which will play harmony parts on the synthesizer in time with the drum machine.

sound module. When you press Stop on the drum machine, the sequencer will also stop. Changing the tempo control on the drum machine will make the sequencer respond with a tempo change.

Isn't technology wonderful? The beauty of the above method is that you don't have to worry about MIDI channel assignments and so on. The units are just responding to clock synchronizing data. One of the problems with the above setup, however, is that in order to change tempo during a piece, you need to manually move the tempo control. These things can be a little touchy, and the tempo change may be too abrupt. Putting the sequencer in charge of things—making it the master—often makes it possible to automate tempo changes. You can program tempo changes into many sequencers.

In order to use the sequencer as master, the drum machine will need to be assigned to a MIDI channel that is not sending note information. That way, the drum machine instruments won't be playing your bass part.

1. Making the sequencer the master means setting its clock switch to the "internal" position. The MIDI OUT of the sequencer needs to be connected to MIDI IN of the sound module or synthesizer.

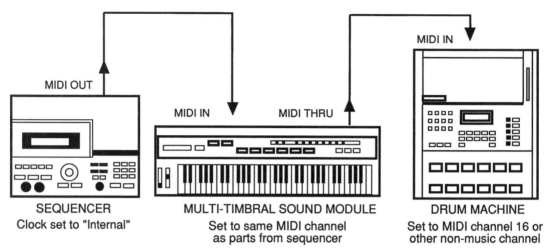

MIDI OUT

MIDI IN   MIDI THRU

MIDI IN

SEQUENCER
Clock set to "Internal"

MULTI-TIMBRAL SOUND MODULE
Set to same MIDI channel
as parts from sequencer

DRUM MACHINE
Set to MIDI channel 16 or
other non-music channel

FIGURE 16-5. Using a sequencer as "master" with a synthesizer and drum machine. When you start the sequencer, the synthesizer and drum machine will play in tempo.

2. MIDI THRU of the sound module or synthesizer should be connected to MIDI IN of the drum machine (Figure 16-5).

3. Set the clock switch on the drum machine to its "external" position. Assuming that your sound module is set to receive MIDI data on Channels 1 through 4, set the drum machine to receive on another MIDI channel—for example, Channel 16. Indeed, if you work a lot with MIDI equipment, get into the habit of assigning your drum machine the same MIDI channel every time. It will save time in the studio. In some workstation keyboards, the drum machine section is permanently assigned to a MIDI channel such as Channel 10.

4. Now, when you press Play on the sequencer, the bass and harmony parts should be played on the sound module, and the drum machine should play whatever parts you've written into its memory. The drum machine will start, stop, and play in tempo. Some machines will even continue from a point in the song after they have been stopped. The *continue* feature means you won't have to start from Bar 1 every time you play the composition.

Using a Drum Machine as a Sound Module with a Sequencer

There are two aspects of using drum machines that make them a little stiff and robotic. First off, tempo changes are difficult to accomplish smoothly. Secondly, the ability to add unique expressions of dynamics and musical nuance to individual measures is sometimes impossible. The reason for this is the way in which the drum machine's memory is divided into patterns and songs. In other words, a complete drum machine composition or song memory (sometimes called a "track") only remembers, "Play Pattern 1A here, now play Pattern 2B, now 1A again, repeat 2B," and so on. If you wanted to compose a thorough, totally varied drum part for a piece 180 measures long, for example, you would need 180 patterns' worth of drum machine memory, and most machines don't have that much. Even if they did, you'd probably have to delete that great reggae piece you worked on for two hours, just to make room for this one composition.

For the utmost flexibility in editing individual measures and its usually greater memory storage capacity, a sequencer is ideal for controlling all the events, while the drum machine is ideal as a passive sound module.

Rather than start from scratch to write all the drum patterns into your sequencer's memory, you can load the basic patterns from the drum machine into your sequencer.

1. Put the sequencer in record mode and assign a track to receive the drum parts.

2. Assign the drum machine a MIDI channel on which to transmit (Channels 16 or 10 are popular with users and makers).

3. Connect the MIDI OUT of the drum machine to the MIDI IN of the sequencer.

4. Press Record on the sequencer and Play on the drum machine. Your song or pattern should now load into the sequencer. When loading is completed, press Stop on the sequencer and on the drum machine.

You may want to load the drum pattern or song after you've already worked a bit on the bass and harmony parts. In that case, you can use the sequencer as the master time keeper, as we mentioned above (Figure 16-6).

1. Connect the MIDI OUT of the sequencer to the MIDI IN of the drum machine. Connect MIDI OUT of the drum machine to MIDI IN of the sequencer.

2. Set the sequencer to run on its internal clock. Assign a track to record the drum parts.

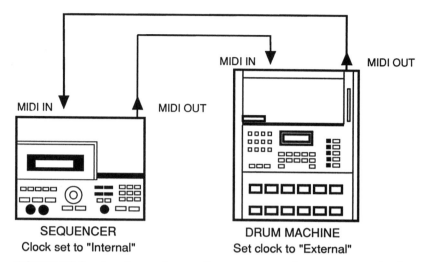

MIDI IN   MIDI OUT

MIDI IN   MIDI OUT

SEQUENCER   DRUM MACHINE
Clock set to "Internal"   Set clock to "External"

FIGURE 16-6. Loading a drum pattern or song onto a sequencer track. The drum machine will play in tempo with melody and harmony parts already on the sequencer.

3. Set the drum machine to run from an external clock, and select a MIDI channel. The sequencer should now stop and start the drum machine.

4. Press Record on the sequencer. The drum machine should run in sync with the bass and harmony parts already on the sequencer. When finished, press Stop on the sequencer.

You can now use the editing features of your sequencer to change individual drum beats and instrument sounds or dynamics. If your sequencer has copy functions, you can use it to duplicate measures or whole sections of the song. You can add notes/sounds by step editing or real-time punch-in or sequencer overdubbing. You can also add rests—periods of silence—as well as tempo changes.

An interesting feature of some drum machines is their ability to receive and play velocity data while their own pads are not velocity-sensitive. These drum machines can be programmed dynamically with a sequencer and a keyboard or other velocity-sensitive controller. The individual drum instruments (bass, snare, and so on) can be assigned individual note values (C–3 = bass, D–3 = snare, and so on; some of the very first MIDI drum machines had permanent notes assigned to the different drum instruments; check the owner's manual for your drum machine). Play these notes dynamically into the sequencer's memory and you will have dynamic playback of the drum instruments later from the sequencer memory.

USING MIDI WITH YOUR MULTITRACK

So what's the big deal? Here's one big answer: After you have composed and recorded your virtual tracks, you may simply attach the audio cables of the sound modules to the mixer inputs of your portable studio and press the Start button on the sequencer. Zap! Great tracks on tape.

Eventually, you may want to overdub sequenced parts on your multitrack. Why not use that multitimbral sound module over and over again to pile up some really thick synthesizer parts? It's possible, the only limitation being your imagination and good taste.

If you want to overdub sequenced music on your multitrack, you need to give your sequencer the "ears" to play its overdubs in sync with its first tracks. Just as a live musician must listen to Track 1 to play in time during overdubs, the sequencer must have a way to listen and respond.

The operation for sequencers begins with the basic track. If you've followed our suggestions, your sequencer or interface has a sync-to-tape feature of some kind. Because MIDI is a non-recordable signal, it needs tape sync, acting as a translator, to allow the recorder and sequencer to hear and understand each other. Whether your tape sync feature is based on FSK or SMPTE, it still translates MIDI into another, recordable, language.

Beware! Functions called *MIDI Time Code, MIDI Clock,* and *MIDI Song Position Pointer* are not recordable signals. We'll talk more about them in a little while.

Basic Recording with MIDI

After you've created something on your sequencer that you'd like to record, start with a fresh tape. Your tape sync signal is the first thing that will go on tape. If you've followed another of our suggestions and gotten a multitrack that will record on all tracks at once, you can record your sequenced parts simultaneously with your tape sync signal (Figure 16-7).

1. Connect the Tape Sync Out to the Buss In connection corresponding to Track 4.

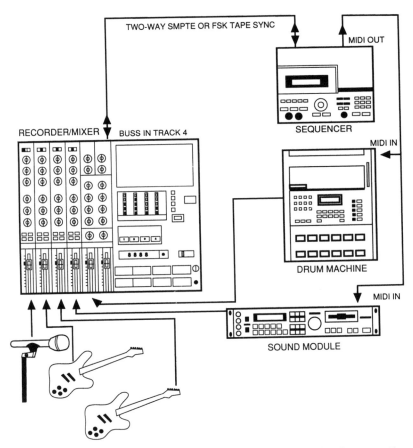

FIGURE 16-7. Basic multitrack recording with MIDI. In a simple setup, the tape sync signal is assigned to Track 4 and the sequencer parts are assigned to Tracks 1 and 2. Live parts can be mixed and recorded on Tracks 1 and 2 at the same time.

2. Some of you have portable studios that are only capable of recording two tracks at once. You will have to make separate passes to record the music and the tape sync. Your first pass, on Track 4, will be the sync tracks. Your sequencer pass will be synced to that track and recorded on Tracks 1 and 2.

3. Connect the audio outputs of your sound modules to the mixer channel inputs of your portable studio. Assign them to Tracks 1 and 2 using the assignment switches and pan controls. If you want to overdub several times before bouncing tracks, you may want to record the first pass on Track 1 only. If so, select parts most appropriate for a mono track. Candidates for a

mono track include bass drum, snare drum, synth bass, synthesizer chord pads, and sound effects. The advantage of recording a mono track is that it leaves Tracks 2 and 3 free for more music.

4. Rehearse the music by playing the sequence and tape sync signal several times. During the rehearsals, set the levels of the various signals using the channel faders and master faders. Unless the owner's manual for your sequencer or interface suggests differently, tape sync signals should not be recorded as hot as music signals. You should record your tape sync signal at about −3 VU or less.

   You should also switch off any noise reduction on the track recording the tape sync. Noise reduction sometimes makes a sequencer unable to read its own tape sync signal. If your machine won't let you turn off the noise reduction on a single channel, you may want to try recording the tape sync signal alone on the first pass with the noise reduction switched off. You can switch it back on to record your music tracks. The expansion side of noise reduction circuits doesn't mess up tape sync as badly as the compression side, so this method should work fine.

5. Put the transport into Record Ready mode for Tracks 1, 2, and 4. Use only Tracks 1 and 4 if you are recording a mono track and tape sync. Use only Track 4 if you are recording only tape sync. Adjust for levels.

   If you want to add some live parts to your sequenced first tracks, rhythm guitar, live drums or cymbals, and electric bass are good candidates. Set up the instrument in a mixer channel and assign it to the mono track or to the appropriate pan position in Tracks 1 and 2. Rehearse the part with the sequenced material and mix the live levels with the sequenced levels using the channel faders.

6. When you're ready, rewind the tape and set the Record Ready mode for the appropriate tracks. Put the transport into Record, and press Start on your sequencer. Your tape sync signal may have five seconds or so of test tone—a steady "beeeeeeeeep"—so don't panic if you hear that first. When the tape sync signal starts, it will sound like high-pitched chatter, kind of like Alvin and the Chipmunks on diet pills. Your sequencer, interface, or tape sync peripheral may have some special procedures for recording test tones, so you should consult the manuals on this. You'll recognize the sound of your sequenced music—at least we hope so.

7. When the sequencer has finished, stop the transport. Congratulations! Technology has just changed your life. Rewind the tape.

MIDI Overdubs

We spent so much time on the logistics of recording the tape sync signal because this is the element that allows you to do MIDI overdubs. When it comes to actually committing the overdubs to tape, you will want to enable your sequencer to "hear" the tape sync track. So . . .

1. Connect the Tape Out jack for Track 4—the tape sync material—to the Sync In jack of the sequencer or interface. Put your sequencer program into its External Sync or External Clock mode, which will *slave* it to the sync track. It will follow the timing information it receives from the sync track on tape, just as a musician might follow the clicks of a metronome.

2. You are now ready to record those additional parts from your sequencer (Figure 16-8). For example, if your first tracks were bass, harmony piano, and drum parts, all assigned to Track 1, you may now want to add your sequenced string and horn parts to Track 2. Assuming these parts are written on different MIDI channels in the sequencer, say Channels 5 and 6, assigning the string and horn sound presets on your sound module will cause these sounds to play from the sequencer. You want to defeat the channel assignments for the bass, drums, and harmony piano, or they will also play when you start the sequencer. Some sequencers let you mute certain MIDI channels. You may find it easier to do this.

3. Now press Start or External Start on your sequencer (sometimes putting the sequencer in external clock mode is all you need to do). The sequencer will wait for a signal from the tape sync track before it will actually begin playing.

   Note that there is an occasional discrepancy in the starting points of various instruments when using tape sync. The sequencer or drum machine will sometimes read the Start command from tape sync as a "Get Ready to Start" command. It will start at the next pulse. This means that some machines start $1/24$ of a quarter note later, which is a pain if you recorded a live track or two while recording the tape sync or if you have several instruments reading the same tape sync and responding differently. If this happens to you, you will have to "stripe" the tape (record your tape sync signal) first, without recording

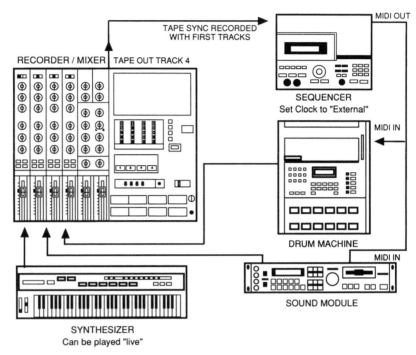

TAPE SYNC RECORDED
WITH FIRST TRACKS

RECORDER / MIXER | TAPE OUT TRACK 4

MIDI OUT

SEQUENCER
Set Clock to "External"

MIDI IN

DRUM MACHINE

MIDI IN

SOUND MODULE

SYNTHESIZER
Can be played "live"

FIGURE 16-8. Overdubbing with MIDI. The sequencer is "slaved" to the tape sync track so that it will play in time with previously recorded material. The new parts are assigned to available tracks.

any music tracks. Since all subsequent material will start with the same delay, your sequenced tracks will be in sync. If you have multiple units reading the same tape sync differently, make one unit the master and slave the others to it. If you have a drum machine and a sequencer responding differently, then you will probably have to sequence the drum parts and let the sequencer "play" the drum machine via MIDI.

4. Put Track 4 in the playback mode with the record function switch for that track off. Turn on the record function for the tracks to receive the sequenced music (Track 2 if the original parts were recorded on Track 1). If you have connected the Track 4 Tape Out to your tape sync input, you won't have to worry about switching your mixer channel for Track 4 to the monitor mode. Your tape sync signal will come directly off the tape head and to your tape sync input.

5. Press Record on your transport. The tape will begin playing. When your sequencer gets the start command from the tape

sync signal, it will play the sequenced material. Let the sequencer do its little musical thing, and when it's done, press Stop on the transport and on the sequencer.

6. You can add live parts along with your sequenced material as we described above in the basic track section. Each time you overdub using your sequencer, you can add as many live parts as you can muster. Make sure you have rehearsed it well, so that you won't drive yourself crazy rewinding, restarting, rewinding, restarting. . . . Use your mixer assign switches and pan controls to get the live material to the same tracks as the sequenced parts.

Be sure to plan your live parts so that they go well with the sequenced parts. If you have a really deep synth bass part, don't play a bunch of unison notes on a piano and record them to the same track. The bass will boom all over your track. It's very easy to get carried away with sequencing power and ruin your tracks by simply putting too much material on them—particularly by putting too much material in the same frequency ranges on the same track.

7. When you have finished recording your first sequenced and synchronized overdub, throw a little party and get ready to do it again. Create some new and overwhelmingly creative parts that will complement your other tracks perfectly. Program them into the sequencer, and prepare to sync them as you did before to the tape sync track. You can record these to any available tracks along with a live part.

Don't get carried away with your sequencing power. Make sure all the parts work and don't clog up the frequency ranges on tape. You can fill up all your available tracks this way, or you can prepare to ping-pong.

Ping-Ponging with MIDI

If you intend to perform track bounces with MIDI and tape sync, you'll inevitably be planning for mono tracks. You should plan your session so that any instruments that will be panned dead center (mono) will be recorded first. Since the tape sync takes up Track 4, you only have two tracks open (1 and 2) before you must bounce to the empty Track 3 (there's not much point in recording stereo on Tracks 1 and 2 only to bounce them to a mono Track 3). You will lose your sync track if you're bouncing to an external machine like your stereo mixdown deck.

An entire track can be panned to any degree left or right, so you can put instruments with the same pan placements together on a single track. For example, bass drums, snare drums, and rhythm guitar or piano could all be recorded to the same track if their stereo image will be dead center. This way you can perform your basic Track 1, overdub Track 2 in sync, and then bounce 1 and 2 to Track 3 while you're adding another sequenced part in sync. Three sequenced parts will end up on Track 3 and you will still have your tape sync Track 4 intact. You can then record over Tracks 1 and 2 with your stereo tracks (Figure 16-9).

If your equipment allows, you can record two stereo sequenced parts in one of two ways. First, record your stereo parts on Tracks 1 and 2. Then record a mono part on Track 3. You can now use your external mixdown machine for a ping-pong. Bounce the three tracks from the multitrack to the mixdown deck while adding a stereo sequencer part in conjunction with the tape sync on Track 4. Afterwards, you can take the results back to the multitrack and

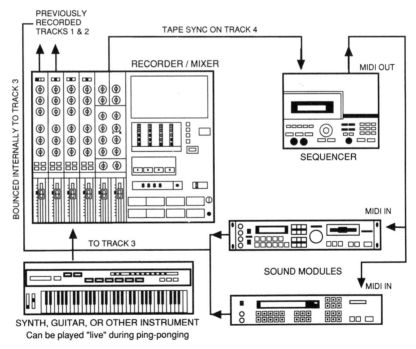

FIGURE 16-9. Ping-ponging with MIDI. Previously recorded Tracks 1 and 2 may be bounced to Track 3. New sequenced and live parts may be mixed in and recorded onto Track 3 at the same time.

use Tracks 3 and 4 for live overdubs of vocals, guitars, or whatever (Figure 16-10).

The second alternative is that you can use your sequencer and your best friends to help you gain stereo tracks. Create virtual tracks on your sequencer, even though you don't have the necessary sound modules to play them all. On the day of the recording, borrow a friend's sound module to record the appropriate parts. As birds of a feather tend to record together, you probably know someone who might lend you a sound module or two for a couple of hours.

A possible third method comes to mind when we think of using your friend's equipment. Borrow a multitrack for a few hours so that you can record the stereo material as you would using the

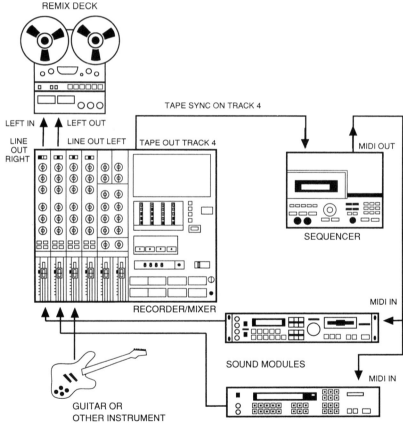

FIGURE 16-10. Ping-ponging using an external mixdown deck. Three tracks, along with a new sequencer part, are mixed to the stereo remix deck. The results can be dubbed back to one or two tracks on the mixer, opening up tracks for new recording.

mixdown deck, but also bounce the tape sync signal to Track 4 of the second machine (assuming it will record on more than two tracks at once). This way, you will have two stereo sequenced parts (Tracks 1 and 2 plus the added part during the ping-pong) and retained your sync track. If your friends don't come through, consult your friendly music store about renting a multitrack for a day. You can have two stereo sequenced parts on Tracks 1 and 2 and still have Track 3 free for some more sequencer madness in mono. Consult the earlier sections of this book for more details regarding the ping-pong procedure.

MIDI Punch-ins

Punching in and out with MIDI equipment can be either very easy or very difficult depending upon whether or not you've recorded live tracks along with your sequenced material. Or, for that matter, whether or not you've already committed the material to tape.

Performing a punch-in with your sequencer happens to be very easy. Simply follow the editing procedures in the sequencer's manual to replace or improve any musical sections. For the complete replacement of tracks on tape, simply follow the overdub procedures and replace them completely.

But what if you have recorded a live part with the sequenced material and you really like the live part? Follow these steps:

1. Isolate the section that is bothering you, and use the sequencer's editing procedures to correct the problems.

2. Play the tape to within several seconds of the desired punch-in point. Use the transport's memory functions or counter to mark the spot.

3. Set the monitor section of your portable studio so that you can hear the music from the tape tracks.

4. Set the channel assign and pan controls in your mixer to send the sequenced material and the live part to the appropriate tracks of the recorder.

5. Rehearse your live part until you feel comfortable enough playing along with the sequenced music that it will naturally flow through the punch-in and punch-out points. Make sure the timbre and tone of your instrument match the track so that the punch-in won't be noticeable.

6. When you feel ready to play along with the part, set the record function switches for the punch-in channel(s) to their On position(s).

7. Rewind the tape. Press External Clock Start on your sequencer and press Play on your transport. Play along with the music and watch your tape counter. As it is approaches the punch-in spot, get ready to press Record or hit the footswitch punch-in pedal for the portable studio (a good investment if you are planning to do a lot of punch-ins on your multitrack).

8. Hit the footswitch again to punch-out or press Stop, Play, or Rewind on the transport. Many portable studios have a return-to-zero function (RTZ) that will automatically disengage the punch-in when it reaches a pre-assigned point. Set the punch-out point in memory for the RTZ function. When the tape reaches it, the transport will automatically go into rewind mode, stopping the punch-in. Some portable studios offer automated punch-in as well. In these transports, you don't have to worry about pressing Record, or stepping on a footswitch. Set the memory locations for punch-in and punch-out. Follow the specific directions in the manual, then play along with the bouncing sequencer. If you have set the memory controls properly, when the punch-in point rolls by, the transport will automatically go into record. When the punch-out point comes up, it will go into play or rewind.

MIDI Mixdown

If you are a keyboardist with a sizeable inventory of sound modules and signal processors, or you're just a newly hooked MIDI-holic with sufficient discretionary income, you may be in a position to compile numerous virtual tracks without having to commit anything to tape until the mixdown process. In such cases, the multitrack will carry the live instruments, vocal, and tape sync tracks, while the sequencer carries the virtual tracks for the MIDI sound modules (Figure 16-11).

The secret is logistics.

1. Do the basic sequencer parts first before you touch a live instrument.

2. Record the tape sync signal to the multitrack.

3. Record your live instrument parts while monitoring sound modules activated by the tape sync track already on the multitrack.

4. Since the live instruments and the tape sync track are the only things on tape, the only ping-ponging or punching-in you'll do on the multitrack will be for these parts. Don't forget to spare

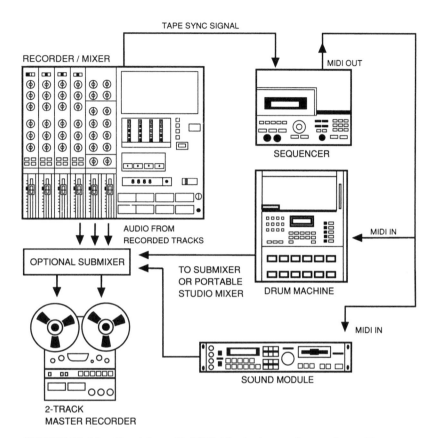

FIGURE 16-11. Remixing with MIDI. Live instruments, vocals, and tape sync take up all tracks of the mixer. They are then mixed down to a stereo master while adding virtual tracks from the sequencer.

the sync track! Since the sequencer tracks are still virtual, you can edit those through the sequencing program.

5. The last thing that actually goes on tape are the vocals. Now you have your live instrument and vocal parts on tape and your MIDI parts on the sequencer. In fact, your MIDI parts won't hit tape until the mixdown itself.

6. Mix the live instruments and the sequenced material in the same way you would perform an external ping-pong: you record them on to the mixdown deck.

This method has some advantages if you have a nice mixdown deck, particularly a DAT mixdown deck. Your virtual tracks lose no fidelity from endless playback and manipulation in the MIDI world, while your live instruments, if bounced carefully, will have still plenty of room sonically on the multitrack tape. And with a track all their own, your lead vocals will stand out sharply. Mixing down this way eliminates those extra bounces that deteriorate the sound quality of your music.

The one disadvantage is that your stereo master is essentially your *only* master tape. If you have opted for a MIDI system with good memory storage (preferably diskette or hard drive), you should be able to re-do the mastering should the need arise simply by calling up the appropriate files and patches.

All of which points out yet another reason for keeping a log of everything you do in your studio: Knowing which diskettes contain which files for which songs.

You may choose to use part of this method, recording some of your sequenced parts to tape and keeping some in the virtual track domain. Or, you may choose to record all your sequenced parts to tape before mixing down in the way described in Chapter Nine.

Whatever your choice, the flexibility and performance of a MIDI system will add tremendous power to the home studio.

CHAPTER 17

Expanding Your Studio

The tape's now rolling on a daily basis and as you become more adept at this "home recording thing," you may find yourself becoming not more comfortable but more restless. Oh, brutal irony! You find yourself furtively hunting catalogs for hard disk recorders and mixers with automation. You're going to the music store on Saturday for a MIDI demonstration when you should be mowing the lawn or watching the Cubs. Your food intake is deplorable: vacuum-packed snacks and generic beverages are the standard as you put aside more money for new studio components. You have gone blissfully over the edge. With skin the pallor of a cave dweller, a lawn that looks like a wildlife refuge area, and the names of your children all but forgotten, your one remaining thought is the MIDI command number for volume.

These are just a few of the symptoms of track fever and MIDI mania. Common enough as afflictions go, these diseases can ravage the host if they go untreated. How do you retain the enthusiasm and energy of MIDI mania and track fever without the unseemly side effects?

First, realize it's natural to want to do more and experiment more. Just as you once only dreamed of your material in terms of a band, you now have a symphony orchestra sleeping in your sequencer and sound modules. And where you had been happy in the good old days to put voice and guitar down on tape, you're now hearing the whole world differently. When you stand on a curb, instead of watching the passing traffic, you're hearing buses panning from hard left to hard right.

You're also getting finicky. When you first got your portable studio, you were knocking off three or four songs a day. Now you can barely listen to those old tapes because they sound so sloppy. To make matters worse, you're hearing tape noise from all those bounces. Oh, if only Mother Nature had come with good noise reduction!

The only answer is: Get more gear!

Which is fine, but it's going to run you a bit more than just taking a few aspirin and going to bed for a few days. Expanding your studio isn't simply a matter of getting more equipment. Your studio is a system in balance; you must evaluate additions on how they will affect the rest of the studio. Bringing an eight-track recorder into the studio may be exciting, but it won't go with your four- or six-channel mixer. Then you get a new mixer; now the patch bay isn't sufficient. In the meantime, your new mixer is so big you have to build a new shelving system and redo the acoustic panels you installed. And you still haven't figured out how to handle your new sound modules. Finally, your overall system has escalated to the point at which you need a serious monitor system with a new power amp and speakers.

A single change can have catastrophic effects on the whole studio. What we need to discuss now are some suggested priorities. These are only suggestions because your priorities will change depending on the type of music you play, your instrument of choice, and your resources.

PRIORITY ONE: MORE AND BETTER MICS AND A MIC PREAMP

For the sake of example, our studio has used a dynamic mic and a PZM mic. As you saw in previous chapters, we often suggested using more than these two microphones. To achieve the most from your acoustic instruments, you may need additional mics. To achieve the most from your voice, or to capture accurately the exceptional tone of your 40 year-old Martin guitar, you may need *better* mics. To utilize better mics effectively, you may need a separate mic preamp.

Start your studio expansion by doubling your mic inventory. Get another dynamic and PZM that are exact duplicates of the ones you have now—the same brand and model. Having matching microphones is essential for stereo and X–Y miking. You'll have a better shot at miking that live drum set. You'll have that extra mic for the backup singer. And you can use two PZMs to mic your acoustic piano. Two PZMs are nice for choral groups or stage plays. Not that these mics will make all the difference, but your studio life will become much easier.

But we're also talking about better mics—the kind of mic that studios keep locked up tight for security. If your music is acoustic or vocally oriented, sooner or later you will be in the market for one of these treasures. Almost 20 years ago the author had his first experience with a mic of this type. In an eight-track studio in Des Moines, the acoustic guitar just wasn't sounding right. The engineer went to the securely locked mic room and brought out a Neumann (I was too young to notice the model number). He just set it in front of the guitar and said, "Play." Later in the control room, when the track was played back, I had the sensation that I was sitting with the guitar in my lap, playing the part. No microphone had ever offered up that sensation before. It was astounding!

We're talking about microphones in the $1,000-plus range, such as the AKG-414, the Neumann U-87 or U-89, or the Shure SM-7. In the last few years, a number of high-quality microphones have been introduced that emulate the performance of these older gems. Mics by CAD, Stedman, Audio Technica, and others can be found in the $700 to $800 range. These mics offer large diaphragms and low-noise FET electronics, but most of all great sound. You may be romanced by a "tube" mic such as the old Neumann's, but you will pay dearly for that tube. So beware.

The problem in our studio ecosystem is that a mic in this class will begin to disrupt the balance a little. Your cassette based-multitrack will have a little trouble appreciating and translating the splendor and sophistication of mics of this type. Short of pitching your multitrack and shelling out for a digital recorder, you might investigate a microphone preamp. These add-on units offer higher-quality electronics than you'll find in the mixer in your portable studio. The output of the preamp can be plugged into a buss or line input on your portable studio.

PRIORITY 2: DAT MIXDOWN DECK

DAT (digital audio tape) recorders are really making their presence felt on the professional and home recording scene. With its pristine audio performance, a DAT mixdown deck offers some real advantages over a cassette mixdown recorder.

Even if you've created all your basic tracks on the analog portable studio multitrack, a digital mixdown deck will make great-quality stereo master tapes. On some professional DAT machines, there are digital outputs that can send to compact disc mastering machines. It's not too likely that you will create an album-quality tape from your portable studio, but you never know. The point is, with a DAT mixdown deck, you have jumped into big-league performance.

If you use a lot of MIDI sound modules and sequencing in a virtual tracking system, then a DAT mixdown recorder becomes even more exciting. By synchronizing your sequencer and portable studio, as described in the MIDI section of the book, you could create some very professional-sounding masters on a DAT machine. Using the portable studio for the acoustic instruments and vocals, everything else in the MIDI domain waits to hit tape until mixdown. If you can avoid track bouncing, getting by with just the four tracks for vocals and acoustic instruments, you will be able to retain all the audio performance your portable studio system can muster. Your acoustic instrument and vocal tracks will be "first generation." The DAT mixdown deck allows you to retain this quality through the mixing stage.

External track bouncing can be more productive with a DAT too. With the increased audio capability, your two-machine ping-pongs will have more clarity and definition. On the downside, you won't be able to bounce your sync track from the multitrack to the stereo DAT any more effectively than by using an analog stereo cassette or open-reel machine. Whether they are analog or digital, two tracks (stereo) are still only two tracks. Several professional DAT machines offer the ability to embed SMPTE time code within their digital data stream, so these machines are synchable. Professional DAT machines are prohibitively expensive for your expansion unless you are planning major upgrades in your multitrack, mixer, and other areas as well.

PRIORITY 3: MORE MIDI

For those of you slightly more afflicted with MIDI mania than other musical maladies, more MIDI may be the first area you will want to expand. Sound modules get the first nod. They can help increase the number of virtual tracks and expand your library of sounds (such as acoustic grand piano). Sometimes they offer higher audio quality than your current sound module provides.

As you progress in your multitrack expertise, you will eventually realize many of the advantages of performing your music using both virtual tracks and multitracks. The addition of another multitimbral sound module will give you just the right amount of flexibility the performance of your music.

It's always handy to have more sounds available, but bear in mind it can be a challenge to use sound modules effectively. Adding more tracks, virtual or tape, simply for the sake of more tracks, can be a very sure road to muddy, crowded music. Some of the most artistically successful music of all time is music that would require very few virtual or tape tracks to record today. Consider Buddy Holly's guitar, bass, drums, and vocal; Bartok's string quartets; Ella Fitzgerald's voice with Joe Pass's guitar; Jimi Hendrix's guitar, bass, and drums; Beethoven's piano music; Julian Bream's guitar; the local Barber Shop Quartet; Tracy Chapman; bluegrass quartets; Gatemouth Brown; John Fahey; Keith Jarrett; Tuck and Patty. The list is quite long, and the point becomes obvious. Effectively using what you have is far preferable to ineffectively using more. More is not better, *better* is better.

Your search for another sound module should, perhaps, focus on the sounds themselves. Do you need an acoustic piano sound under MIDI control? Is it an important ingredient in your music? Then a sound module that offers great acoustic piano sounds, even though it does little else effectively, might be the best investment for your expansion budget.

If your existing sound module is a synthesizer, you should consider a sampler for your second module. As noted before, synthesizers and samplers make their sounds differently. As a result, they have different strengths and weaknesses when it comes to the sounds they produce. Synthesizers usually offer greater polyphony (the number of notes they will play simultaneously), and greater multitimbral capability. Synthesizers usually cost much less than samplers. As producers of sounds "from the ground up," synthesizers can provide many timbres. Some synthesizers are able to emulate certain natural instruments, although this is not a strong suit.

Samplers, on the other hand, are very exciting because of the realism they offer. As purveyors of digitally recorded sounds, samplers can provide great percussion, human voices, and sound effects, to cite just a few examples. There are also sample playback units. Though incapable of recording their own samples, they can play back the samples created by the factory. The samples themselves are permanently loaded into the unit's internal memory system, or are available on some storage medium. Some of them offer a very limited number of sounds, but with very high quality (several, in particular, offer great acoustic piano sounds at very reasonable prices). So, again, if your first sound module is a synthesizer, you should strongly consider getting a sampler or sample player to add to your system.

The audio quality of your sound modules may be your primary area of concern. Inexpensive sound modules that seem very attractive in the music store have a way of sounding noisy at home. This phenomenon becomes more pronounced as time passes. Your ears become more attuned to the qualities of your sound on tape, and sound modules that were great when you started seem deficient later on. In the music manufacturing business, like every other business, there are no bargains except quality.

In order to make a multitimbral sound module with a zillion sounds in one little black box that sells for half the price of everything else, the manufacturer had to "shave the baby" somewhere. The audio circuits are probably one of the places that got a good shaving. Few things are more annoying than working hard to get a sequence figured out only to commit your music to tape and hear a constant hissing from your sound module. The noise only gets worse as you use the module in overdubbing and track bouncing.

Other than price, there are few indicators of a sound module's audio quality. It is often difficult to hear the hiss in a busy music store. A module that sounds good in the store might be a snake when you get it into the home studio. So make sure that you have the option of bringing the module back the next day if you get it home and it reveals a noise problem.

This brings us to a topic discussed earlier: the value of a local dealer who sincerely helps you get the quality you need. The search for audio quality may mean you will spend more money than you planned, but the hours of unhappiness created by bad audio from a sound module is a far steeper price to pay. Support those local dealers who spend the money to have quality people on their sales floors, whose business practices focus on getting you what you need. These people deserve to make a buck or two more than the slock rock houses. And, in the long run, you will receive more value from the instruments you buy from honest traders.

Adding more sound modules has only one real downside. Your mixer may not be able to handle the increased number of audio inputs, particularly if you are running many separate audio outputs from a sampler or drum machine. If this becomes a problem, investigate several of the fine line-level mixers available. Remember, you don't need much EQ at all for synthesizers. They have sophisticated filters and other controls that are far more powerful than most EQ systems. So a rack-mount line-level mixer without EQ circuits is the perfect low-noise solution to a shortage of mixer channels. You can use it as a submixer, connecting its outputs to the buss inputs of your portable studio.

PRIORITY 4: MORE SIGNAL PROCESSING

You will almost immediately feel the need for more signal processing when you get serious about your recordings. In addition to the more obvious effects of reverb, chorus, flanging, delay, and pitch shifting, you will find a use for compression (or limiting), audio enhancement, gating, and possibly more EQ than is available in your mixer. As a performer, you may not have had much need of these processors, but as a recordist you will find that they can really enhance the quality of your tapes.

We mentioned compression often during the discussions of recording the various instruments. In earlier chapters we also explained that a compressor is a dynamic effect that works on the relative loudness and softness of the music. A compressor helps a tape recorder by controlling transients. While an engineer can usually just ride the channel fader or input trim control to reduce the signal of an extended loud passage, very short bursts of sound are too much for the tape and electronics. This is where the compressor comes in. If properly set, a compressor can recognize and reduce only those bursts of sound.

Compressors and limiters help you retain sufficient canvas for your audio paint. As you record more and more tracks, you quickly fill up the available tape capacity. On a small-format tape such as our cassette-based portable studio, you'll find yourself running into problems such as tape saturation and cross talk. While you might use your compressor in the ways suggested in earlier chapters, you may also find it useful when you are bouncing tracks of music that have a lot of dynamics.

The compressor you buy should be stereo and have controls for threshold and ratio adjustment. It should not add noise or "color" the sound of your music too much. If a fully operable compressor is too much for your budget, you might consider a soft-kneed limiter. Several companies make stereo versions of these at very affordable prices (see Chapter 4 for further details on compressors and limiters).

After you have recorded a track, or bounced several tracks together, you may have a funny feeling when you play them back.

They sound different, don't they? A little like "tracks under glass." We sometimes lose the zip and sparkle in our sound when we commit the music to tape. Ping-ponging tracks is a process notorious for creating this sensation. What do we do about it?

In our general tips section and the discussion of processing specific instruments, we suggested some uses for EQ that will help. But there are times when it seems you've done everything right, yet the tape still doesn't retain the music's original zing. This is where the products known as *exciters, enhancers,* or (get this!) *psycho-acoustic processors* might find a place in your studio. To simplify the present discussion, we'll call all of the above enhancers.

Enhancers add their zing in a couple of different technical ways. Because the human ear is a highly biased listening instrument, enhancers are designed to take advantage of these biases. They stimulate the brightness controls in our listening systems. As a result, they can rectify somewhat the effects of recording processes that diminish brightness.

Don't expect the thing to knock you over in the music store. The effect is too subtle for that. But using an enhancer when you bounce tracks, record vocals, or record some virtual tracks to tape will really help your tapes sparkle. They will have that little something extra that may be enough to set them above the crowd on the music executive's desk.

Having an extra, stand-alone, equalizer can also come in handy as you expand the studio. Any equalizer can help add brilliance, eliminate rumble, and combat noise, but a parametric EQ can really zero in on problem areas. An instrument or microphone that produces an annoying timbre can be fixed by using a parametric to notch out the offending frequency. Simply dial in the offender, cut the frequency back (and set the Q very narrowly), and the killer buzz dies without affecting the living frequencies around it. With only the EQ section of your portable studio to work with, you may have found it difficult to perform some of the EQ tips in the sections on recording specific instruments. An extra EQ can be just the way to "fix it in the mix."

We mention the gate as our last of the subtle but very useful processors that can be added to the home studio. A gate works in the opposite way a compressor or limiter does. It is a dynamic processor like a compressor or limiter, but it affects everything *below* its threshold. If a signal doesn't knock loud enough—a signal such as a noise—the gate won't open to let it through. Gates are useful with noisy electric guitars like old Stratocasters and Telecasters. Some older analog synthesizers can also benefit from gates. And some newer multitimbral synths are about as noisy as anything ever made. If you are using an array of little-black-box multitimbral synths, then a stereo gate dedicated to processing them may be a great addition to your studio.

An unfortunate side effect of adding these processors may be the bad back you'll get from crawling around plugging and unplugging them, so we'll reiterate our praises for the patch bay to bring all those inconveniently located inputs and outputs to a single panel that can be mounted right next to your portable studio. Most patch bays offer some kind of "normaling," which simply means that you can set up the usual routing patterns via the connections on the backside of the patch bay. Any time you want to change a setup, you simply use the front connectors to reroute the signals.

PRIORITY 5: MORE MIXER

The mixers in portable studios—even digital portable studios such as the Roland VS-880 or Fostex DMT-80—make some compromises that may begin to pinch your creativity as you expand other areas of your studio. You may want to consult Chapter 2 for details on the features mentioned in the next few paragraphs.

Many portable studios offer only high-impedance, unbalanced inputs, or they only allow you to use a few inputs at a time. As you use more mics and better mics, you will want to optimize the mic's performance by having the properly balanced low-impedance input at the mixer (you may decide to add a mic preamp as mentioned in Priority Two). You may need to switch from mic to line inputs, and so on. And you may want better channel equalization.

Adding signal processors will give rise to a need for more aux mixer systems, and will have to be very flexible in their routing capability. Individual channel insert points may become a priority for dropping in a processor on a single channel. You may need direct outputs or aux mixes to create cue mixes or for routing your virtual tracks to tape.

If you add a larger multitrack to your studio, you will need a mixer with more busses, more tape returns, and/or a larger monitor section, complete with more meters, LED peak readouts, and so on. As your whole studio grows, features that seemed unimportant may become very handy indeed. Such things as talkback, slating, built-in patch bays, or increased patch points in the channels and busses will all take on new relevance.

The move up to a bigger mixer is an expensive proposition that usually takes place when you've also invested in a larger multitrack recorder. The brutal question, the one you have to be totally honest about, is if you *really* need more tracks. Smaller submixers, as suggested earlier, are the way to go if you're simply adding more virtual tracks. If increased demands made by signal processors, virtual tracks, monitoring needs, better mics, and more creative ideas are pushing you to look at more mixer, then we suggest that you also look at more tracks.

If financing is an issue, you may be able to work out a package deal with your dealer. And if the total package means payments over three or four years, you had better plan on the kinds of things you're going to want to add during those three or four years so that you can finance them together.

PRIORITY 6: MORE SPACE OR BETTER SPACE

The original idea was to put the portable studio in the hall closet, the mics in a box under the bed, and the instruments neatly away in their cases somewhere. Now you've found that it takes you half an hour to set up your gear, and half an hour to tear it down. Most days you're lucky if you have an hour to spend with your music. And so, most days, you simply don't have time to drag it out and set it up. You need a space where you can keep things set up and ready to go when that great idea pops up.

At first you didn't mind the noise of an occasional car passing by or the furnace or air conditioner as they turned on in the middle of your punch-in. And it really was kind of cute to capture the sound of your three-year-old on tape during the acoustic guitar solo.

In other words, through inexperience or exuberance, you can let many imperfections slide by. But as you get your recording chops in shape, you will find these petty issues start looming large. It may very well be that the time has come to do something about your working space.

You'll find some ideas for carving a permanent and effective space for your recording studio in Chapter 9. Even if it's a garage, basement, or utility room, you will be much happier and more effective if your studio has its own space.

PRIORITY 7: MORE TRACKS

The decision to jump to a larger-format multitrack is a big one that will mean carefully considering many issues. By the time you do make the jump, you should have quite a few recording hours under your belt. This will help—and so will some patience and research.

The jump from four-track cassette-based portable studio should force you to take a psychological and emotional inventory. Where are you going with the studio? Has your basic purpose changed? Are you now aiming to produce a professional-level product for broadcast or the commercial music business? Do your "customers" want your product delivered on a particular medium (ADAT, DAT, computer disk, or something else)?

Although multitrack machines such as the ADAT have blurred the line between what was once called semiprofessional and professional, there is still a pretty clear line drawn between stores selling semiprofessional product and professional audio shops. When you talk to salespeople in a professional shop, they will talk to you as a tool salesperson would to a tradesperson. They will stress performance, absolute performance. They will talk about transport strength and speed. They will talk about minimizing "down time" and maintenance. Of course, there will be the usual pitch words and the exaggerations (after all, marketing hyperbole is a way of life in America). But you will get the definite notion that you're entering a world where the worth of a machine is judged by how well it will earn money for its owner— a professional's tool.

Semiprofessional might also be called semiamateur—the glass may be half full, but it's also half empty. These are machines that are "technological breakthroughs," the "it wasn't possible until now" unit, or the "professional performance at an affordable price" machine. Semiprofessional products are often created by stretching the performance of consumer machines or by modifying a professional machine to make it cheaper to produce and sell. Sometimes they are truly unique solutions to problems found by companies from other fields (such as synthesizer makers) who have taken a very different but creative path. Just as often, they are yesterday's professional technology that the company is trying to get some more sales for by lowering its price into the semiprofessional area.

Professional machines are aimed precisely at a specific professional task. Semiprofessional machines, by definition, are compromise machinery. It is always more difficult to shop for the compromise machine. Limited by budget, you are trying to understand the nature and boundaries of the compromise. Just how did they shave this baby to get it out at this price? Will its limitations give me enough room to do my work? Can this new technology really perform as well as the brochure says it will? Is this meaningful new technology or a marketing attempt to fool consumers and seduce the dollars from our wallets?

These are tough questions without easy answers; your personal inventory will be the place to start. If you're tough with yourself, you will have a pretty good idea of exactly what level of performance you really require. If you are going to make a *big* investment, you want something that will satisfy your track fever for a couple of years. If you know you won't be happy with the machine you're looking at for at least two years, then don't buy it.

There are new and used machines around in both the semipro and professional categories. Unless you know the history of a used semipro piece very well, you should probably pass on it. Semipro machines require good maintenance habits to live long, useful lives. They aren't built for abuse, yet they are used by people who, as a rule, don't know how to maintain them properly. They are the most abused machines on the block. Even digital machines require maintenance and care—after all, many modular digital multitracks (MDMs) are based on consumer video-cassette-recorder transports. All of us by now have probably had to junk a VCR or two because its transport just wore out.

New semipro machines can be a very fine investment. Science *does* march on, revealing new and wonderful things to help us in our struggles to do more with our music. New metals are found that make heads last longer, or hold a tighter tolerance at the head gap. Other metals may make possible motors with lower mass and higher magnetic energy. More tracks can be fit on smaller tape formats. Digital sound processing can be resident in less expensive mixers. MIDI control can mute channels and throw transports into record or stop.

The rapid maturation of the digital multitrack is a perfect example of technology's march. It wasn't long ago that stationary-head digital multitracks carried six-figure price tags. Now a wide array of multitracks based on either the video cassette transport or computer hard disk are available for under $2000.

The recorders to consider for your expansion would be the new breed of MDMs such as the ADAT or TASCAM DA-88. Hard-disk-based multitracks by Roland, Vestax, Emu, and others are also worth investigating. Hard disk systems offer sequencer-like editing capability in addition to superb digital audio. As hard disk storage prices have plummeted, hard disk recorders have become real bargains. Many of them offer workstation features like waveform editing, built-in digital effects, digital mixing, and so on.

MDMs, on the other hand, have become a de facto standard "delivery medium." That is, studios have taken to transporting ADAT or DA-88 tapes back and forth. If the people you work with on a regular basis use MDMs, then that may be reason enough for you to go that direction.

PRIORITY 8: MORE SYNC

In the MIDI chapter, we talked about adding sync capability in our sequencer or computer sequencer set up. This allows the sequencer and its virtual tracks to follow the tape transport. The tape machine is always the master, while the sequencer always is the slave following the commands from the transport.

But what happens when we try to make the transport follow the sequencer? Nothing. What would happen if we tried to get another tape machine to follow our multitrack or sequencer? Again, nothing. What's missing?

Though transports have the ability to "hear" our sync codes, FSK, or SMPTE Time Code, because they can record and play them back, they haven't the foggiest idea what the codes are saying. Your sound material is recorded on tape, and the only way to hear tape is to get it to the head on time. If the section of tape that you want to hear or synchronize to another machine is not in front of the head, it may as well be in another country.

Somehow, the transport must be told how to roll that section of tape up to the head. This may mean telling the transport, "Go into fast-forward, okay here comes the part, slow down, there you go, now stop!" It may mean rewinding, stopping, and then going into play mode. When one transport is doing all this running around trying to find a spot on the tape that will match up with a spot on another transport's tape, the process is called *chase,* or *chasing.* When the transport that is chasing finds the spot, it must be able to stop and then play in absolute sync with the master transport. This process is called *lock* or *locking.*

We need two things to get this chase and lock process to take place. We need something that speaks "transportese." And we need a reference on tape that will tell us where we are. The translator of transportese is called a *synchronizer*. The reference on tape is our old friend SMPTE Time Code.

When we want a tape transport to chase and lock to another transport, both transports must have SMPTE Time Code recorded on them. The synchronizer is then able to "read" the time code from both machines. With the synchronizer's control panel you say, "I, the controller, want you, the synchronizer, to find these two specific spots, as identified by their SMPTE Time Code location markers. You will then sync them together by getting the slave machine to chase and lock to the master machine." Further, "You will then continue to monitor the two tape transports so that they remain in sync, making any adjustments as they are necessary" (Figure 17-1).

The synchronizer must read at least two time code strips, compare them, and then command the transports to chase and lock. The problem is another one of translation. There are as many dialects of transportese as there are different kinds of transports. Transports are complicated mechanical and electronic devices. Each manufacturer creates its own from the ground up. You may find transports by the same maker that speak the same dialect, but you will never find transports by different makers that speak the same language. And since you may be syn-

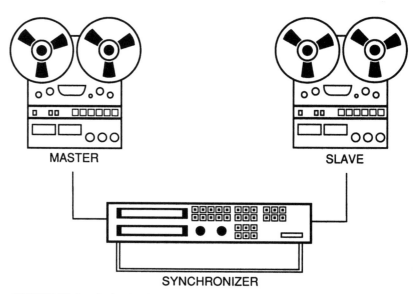

MASTER   **SLAVE**

SYNCHRONIZER

FIGURE 17-1. A simple chase lock synchronizing system. The synchronizer "reads" SMPTE Time Code from both tape transports and uses it to match specific locations on the two tapes. It then instructs the slave machine to *lock to* (play in sync with) the master machine.

chronizing an audio multitrack transport to a video transport, you can see that the transports may be made very differently. In short, your synchronizer must be multilingual.

Some synchronizers have been made with the dialects of many transports in their memory banks. These synchronizers can just be told by their command panels via a few button pushes what the specific transports are that they are controlling. Others can "diagnose the transport's ballistics"—that is, they can listen to the transport go through its commands and figure out the dialect of its transport. Still others, usually less expensive units, must be purchased and configured with specific transports in mind. However they do it, synchronizers must be set up so that they can speak to, and control, the transports you will be using.

The transports that you are using must have the necessary synchronizer connection points on them too. These are not audio connections. So don't confuse them with something labeled "sync" that may be for recording or playing back FSK or SMPTE signals. A synchronizer connection jack will probably be a multipin connector that looks like something that should be found on a big computer or a jet plane. Some of the more expensive portable studios have these connection jacks.

You will soon notice that the two machines you want to sync together probably don't have the same kind of jacks. Now you know that you will need the proper cable kits for your synchronizer and all the transports that you intend to use.

Here's an inventory list of what you will need for the basic synchronized operation of several transports.

1. Audio and video transports that have sync jacks

2. A synchronizer that reads SMPTE (all forms of longitudinal time code and possibly the vertically integrated time code used in video) from the transports and speaks their particular dialects to command them

3. A controller for the synchronizer so that you can set the "offsets" and other data needed to tell the transports where you want them to go and what you want them to do

4. Something that writes SMPTE Time Code (all longitudinal forms)

5. The cables necessary to hook everything up

Is it worth the trouble and expense? Maybe. Does recording soundtracks for videos, films, or television commercials appeal to you? Would you like to expand your audio tracks to 10 (a four-track and an eight-track minus the two SMPTE tracks)? If your artistic direction is taking you in the direction of audio for video or film, you will have to begin preparing yourself for the world of synchronizing.

The good news is that many of the digital multitracks have the ability to process MIDI information. Since they are not analog, their tape (or disk) is not required to hear and record MIDI's 32 kilobaud signal. The electronics of the recorder listen and decipher relevant MIDI information such as MTC (MIDI Time Code), MCC (MIDI Continuous Controller to operate variable controls such as mixer faders), and MMC (MIDI Machine Control designed to signal transport functions such as stop, start, rewind, and the like). These machines are able to sync to one another using MIDI cables and the appropriate software. As more and more machines implement MIDI transport control, synchronizing will get easier and easier.

In the meantime, growing more and more popular are accessory cards and boxes that translate MTC and SMPTE. Since the professional video and film business still uses SMPTE almost exclusively, these accessories can really help musicians and audio pros who want to work with pictures.

If you simply want more tracks, look higher up on our priority list to adding virtual and tape tracks. Unless somebody gives you a new multitrack, it isn't likely you will be able to sync two audio multitracks together more cost effectively than buying another, bigger multitrack.

SUMMARY

The above priority list is a suggested way to look at things. A few other things could also have been included, such as improved monitor speakers, amplifiers, and headphones. These are important and deserve attention. You can't fix it if you can't hear it. Why didn't we cover it? Because the improvement in your monitor system will probably be an extension of one of the above priorities. The addition of better microphones, or a DAT mixdown deck, or the improvement of your acoustic environment may point out the weaknesses in your monitor system. As mentioned in the introduction to this section, one seemingly minimal change may throw the whole system out of balance.

While the order of our list may seem backward to many of you just getting your first serious bout of track fever, please consider the expansion of your studio in the order we suggest. Most people will run out right away and look at bigger multitracks, DAT machines, or synchronizers. It takes a serious level of involvement to justify these expenditures. Get to that level of involvement the logical way. Get to be really good at making great recordings with what you have. Get so good that you know you can't wring another dB of performance from what you have before you start the wholesale replacement of the foundations of Home Studio, Inc. Improve the mics, add some processing, add some virtual tracks, improve your acoustic space, then you can worry about more tracks and the fancy stuff.

This book has taken you on a long and involved journey. We hope that it enabled you to accomplish at least some of your musical and recording goals. But we also hope that you have not become so enmeshed in the technicalities of the tools that you've lost sight of the reason for getting them in the first place. Music should be joyful; it should be fun. Recording music successfully should be like taking great pictures: they evoke the joy of the time they were taken and create new and enjoyable experiences with each viewing. In music, the pleasure that goes into creating and recording music can, if supported by skill and talent, translate into many years of good listening.

A P P E N D I X

SPECIFICATIONS

Stop! Before we go on, here's your chance to avoid ever dealing with the complex and confusing issue of specifications. Just live by this golden rule: Always trust your ears and your instincts when you evaluate a piece of equipment. Never put numbers ahead of actual sound on your priority list. But some of you, by personal inclination or because you are constantly interacting with specs-hounds, may feel compelled to learn more about specifications that apply to audio equipment. A certain amount of specs knowledge is necessary for survival when you are surrounded by merciless salespeople armed with the latest razor-sharp data.

For those of you so motivated, here's a rundown of the primary specs relating to the equipment you've assembled for your studio. For the rest of us, just put the book down and step slowly back from the microphone.

First, learn your specs from a reliable source. Don't let a salesman lead you into the deep, dark cave of numbers. He has read the brochures and been given the hype, but he may not know any more than you do about how to look at specifications. If you don't understand some techno-babble, ask the salespeople to stop and explain. If they can, they won't be offended. They spent some time learning this stuff too. If they can't, they may try to make you feel stupid. It just means they don't know it themselves. Hitch up your wagon and find another place to shop.

DECIBELS

Remember when your math teachers first tried to explain pi to you? What kind of number is that? Most of us still don't understand pi, but we know that at certain times we have to use it. Well, the infamous dB (decibel) is the pi of our audio experience.

Decibels are units of measuring signal level or sound pressure that are expressed as ratio numbers—actually, it's the logarithm of the ratio, so that big differences in levels can be measured by manageable numbers. In the real world, the numbers tell you how loud the sound level is or how much signal there is (Figure A-1). As ratio numbers, they tell you how far they are (relatively speaking) from another number. For instance, +4 dB is four units larger than whatever is used to define zero; –3 dB is three of those units smaller than zero. A dB number, by itself, means nothing without a corresponding zero value. A letter often

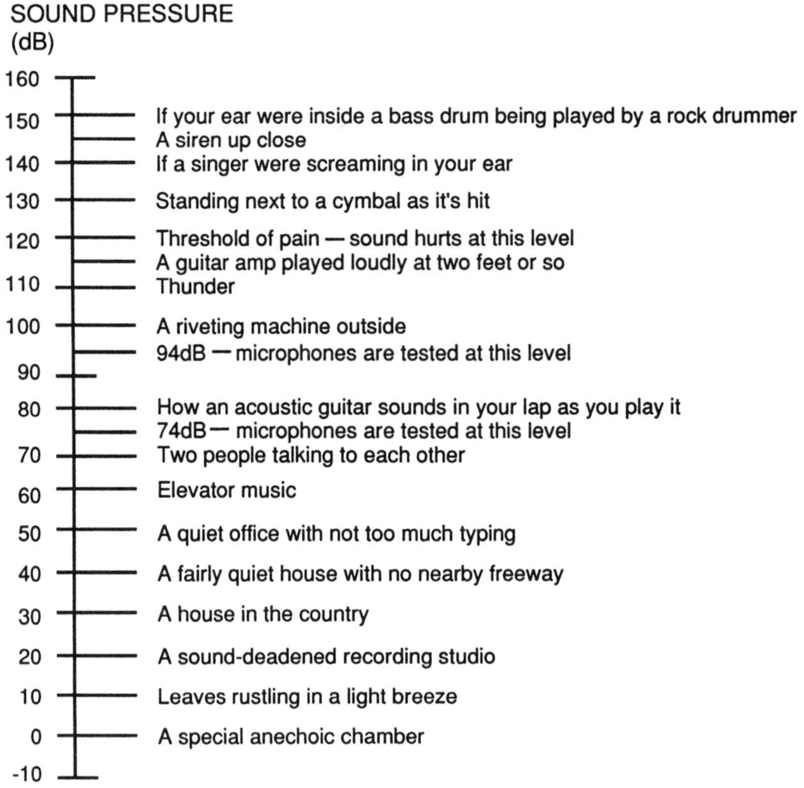

SOUND PRESSURE
(dB)

dB	
160	
150	If your ear were inside a bass drum being played by a rock drummer
	A siren up close
140	If a singer were screaming in your ear
130	Standing next to a cymbal as it's hit
120	Threshold of pain — sound hurts at this level
	A guitar amp played loudly at two feet or so
110	Thunder
100	A riveting machine outside
	94dB — microphones are tested at this level
90	
80	How an acoustic guitar sounds in your lap as you play it
	74dB — microphones are tested at this level
70	Two people talking to each other
60	Elevator music
50	A quiet office with not too much typing
40	A fairly quiet house with no nearby freeway
30	A house in the country
20	A sound-deadened recording studio
10	Leaves rustling in a light breeze
0	A special anechoic chamber
-10	

FIGURE A-1. The effects of various sound pressure levels measured in dB.

appears after the dB to tell us what that reference number is.

If you are talking about electronic signal levels, the zero figure will be referenced to voltage, which is the nomenclature of electrical energy. If you are talking about sound pressure, then the zero will be expressed in *dynes* or *bars,* which are the units of measurement used with air pressure. It's just like anything else—you don't say that the tree is four gallons tall, or that the jug holds 10 pounds of cranberry juice; you must use the appropriate units of measurement.

When dealing with the strength of an electronic signal, we are confronted with a variety of decibel references (Figure A-2). Because of the way that the audio, telephone, and telegraph technologies have evolved through the years, we've now got too many reference "zeroes" for comfort. For example, dBm is referenced to a zero of 1 milliwatt. Because all electrical signals have resistance, and because the phone company wanted to standardize both the signal levels and the resistance factors, 0 dBm became one milliwatt produced by 0.775 volts of electrical energy with 600 ohms resistance.

Another common dB reference, dBV, is referenced to 1 volt of current without any regard for impedance. Since most audio gear uses very high impedance levels, someone thought it easier to drop the 600 ohms reference. Even if we disregard impedance, as vital as it is, we still have a discrepancy between our dBm and dBV: 0 dBV will be more signal than 0 dBm—it will be 2.2 dB more.

So, along comes another dB, dBu (also sometimes written as dBv), which is referenced to 0.775 volts without regard for a standardized impedance (such as 600 ohms). More than a little con-

dB	VOLTAGE	dBm
+6dB	2 Volts	+8.2 dBm
+1.78dB	1.228 Volts	+4dBm
0dB	1.0 Volt	+2.2dBm
-2.2dB	.775 Volt	0dBm
-6dB	.5 Volt	-3.8dBm
-8.2dB	.388 Volt	-6dBm
-10dB	.316 Volt	-7.8dBm
-12dB	.250 Volt	-9.8dBm
-12.2dB	.245 Volt	-10dBm
-20dB	.1 Volt	-17.8dBm

FIGURE A-2.   Comparing dB and dBm levels to actual signal voltage.

fusing, isn't it? The basic lesson is: Don't compare dBv to dBm, it's like comparing three and five. Don't let that audio salesperson rap off a "dB" without telling you what kind of decibel he's talking about. Perhaps you're beginning to see the absurdity of a salesperson's reference to "2 dB better than . . ." if we don't know how it is being referenced.

How Much Is That dB?

The infamous dB is measured on the logarithmic scale; increases and decreases are "geometric," not nice and linear. Using the dBm scale, which includes impedance so that we can get a "power" figure, 3 dBm is two times the power of 0 dBm. But 10 dBm is 10 times the power of 0 dBm. And 10,000 times the power of 0 dBm nets a reading of +40 dBm. Doubling a signal's level nets an increase of 6 dBV. This is because signal is proportional to voltage squared. You need a calculator for this stuff. Not just any calculator either, you need one of those scientific calculators with all the funny-looking buttons on it to get down and dirty with the dB.

Using sound levels as an example, we will give you a common reference for the dB. A 3 dB difference in sound level is a difference anybody can hear. A 1 dB difference requires the ears of an experienced audio engineer to hear. A 6 dB difference your half-deaf grandmother could hear. So, when someone says that the signal is "3 dB down," this is something we can hear as a slight loss of sound power or energy.

Signal Levels

"This thing has both +4 dB and −10 dB inputs and outputs." What does the well-meaning salesperson mean by this? In the first place, he should have said, "This thing has both +4 dBm and −10 dBV inputs and outputs." Whatever the piece of gear is, it has two sets of both inputs and outputs that are rated at two different signal levels. We know that we try to match levels and impedances, don't we? Why are there so many levels and no apparent standardization? The proliferation of various input and output levels has to more to do with the spotty evolution of the audio industry than anything else.

Low-impedance equipment was designed by the phone company to transmit telephone signals over many miles of cable. Low-impedance instruments are still better at long cable runs. The +4 dBm (remember the "m" means it is referenced to the low impedance of 600 ohms) signal level evolved from the early studios. In those days, recorders and consoles were not as efficient as they are now. The signal level +4 dBm was deemed to be about the absolute that could be handled by the recorders and mixers without involving distortion. It was, therefore, picked as the standard for a zero reading on the meters. "0 VU" on the meter equaled a signal level of +4 dBm. Most broadcast and professional recording studios still use the +4 dBm standard. In Europe, many studios have pushed the signal level up to +8 dBm.

So where did the other signal levels come from? The levels –10 dBV and –20 dBV are products of the home stereo business. When equipment got more efficient, it was no longer necessary to generate as much overall signal level. There were many advantages to lower signal levels, including less expensive power supplies, and lower heat and distortion generated. The recorders and mixers you will use in your home studio will probably use the –10 dBV standard levels.

Makers of musical instruments throw us more levels. The level 0 dBu sometimes shows up as the input and output levels of some devices used as effects for musical instruments, even rackmount effects. The instruments themselves tend to put out various levels. Synthesizers and electric pianos tend to have 0 dB levels for outputs. Electric guitars and basses have outputs much less than this, usually around –30 dBu. Microphones tend to put out very low signals in the –40 to –60 dBu area (Figure A-3).

You can see why there is such a thriving business for level-matching devices, direct boxes, and impedance transformers. You can also see why it is so important to consider the levels of your equipment before you buy it. How important, or tragic, are these level differences?

We can loosely group levels, regardless of impedance, into four categories: *mic levels, line levels, instrument levels,* and *speaker levels.* Mic levels, as we've said, are very low. The good news is that mic levels are pretty consistently low so "mic" inputs in mixers are ready to accept and boost these levels. A specially designated microphone input can handle the level of any mic. We are disregarding impedance and XLR/phone connector problems—these can be handled with transformers and direct boxes.

Line levels are the +4 dBm, –10 dBV, or –20 dBV inputs and outputs you'll see on your recorders, mixer, and signal processing effects. The most common mismatch will be the –10 dBV and +4 dBm—a mismatch of both impedance and level. Going from a +4 dBm output to a –10 dBV input will be less of an impedance problem because outputs like to "look up to inputs" in terms of imped-

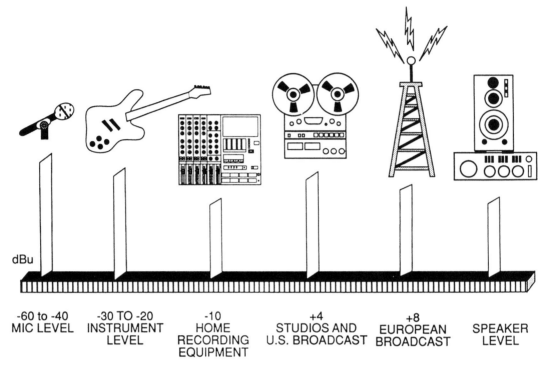

FIGURE A-3. Comparative signal levels on a dBu scale.

ance. The level difference can be compensated for if there is some kind of pad, trim, or level control on the input. Going the other way, −10 dBV to +4 dBm, may be more of a problem. It may require a professional level and impedance-matching device manufactured by various recording equipment companies. Some signal processing makers are solving this problem by supplying two sets of inputs and outputs, possibly with a selection switch.

Speaker levels are the much amplified current levels that are sent to loudspeakers. These are incredibly hot—the output of a 15 or 20 watt amplifier is plenty hot enough to charbroil the best input amplifiers of a mixer, recorder, or signal processor. *Never, ever* hook up an output intended for a speaker to your other equipment!

Instrument levels are a problem. There is absolutely nothing that we can say for certain. Instrument levels run from near-record-low mic-stature of −40 dBu to near record highs of +4 dBm or even higher. Electric guitars and basses tend to be very low level unless they have some kind of "active" electronics. Synthesizers sometimes send fire out their output holes. The output levels of synthesizers is sometimes dependent on the nature of the patch or sound they are playing at the time. Be very careful to monitor the levels you are sending from synthesizers or drum machines. Check the output specifications in the owner's manuals of your electronic instruments before you get too far along in the recording process.

IMPEDANCES

Every piece of audio equipment has impedance at its inputs and/or outputs. A typical home studio has quite a few components all connected from outputs to inputs. The impedance relationships between these pieces is very important to the efficiency of the current flow through the system. An input impedance must be higher than the output impedance of the source it receives. Impedance is measured in *ohms,* sometimes called simply Z (denoting resistance).

At first glance, this principle that input impedance must be higher than output impedance seems backward. Remember that we have current already in motion, applying pressure from the output upon the input. If the input impedance were lower than the output, there would be no control of the signal flow from one device to another. Much like a balloon puncture, we would have unrestricted flow of energy and movement from one to the other.

Having too low a resistance causes an input literally to draw the current from the outputs of the source feeding it. The source doesn't have an infinite supply of current, so you could just plain use up the energy available. Just as the balloon goes pop as its air pressure is drawn too quickly through the puncture, too low an input impedance will create destructive energy in the form of heat that will burn up your circuits. This is why audio professionals call a decrease in input impedance an "increase in load." The output amplifiers keep trying to generate more and more energy to send out the hole, but as fast as they can generate it it's gone, because there is insufficient resistance to it. So the low-input impedance is "loading" the work on the poor output amplifier to the point that it will burn out under the stress.

Output impedance, on the other hand, must be as low as possible. We have to get the air flowing from the balloon. Too high an impedance at the output keeps the current in the device, just as the air stays in the nonpunctured balloon. Once the current is moving, we have to control its movement with the input impedance of the device it's going to, so output impedance numbers expressed in ohms need to be low and input impedance numbers in ohms need to be high (10,000 or 20,000 ohms or more is common).

What about those microphones—didn't we stress always plugging low-impedance microphones into equally low-impedance mic inputs? Yes! Here comes the proverbial exception to the preceding rule. Microphones generate such a small amount of energy that the primary concern is the efficient transfer of the available power, without the introduction of noise, from the mic diaphragm through the mic input on the mixer. In other words, a little pop from our mic-balloon isn't such a bad thing. The current is so low that we need the input to draw from the mic. Low-impedance microphones should see a low-impedance input. Some of the technical explanations for this exception are just too complex for this book , so if you are an engineer, please bear with our simplifications.

FREQUENCY RESPONSE

If you've been reading this book more or less from page one straight through, you've already found out that frequency is related to what musicians would call pitch and tone. Frequency response is a measure of how well an instrument or machine is able to reproduce or process sound from the lowest pitches through the highest and right on up through the harmonics that help create tone. It's a pretty important specification, but it is often stated on specifications sheets in a way that's a little misleading.

You will most often see frequency response with a set of numbers that tell how low and how high the machine will go, for example, from 20 Hz to 20 kHz (Figure A-4). You will also see a number that states the variance from absolutely level performance across its range. This number will be stated in dB with the tag "plus or minus," which is like saying "give or take X dB." The number most often used to express variance from "flat" frequency response is 3 dB.

This is where most specs sheets stop. Is it enough? No! We need to know at what level of signal the frequency response is measured. As you can see from our chart, measuring response at −20 dB, as some consumer audio makers do, will give an inflated figure for response. We should see the figure referenced to "0 dB."

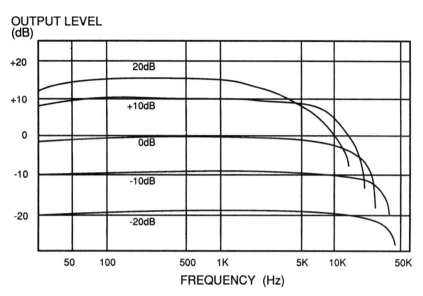

FIGURE A-4. The approximate frequency response of a quality home recording multitrack.

So your complete frequency response numbers would look something like this: 20 Hz to 20 kHz +/− 3 dB at 0 dBV.

What kind of numbers can you expect to see? You'll see measurements for electronic components and also such things as the recorder's record/reproduce response. Expect great-looking numbers from today's electronics, such as 20 Hz to 20 kHz +/− 1 dB. If you can, when looking at mixers, get the numbers showing response with all channels sending signal to one buss. This will help evaluate the electronics when everything is cooking and the power supply is under stress.

Recorders are different beasts entirely. The process of changing electrical energy to magnetic energy on tape is very inefficient. Tape has to be hit fairly hard with a lot of signal for even a little of it to "stick." For this reason the record amp circuits in tape recorders are very powerful and the playback amp circuits are very sensitive and are capable of high gain. We will be referring to this principle again, but what it means for our purposes here is that you can expect the numbers to be significantly less for a recorder's response than they are for electronics. For a cassette-based machine, expect 40 Hz to 15 kHz, +/− 3 dB. Open-reel machines can be expected to respond from 30 Hz to 22 kHz, +/− 3 dB.

A bit of trickery sometimes occurs when specifications are

given for a recorder's response. A measurement is taken of only the electronic portion of the recorder by passing a signal through it. What we are interested in is the "record/reproduce" frequency response. To get this number, a signal must be recorded on tape and then measured on playback from that tape (on the same machine, we hope).

Since we are converting electrical energy to magnetic energy through the recording process, we need a reference point that is measured in the units of magnetic energy called *Webers*. Since they are small units, they are usually expressed as nano-Webers, abbreviated as "nWb/m," which means nano-Webers per meter. A standard reference level for open-reel recorders is 250 nWb/m, while cassette recorders use 160 nWb/m. Tape-noise-reduction systems tend to use 200 nWb/m as a reference. On a specifications sheet, any variance from these references, or the total omission of a flux (magnetic energy) reference, should be reason enough to be suspicious. These references were established by the National Association of Broadcasters (NAB) so that their engineers would have standards of comparison.

SIGNAL-TO-NOISE RATIO

Assuming that there will always be a certain amount of noise present in the signals that we're using, we need to know how well our equipment will perform relative to it. This relationship is called signal-to-noise ratio, or S/N for short. It defines how much good we have (the signal), versus how much bad (the noise). The number is expressed in dB, and the higher it is, the better.

To measure S/N, test engineers send a simple mid-range tone, 1 kHz, through the electronics, or they record and play it back on a recorder. This tone is sent at a level that produces an amount of distortion that is easily perceived: 3 percent total harmonic distortion. The output is then measured to see how much noise is present relative to the clean signal. What could be simpler? As usual, there are some snakes in the cave.

S/N is most often measured using some kind of weighted curve. The human ear is a very complex device that is connected to an even more complex device called the brain. These two human sensors tend to perform millions of biased calculations regarding anything they hear. The ear/brain combo doesn't work in a nice, linear, easily measured sort of way. The weighted curve is the engineer's way to emulate the performance of the ear.

These curves are standardized by associations such as NAB.

Just as in Frequency Response measurements, some people get tricky when measuring a recorder's S/N. They route the signal through the electronics without actually recording it and then playing it back. By testing without the transport in motion so that any clunks or scraps it generates might be picked up, and by not transducing the energy to magnetic flux and back, they get stellar S/N figures. Very tacky!

A filter is sometimes used on the output so that certain frequencies don't make it to the test gear. Guess which frequencies those are. Right—just the ones where some of the most annoying noises exist. A bandwidth figure that looks like the frequency response figure should be given to tell you whether you're getting the complete picture.

A usable S/N number should look like this: "Record/reproduce S/N XX dB, A-weighted, referenced to 3 percent THD at 1 kHz (20 Hz to 20 kHz)." If the unit you are considering has noise reduction, then you need the figures with and without noise reduction operating.

TOTAL HARMONIC DISTORTION (THD)

Even those maniacs who compete in triathlons sometimes reach a point were they just can't run, bike, or swim another foot. Before one of these athletes falls down unable to move any further, they reach what is sometimes called "the wall." It is a measure of bravado and determination to keep going right through the wall.

The tape we record on and the electronics used to transport signals around our system also have little walls of their own. They have a point at which they simply can't move, and they have their point just before that at which they need to sit down and take a rest. The wall occurs between 5 dB and 10 dB before complete saturation of the tape or overload of the circuits. This level is 3 percent THD, and it can be easily heard by the average listener.

Harmonics are an integral part of the audio world. Remember we talked about them related to microphones and frequency response? We spent some more time on them when we learned how to use EQ properly. For our purposes, just know that harmonics can be generated by the improper interaction of signals and the components of our system. One of the most annoying and prominent of these harmonics generated is the *third harmonic*. For this reason, it is the third harmonic that is usually measured to get a THD spec.

A usable THD specification will tell you the signal used as a test, usually 1 kHz, that 3 percent THD was reached at X dB above 0 VU (zero on the meter), and that 0 VU is equal to X nWb/m. Sometimes, you will see the percentage of THD that occurs at 0 VU with a referenced signal and fluxivity. If there are noise-reduction circuits on the machine, the manufacturer probably used them to make the spec look better, but should tell you if noise reduction is used. A good spec might be: 3 percent THD at 15 dB above 0 VU (250 nWb/m) with dbx.

DYNAMIC RANGE

You will often hear people throw around the phrases *dynamic range* and *headroom*. Dynamic Range is the area between the noise floor and 3 percent THD. As such, you can get this figure by adding the dB numbers for Signal to Noise Ratio and 3 percent THD to get Dynamic Range. Headroom is essentially the same as 3 percent THD; it is the area, measured in dB, between 0 VU and the occurrence of 3 percent THD (Figure A-5).

Dynamic Range is your complete sonic drawing board—from softest whispers, which can just be heard above the noise floor, to the explosions and crashing guitars that push it over the edge of loudness and distortion. While recording along at 0 VU on your meters, occasionally along comes a little thunderstorm of music that demands more dynamic room on your tape. Headroom is the space you have available for these cloudbursts of sound.

CROSSTALK

Crosstalk, the last of the vital performance specifications, is essentially a leakage of sound from its intended pathway into another. It happens when the signal going down channel 1 of your mixer bleeds through to also go down channel 2 a little. And it happens in the recording and reproducing process on our recorders.

What difference does a little crosstalk make? You may not want bass drum sounds on your vocal track, particularly after

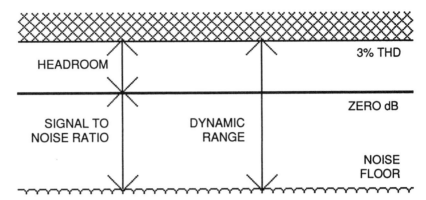

FIGURE A-5. The dynamic range is your complete sonic drawing board—the area between the noise floor and 3 percent total harmonic distortion.

you have put some reverb on that track. Crosstalk can create all kinds of havoc when you are ready to start adding effects to or panning your mix. As you record more tracks and start bouncing them, you may run into problems as these leaking signals create effects of their own. As you may recall, many effects are created by slightly delaying signals or combining them in different ways. Through crosstalk, you may end up creating effects you don't want. In short, you are losing control of your mix and recording.

Crosstalk is really tough to prevent in recorders. The reasons for this have to do with the relative "deafness" of audio tape. Record amps are really hot. They pound a lot of signal into the tape. The tape retains relatively little of it, so playback amps are really sensitive and heavily amplify anything they can pick up off the tape. In a multitrack, you often have one track in the record mode while the adjacent track is in the playback mode. With these two high-gain amps pumping away right next to each other, it's pretty easy for them to start mixing up the signals. This is where you'll get your crosstalk in the recorder.

Crosstalk is expressed as a ratio number—surprised? For a recorder, expect to get numbers around 50 dB or better without any noise reduction. With noise reduction, you should see numbers more like 70 dB. If they don't tell you whether they're using noise reduction, they probably are, as we have learned. Expect really high numbers for crosstalk in mixers and other electronics.

Manufacturers use a test signal to measure crosstalk just like they do everything else. They should tell you what it is. It will probably be a nice, easy-to-handle, mid-range signal about 1 kHz. They should tell you how hot this test signal was, particularly for record/reproduce figures. It should be 0 VU.

OTHER RECORDER SPECIFICATIONS

There are a couple of other numbers that you will see specified including wow and flutter, and erasure. These are recorder specifications. *Wow and flutter* has to do with the noise level that the transport itself generates. It should be a very low number, less than a tenth of a single percentage point. Look for something like 0.05 percent (NAB weighted).

Erasure has to do with how well your recorder wipes away old signal from tape before recording new signal in its place. This number should be around 70 dB measured at 1 kHz.

DIGITAL SPECIFICATIONS

Many of the specifications we've just elaborated simply don't apply to digital technology. Once converted in the digital process, your music is carried along through the digital audio chain as binary digits (bits—a numerical series of zeroes and ones). As such, digital audio remains immune to the problems of analog distortion and noise.

While free of these analog restraints, digital brings problems of its own, such as those inherent in representing the infinitely variable fluctuations of amplitude with finite numbers. There is no way to do this without the compromise of approximation.

An *analog to digital converter* (ADC) uses time *sampling* and amplitude *quantization* to transform music from the analog domain to the digital. Inherent in these two processes are the two primary anomalies of digital audio: the sampling of wrong frequencies known as *aliasing* and errors in the quantization of analog waveforms. Both of these errors come from digital's need to approximate analog waveforms.

A sample can best be thought of as an audio snapshot. A series of samples are taken of an incoming analog waveform, similar to the way that a film is a series of still frames. In the same way that the playback of a film doesn't appear to be a series of single frames but a continuous flow, if a sufficient number of samples-per-second are played back, the audio will retain its flow.

While the eye can be fooled into flow with a speed of between 24 and 30 frames per second, the ear is considerably more discerning. The Nyquist theory of sampling suggests that a sampling speed/rate of at least twice the frequency to be sampled must be used for accuracy. This means a 20 kHz tone requires a sampling frequency of at least 40 kHz! That's 40,000 samples a second.

Assuming a sample rate of 40 kHz, the attempt to sample a tone higher than 20 kHz would cause the distortion called aliasing. For this reason, analog-to-digital converters employ low-pass filters (sometimes called anti-aliasing filters) in their earlier stage to block frequencies that are high enough to cause problems from getting through.

The theoretical limit of human hearing high frequencies has been placed between 20 kHz and 22 kHz. For that reason, the audio industry standardized a sample rate of 44.1 kHz for compact discs. Although there has been considerable argument for raising this rate, it has proven to give reasonable performance.

If sampling is the capturer of time in digital recording, then quantization is the capturer of amplitude. The accuracy of a systems quantization is limited by its *resolution*. The resolution of a digital system relies on the number of bits available to it. The more bits available, the higher the degree of resolution and accuracy.

Sound in nature is very complex. Even the simplest bird call can present nearly infinite fluctuations of amplitude. For this reason, there are always errors present in any digitized approximation of waveforms. The question is: Is the approximation close enough to fool the ear?

As we said, the more bits, the greater the accuracy. The resolution increases logarithmically as well. For example, an 8-bit system offers 256 increments of resolution. A 16-bit system, by contrast, offers 65,536. An 18-bit system offers 262,144 increments, and a 20-bit system comes in at an incredible 1,048,576 increments. The theory is that at some point quantization error can not be heard by the human ear. The industry has established 16-bits as an adequate bench mark.

Most digital systems also use analog noise to help mask quantization errors. This white noise is called *dither*. An extended discussion of dither and quantization error is not warranted. But you are encouraged to remember that digital systems have their problems too. As a simple example, we could question the quality of the low-pass filters used at the input stage of the ADC. What kind of phase anomalies is this filter introducing into the system? Unfortunately, a treatment of these subjects would require another book-length manuscript.

Once signal is in the digital format, it must be brought out again to be heard via analog amplifiers and speakers. This process requires the *digital-to-analog converter* (DAC), which determines how well the digital signal is restored to analog on playback. Output systems of digital machines also employ low-pass filters and often sample-and-hold circuits just as input systems do. Digital filters employing *oversampling* techniques are often used to decrease potential phase shifts and to improve signal-to-noise performance. Oversampling at the output helps to decrease quantization noise dramatically by decreasing the ratio of its appearance versus the signal and pushing toward the absolute noise floor.

Features to look for in your digital toys are: high sample rates (44.1 or higher), high resolution for both ADCs and DACs (16-bit or more), oversampling at outputs, and high rates for internal processing in the digital domain (24-bit or better). The suggestions of 44.1 kHz, 16-bit, oversampling, and 24-bit internal processing are really minimal to realizing the serious advantages of digital audio. Expect to see machines with significantly higher specs in the near future. Don't assume that because it's digital it's perfect. Strive for the best-performing machines you can get.

SUMMARY

Numbers are the playthings of engineers. If you are an engineer, have fun! If you are not, then be wary of numbers. The preceding paragraphs are here because numbers often become the weapons of the marketers and salespeople. Sometimes this is quite unintentional—most marketers and salespeople are just trying to make an honest buck. If we weren't certain that you would be confronted with a barrage of these numbers, the preceding explanations would have been left out.

Whenever you are in doubt about a piece of equipment, let your ears and your instincts be the judges. Usually, a couple of dB are not going to make much difference. If it sounds good to you, and it feels right to you inside, then it probably is right for you. Use those beautiful test instruments flapping on the sides of your head. After all, you've trusted them enough to take you deeply into the world of home audio recording.

INDEX